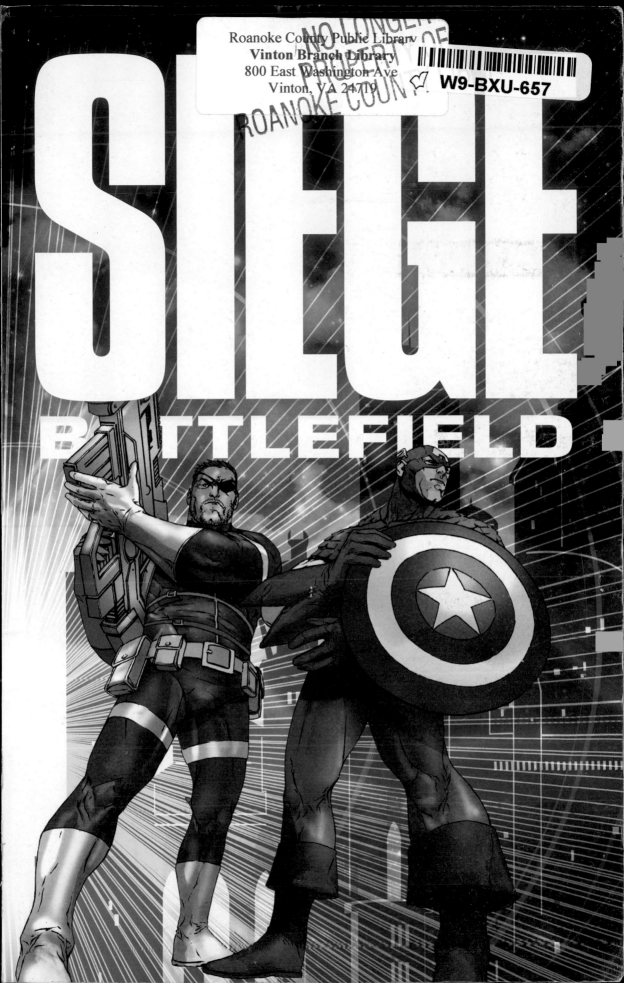

SIEGE
BATTLEFIELD

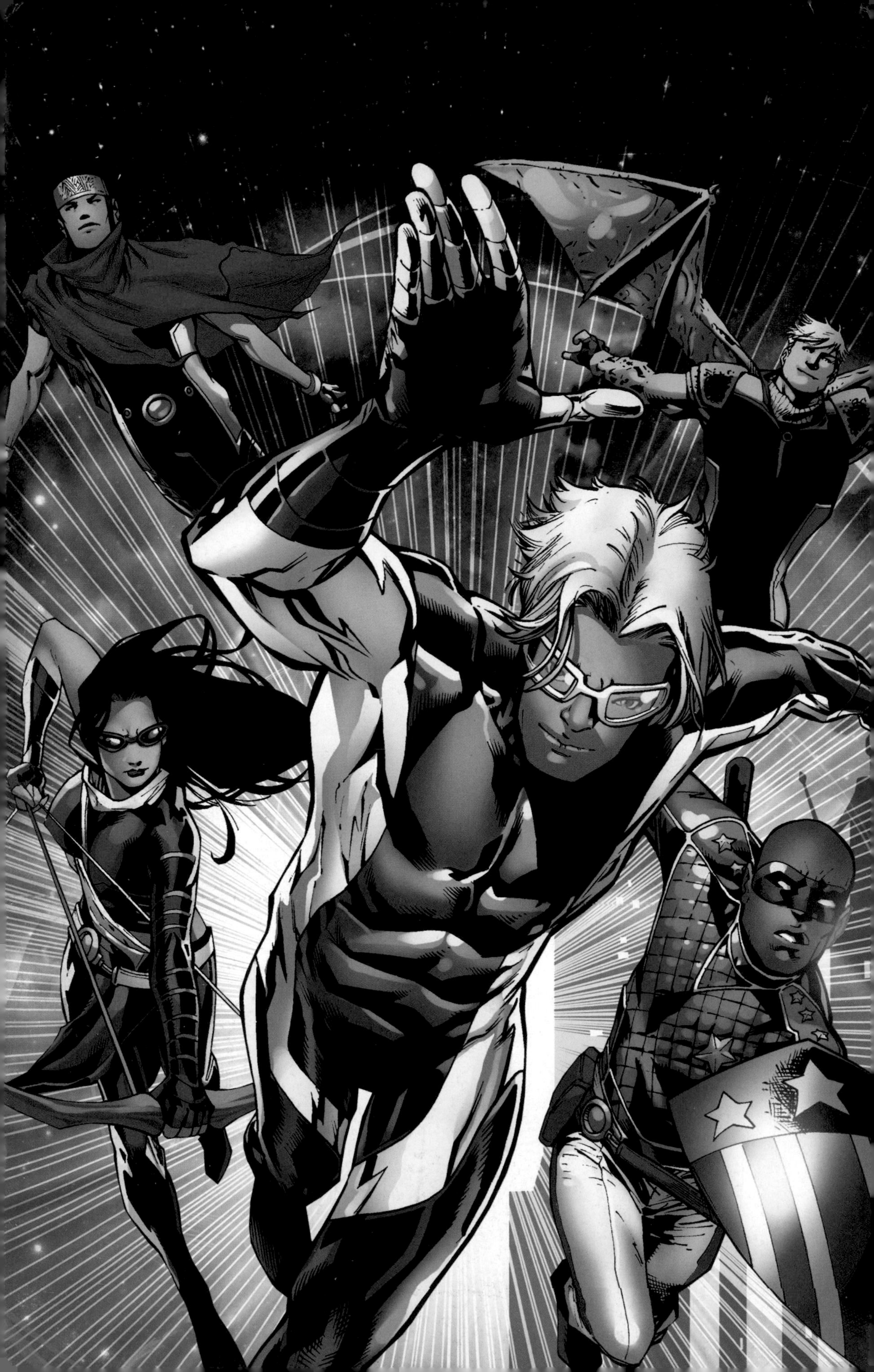

SIEGE
BATTLEFIELD

WRITERS: **KIERON GILLEN, BRIAN REED, CHRISTOS N. GAGE, SEAN MCKEEVER** & **JONATHAN HICKMAN**

ARTISTS: **JAMIE MCKELVIE; MARCO SANTUCCI; FEDERICO DALLOCCHIO; MAHMUD A. ASRAR, SCOTT HANNA** & **VICTOR OLAZABA;** AND **ALESSANDRO VITTI**

COLOR ARTISTS: **NATHAN FAIRBAIRN, CHRIS SOTOMAYOR, GIUILA BRUSCO, ROB SCHWAGER, MATT MILLA, JORGE MAESE** & **JOSE VILLARRUBIA**

LETTERERS: **JOE CARAMAGNA, DAVE SHARPE** & **DAVE LANPHEAR**

COVER ARTIST: **MARKO DJURDJEVIC**

ASSISTANT EDITORS: **ALEJANDRO ARBONA** & **RACHEL PINNELAS**

EDITORS: **RALPH MACCHIO, TOM BRENNAN, STEPHEN WACKER** & **BILL ROSEMANN**

EXECUTIVE EDITOR: **TOM BREVOORT**

COLLECTION EDITOR: **JENNIFER GRÜNWALD**

EDITORIAL ASSISTANTS: **JAMES EMMETT** & **JOE HOCHSTEIN**

ASSISTANT EDITORS: **ALEX STARBUCK** & **NELSON RIBEIRO**

EDITOR, SPECIAL PROJECTS: **MARK D. BEAZLEY**

SENIOR EDITOR, SPECIAL PROJECTS: **JEFF YOUNGQUIST**

SENIOR VICE PRESIDENT OF SALES: **DAVID GABRIEL**

BOOK DESIGNER: **RODOLFO MURAGUCHI**

EDITOR IN CHIEF: **JOE QUESADA**

PUBLISHER: **DAN BUCKLEY**

EXECUTIVE PRODUCER: **ALAN FINE**

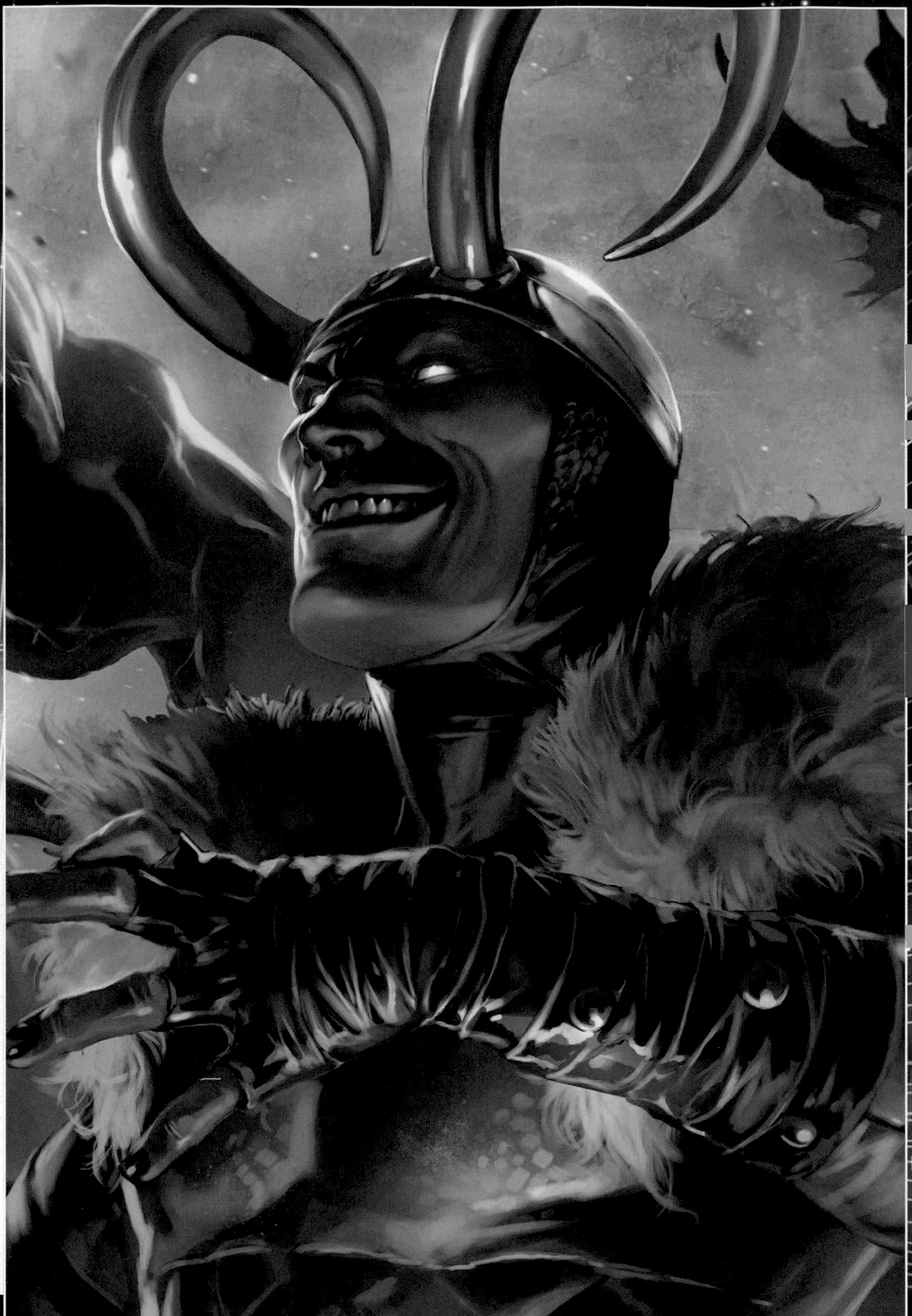

LOKI

PREVIOUSLY...

HAPPY DAYS HAVE COME FOR THE GOD OF MISCHIEF.

THROUGH LOKI'S MANIPULATION, HIS OAFISH, NAIVE BROTHER, THE NOBLE THOR, WAS CAST OUT OF ASGARD, INTO EXILE. IN THOR'S ABSENCE, THEIR BROTHER BALDER WAS PLACED ON THE THRONE...WITH LOKI AS ADVISER, WHISPERING WONDERFUL MALICE IN THE KING'S EAR.

UNDER LOKI'S GUIDANCE, BALDER WAS PERSUADED TO MOVE THE POPULATION OF THE SHINING CITY TO A NEW HOME, IN THE MONARCH DR. DOOM'S WINTRY NATION OF LATVERIA. DOOM INTENDED TO EXPLOIT AND KILL ASGARDIANS TO SUIT HIS OWN SINISTER ENDS, BUT HIS PLOT WAS EXPOSED. USING SLY LIES AND TRICKERY TO CONCEAL HIS ALLEGIANCE TO THE TYRANT, LOKI REMAINED IN BALDER'S GOOD GRACES, AND RETURNED WITH THE ASGARDIANS TO THEIR PREVIOUS HOME IN THE PLAINS OF OKLAHOMA.

BUT IT ISN'T MERELY BALDER WHO FELL UNDER LOKI'S INFLUENCE. THE TRICKSTER CONVINCED NORMAN OSBORN FORMERLY THE VILLAINOUS GREEN GOBLIN, NOW THE POWER-MAD DIRECTOR OF THE LAW ENFORCEMENT AGENCY H.A.M.M.E.R.– THAT ASGARD MUST BE REMOVED...

KIERON GILLEN
WRITER

JAMIE McKELVIE
ARTIST

NATHAN FAIRBAIRN
COLORIST

MARKO DJURDJEVIC
COVER ART

VC'S JOE CARAMAGNA
LETTERER

ALEJANDRO ARBONA
ASSISTANT EDITOR

RALPH MACCHIO
EDITOR

JOE QUESADA
EDITOR IN CHIEF

DAN BUCKLEY
PUBLISHER

ALAN FINE
EXEC. PRODUCER

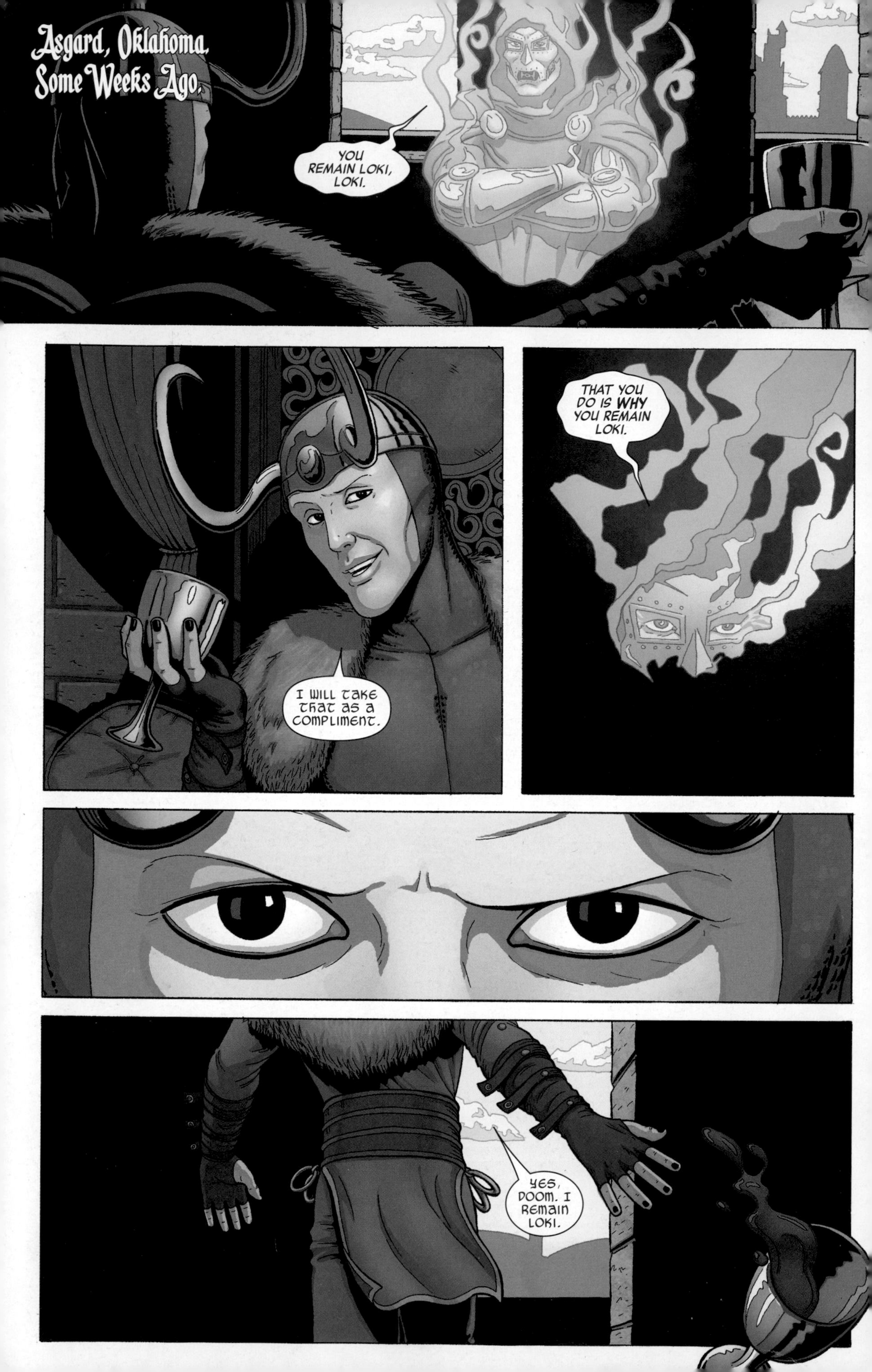
Asgard, Oklahoma.
Some Weeks Ago.
YOU REMAIN LOKI, LOKI.
I WILL TAKE THAT AS A COMPLIMENT.
THAT YOU DO IS WHY YOU REMAIN LOKI.
YES, DOOM. I REMAIN LOKI.

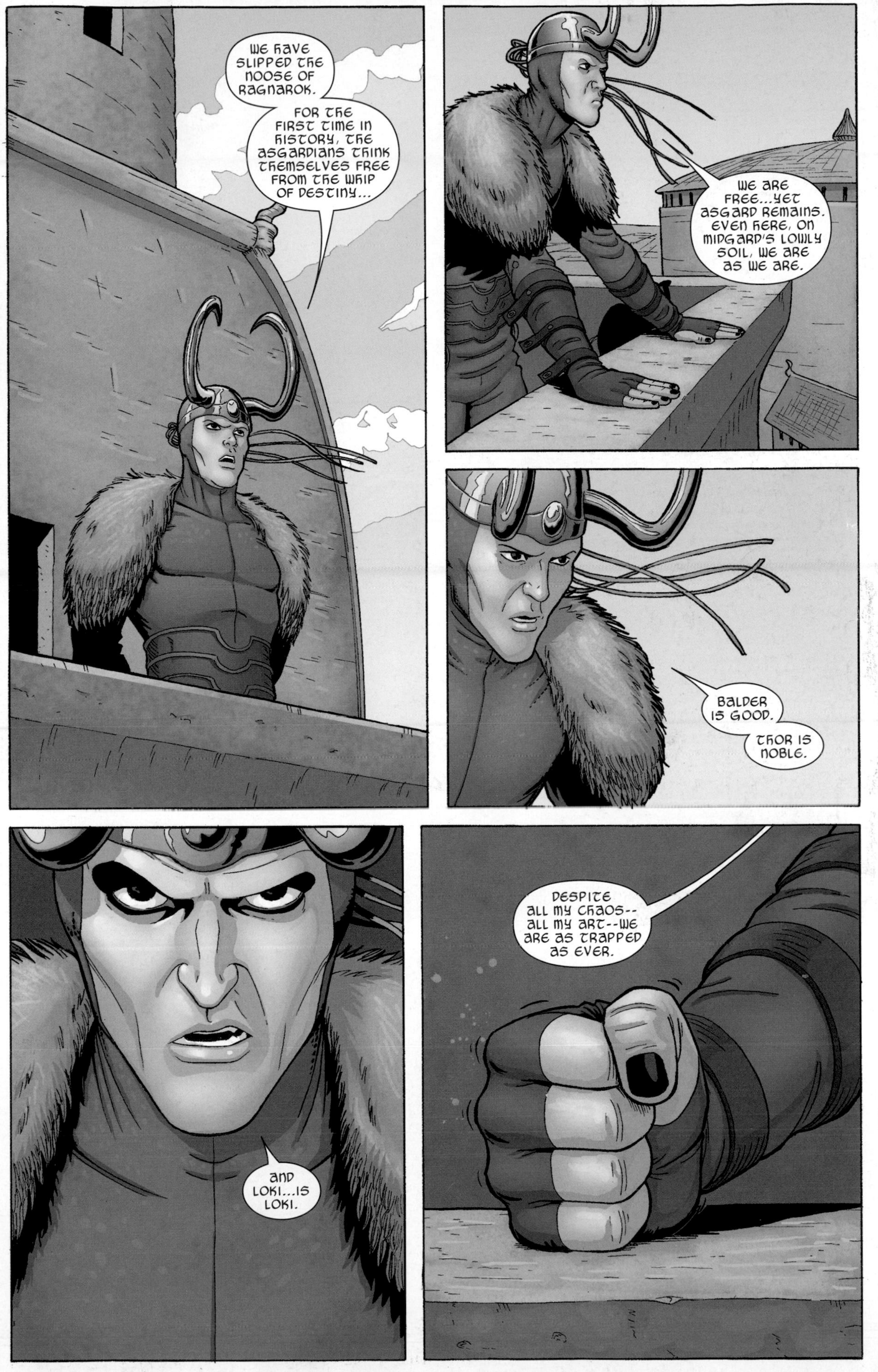
WE HAVE SLIPPED THE NOOSE OF RAGNAROK.
FOR THE FIRST TIME IN HISTORY, THE ASGARDIANS THINK THEMSELVES FREE FROM THE WHIP OF DESTINY...
WE ARE FREE...YET ASGARD REMAINS. EVEN HERE, ON MIDGARD'S LOWLY SOIL, WE ARE AS WE ARE.
BALDER IS GOOD.
THOR IS NOBLE.
AND LOKI...IS LOKI.
DESPITE ALL MY CHAOS--ALL MY ART--WE ARE AS TRAPPED AS EVER.

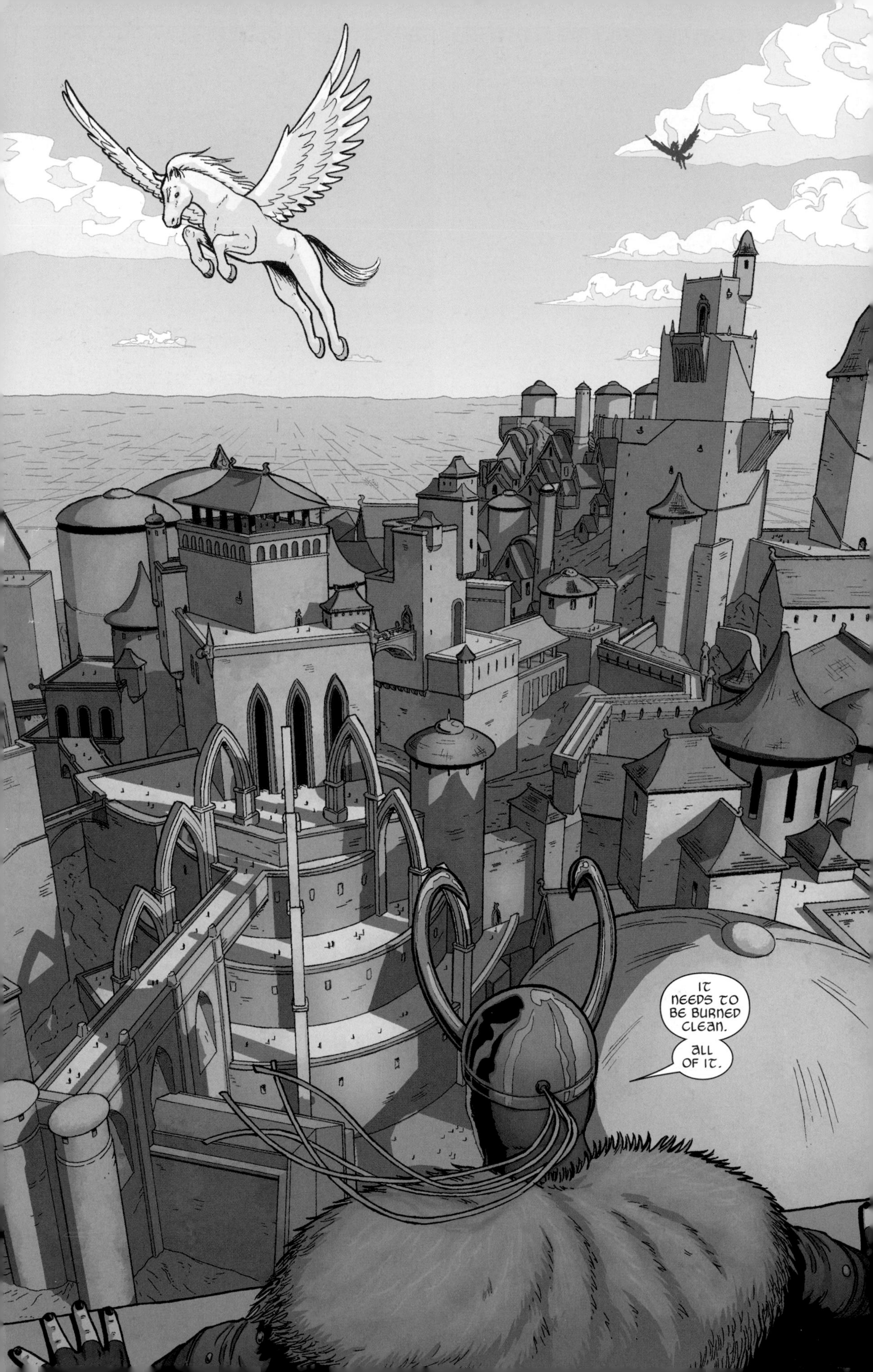
IT NEEDS TO BE BURNED CLEAN.
ALL OF IT.

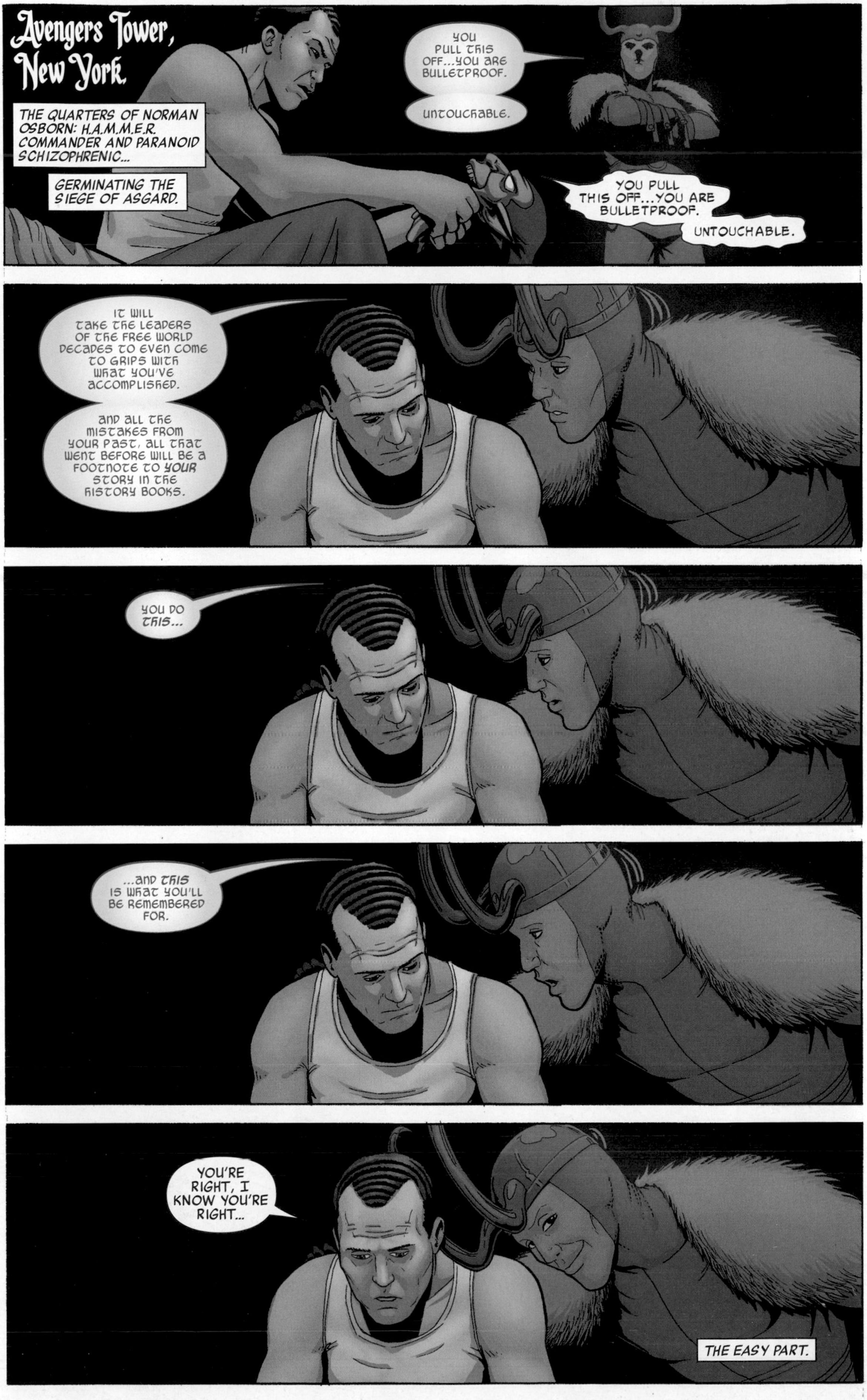
Avengers Tower, New York.
THE QUARTERS OF NORMAN OSBORN: H.A.M.M.E.R. COMMANDER AND PARANOID SCHIZOPHRENIC...
GERMINATING THE SIEGE OF ASGARD.
YOU PULL THIS OFF...YOU ARE BULLETPROOF.
UNTOUCHABLE.
YOU PULL THIS OFF...YOU ARE BULLETPROOF.
UNTOUCHABLE.
IT WILL TAKE THE LEADERS OF THE FREE WORLD DECADES TO EVEN COME TO GRIPS WITH WHAT YOU'VE ACCOMPLISHED.
AND ALL THE MISTAKES FROM YOUR PAST, ALL THAT WENT BEFORE WILL BE A FOOTNOTE TO YOUR STORY IN THE HISTORY BOOKS.
YOU DO THIS...
...AND THIS IS WHAT YOU'LL BE REMEMBERED FOR.
YOU'RE RIGHT, I KNOW YOU'RE RIGHT...
THE EASY PART.

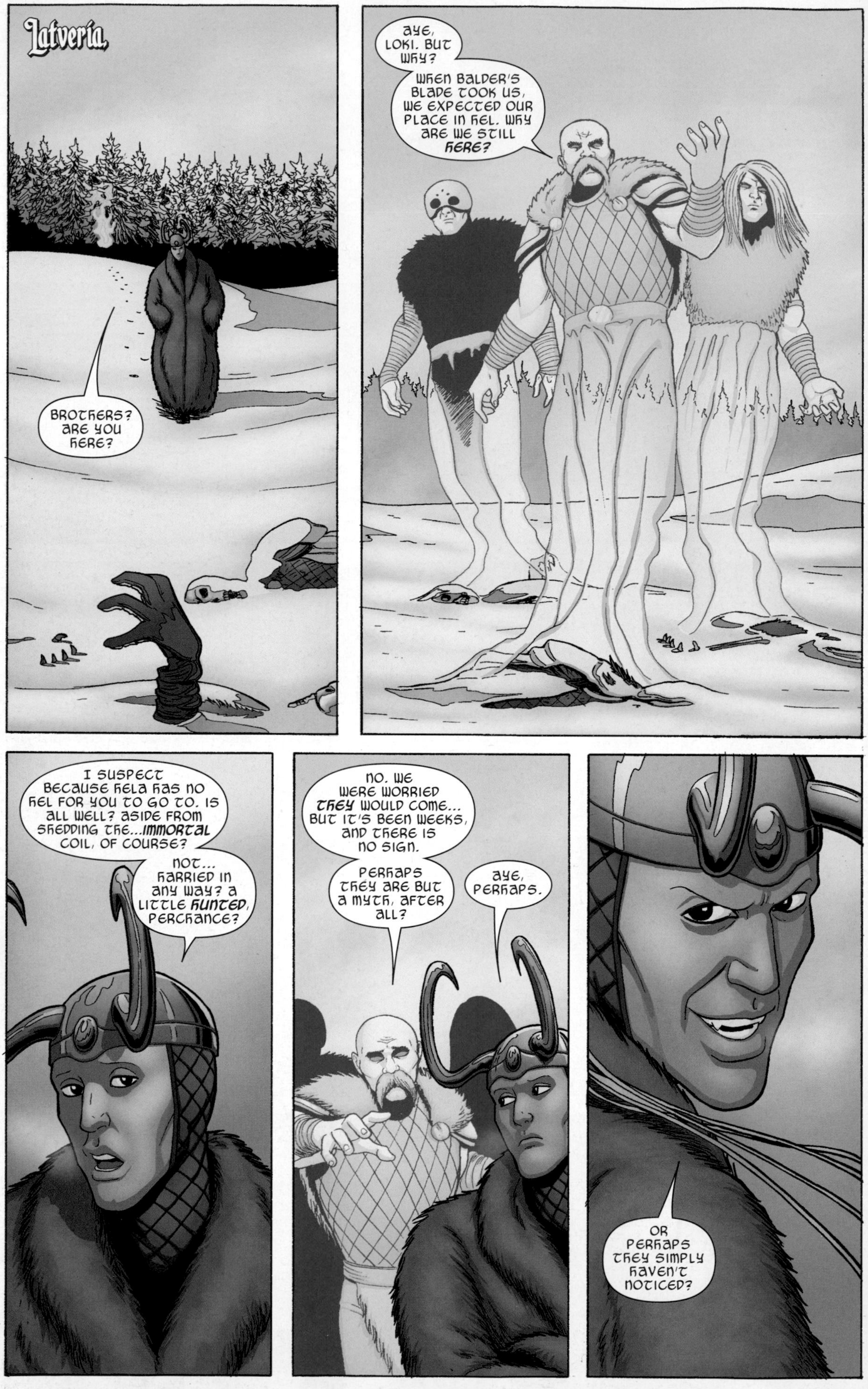
Latveria.
BROTHERS? ARE YOU HERE?
AYE, LOKI. BUT WHY?
WHEN BALDER'S BLADE TOOK US, WE EXPECTED OUR PLACE IN HEL. WHY ARE WE STILL HERE?
I SUSPECT BECAUSE HELA HAS NO HEL FOR YOU TO GO TO. IS ALL WELL? ASIDE FROM SHEDDING THE...IMMORTAL COIL, OF COURSE?
NOT... HARRIED IN ANY WAY? A LITTLE HUNTED, PERCHANCE?
NO. WE WERE WORRIED THEY WOULD COME... BUT IT'S BEEN WEEKS, AND THERE IS NO SIGN.
PERHAPS THEY ARE BUT A MYTH, AFTER ALL?
AYE, PERHAPS.
OR PERHAPS THEY SIMPLY HAVEN'T NOTICED?

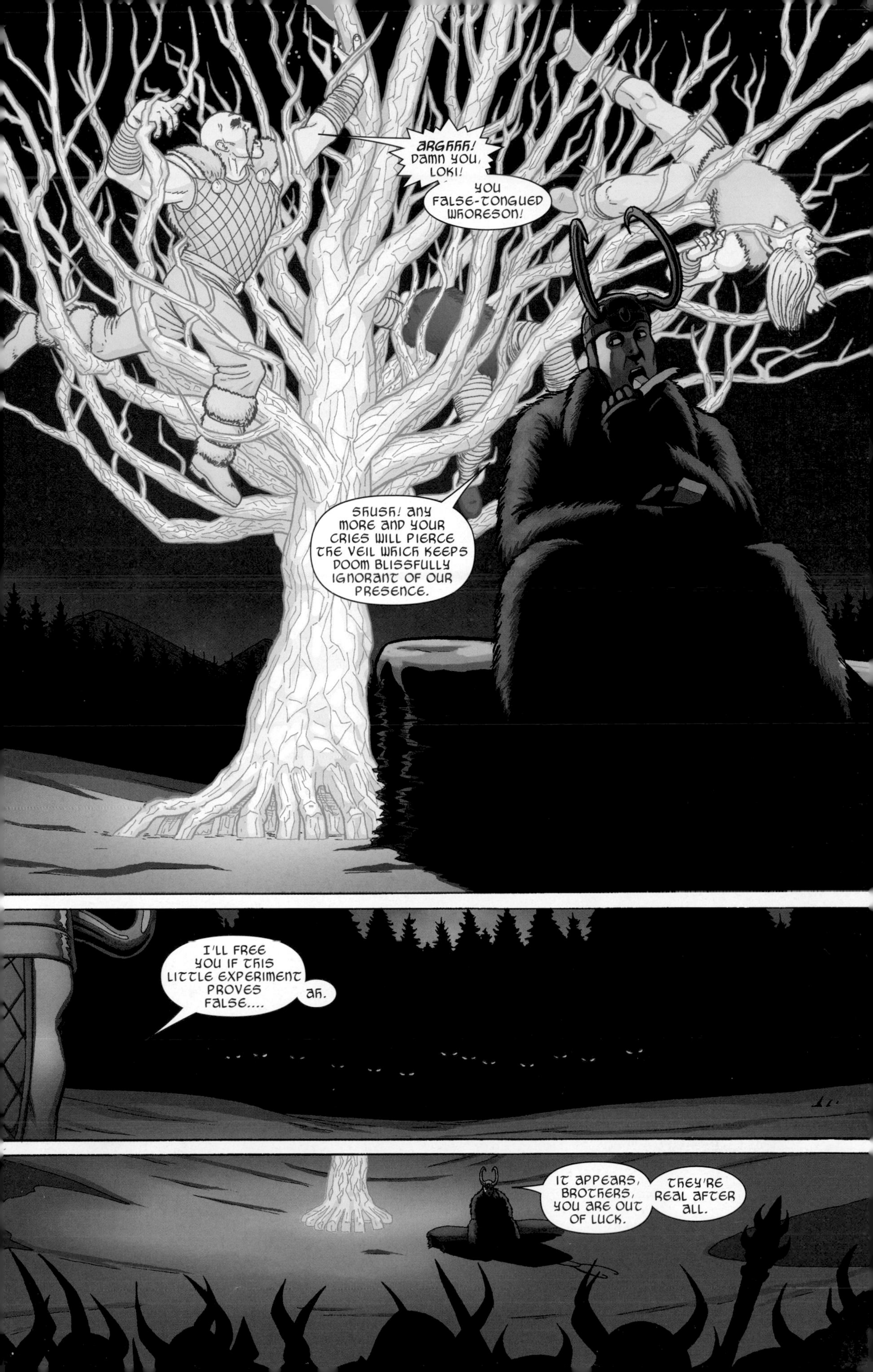
ARGHHH! DAMN YOU, LOKI!
YOU FALSE-TONGUED WHORESON!
SHUSH! ANY MORE AND YOUR CRIES WILL PIERCE THE VEIL WHICH KEEPS DOOM BLISSFULLY IGNORANT OF OUR PRESENCE.
I'LL FREE YOU IF THIS LITTLE EXPERIMENT PROVES FALSE....
AH.
IT APPEARS, BROTHERS, YOU ARE OUT OF LUCK.
THEY'RE REAL AFTER ALL.

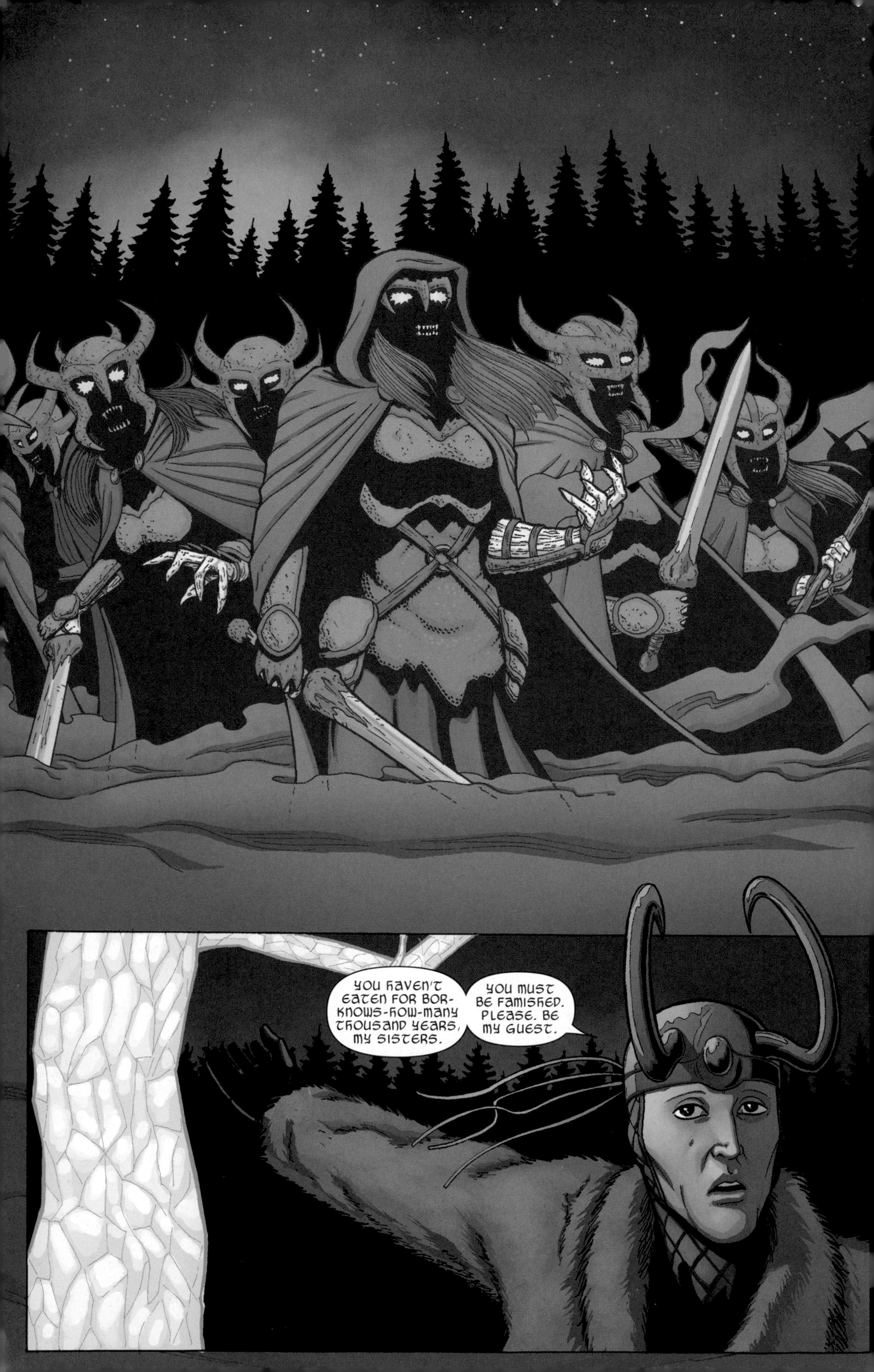
YOU HAVEN'T EATEN FOR BOR-KNOWS-HOW-MANY THOUSAND YEARS, MY SISTERS.
YOU MUST BE FAMISHED. PLEASE. BE MY GUEST.

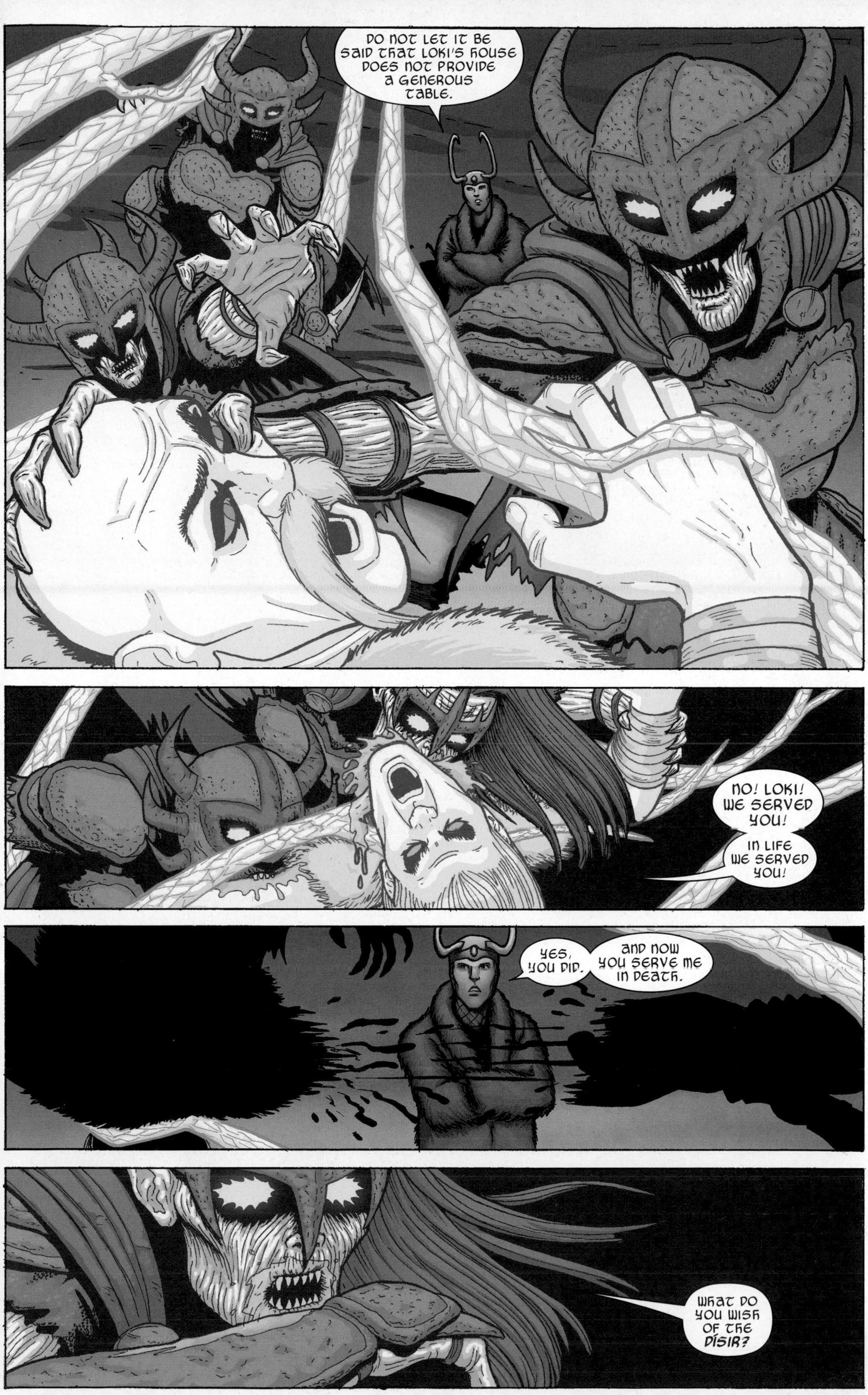
DO NOT LET IT BE SAID THAT LOKI'S HOUSE DOES NOT PROVIDE A GENEROUS TABLE.
NO! LOKI! WE SERVED YOU!
IN LIFE WE SERVED YOU!
YES, YOU DID.
AND NOW YOU SERVE ME IN DEATH.
WHAT DO YOU WISH OF THE DÍSIR?

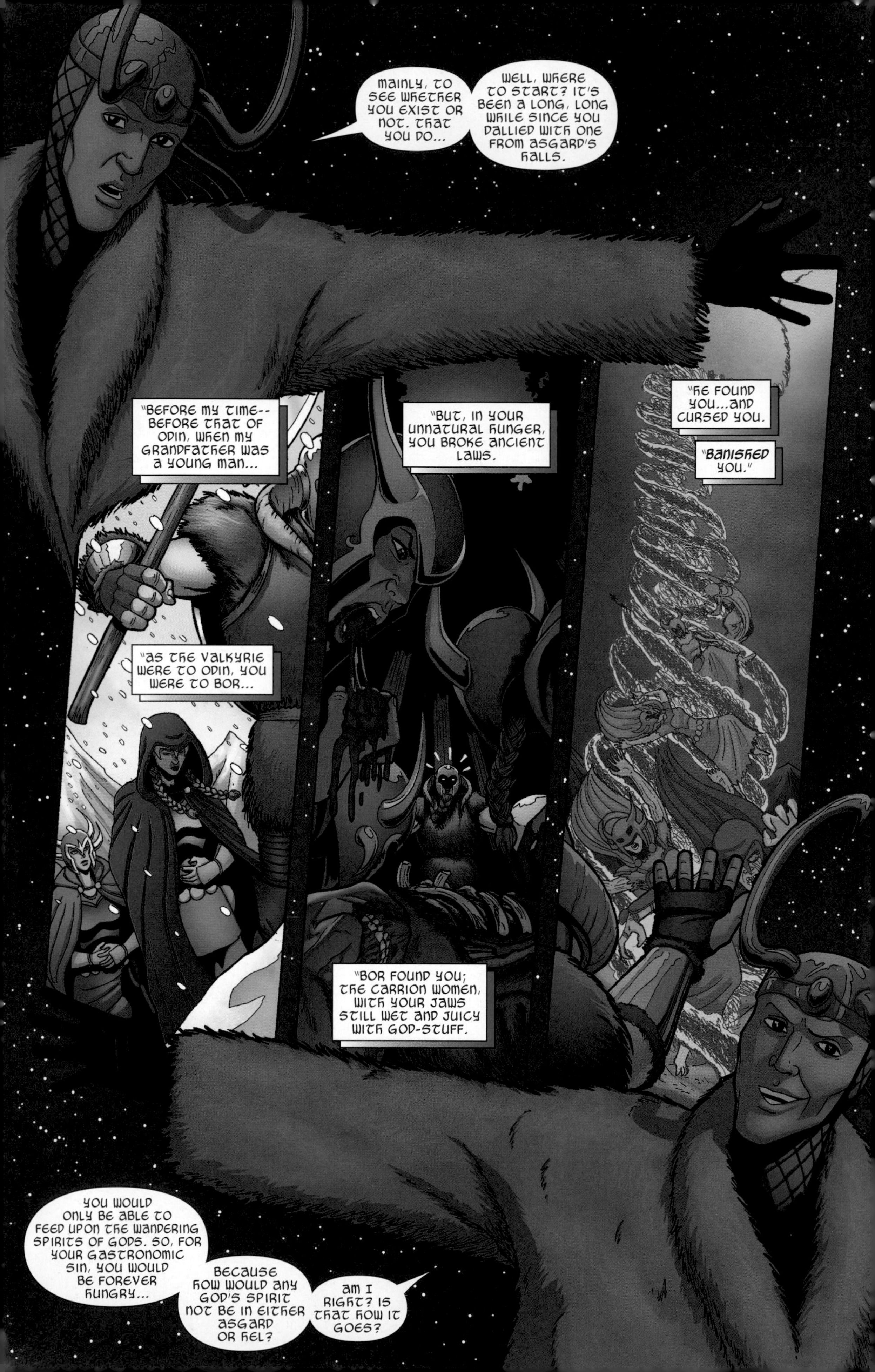
MAINLY, TO SEE WHETHER YOU EXIST OR NOT. THAT YOU DO...
WELL, WHERE TO START? IT'S BEEN A LONG, LONG WHILE SINCE YOU DALLIED WITH ONE FROM ASGARD'S HALLS.
"BEFORE MY TIME-- BEFORE THAT OF ODIN, WHEN MY GRANDFATHER WAS A YOUNG MAN...
"AS THE VALKYRIE WERE TO ODIN, YOU WERE TO BOR...
"BUT, IN YOUR UNNATURAL HUNGER, YOU BROKE ANCIENT LAWS.
"BOR FOUND YOU; THE CARRION WOMEN, WITH YOUR JAWS STILL WET AND JUICY WITH GOD-STUFF.
"HE FOUND YOU...AND CURSED YOU.
"BANISHED YOU."
YOU WOULD ONLY BE ABLE TO FEED UPON THE WANDERING SPIRITS OF GODS. SO, FOR YOUR GASTRONOMIC SIN, YOU WOULD BE FOREVER HUNGRY...
BECAUSE HOW WOULD ANY GOD'S SPIRIT NOT BE IN EITHER ASGARD OR HEL?
AM I RIGHT? IS THAT HOW IT GOES?

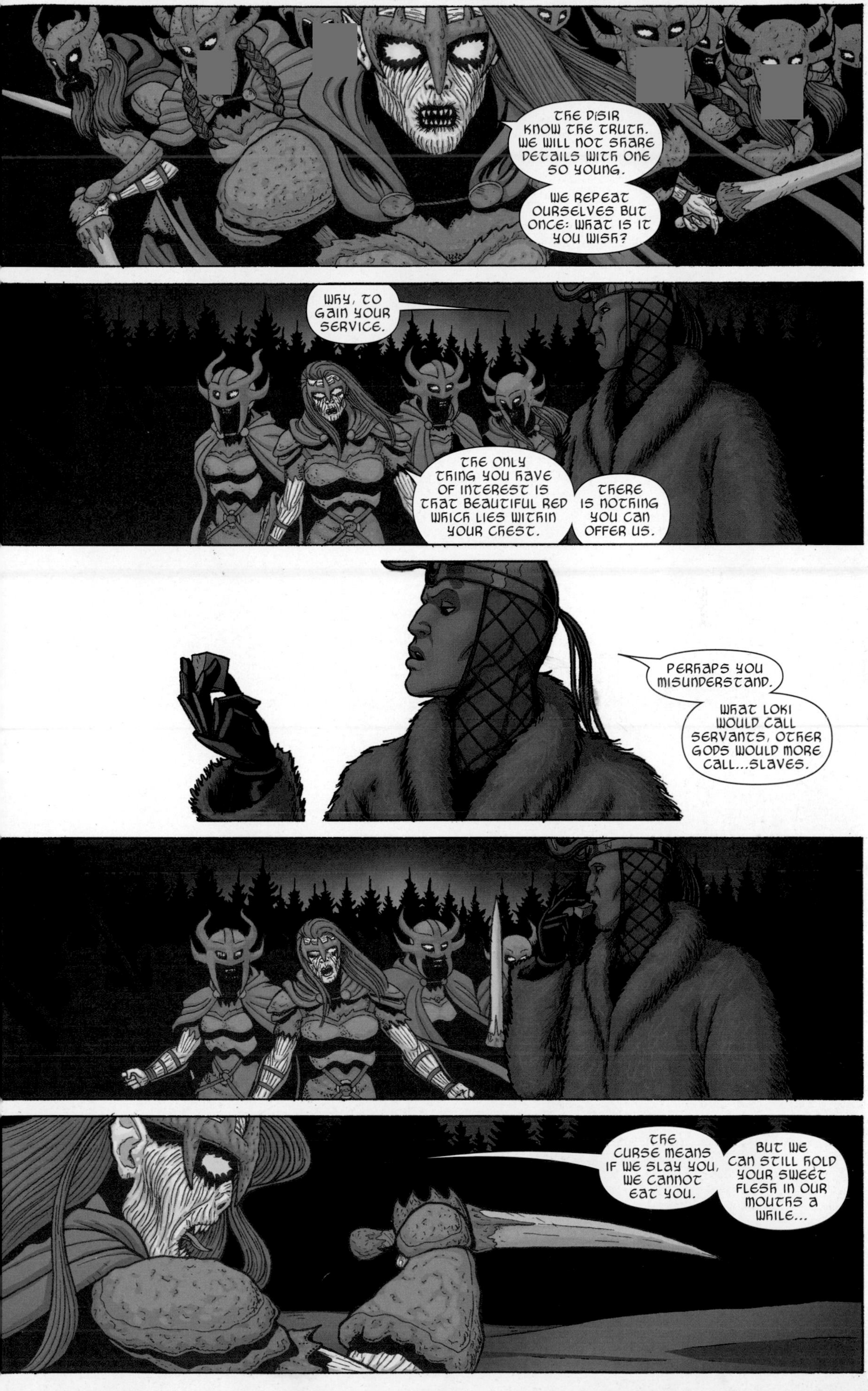
THE DISIR KNOW THE TRUTH. WE WILL NOT SHARE DETAILS WITH ONE SO YOUNG.
WE REPEAT OURSELVES BUT ONCE: WHAT IS IT YOU WISH?
WHY, TO GAIN YOUR SERVICE.
THE ONLY THING YOU HAVE OF INTEREST IS THAT BEAUTIFUL RED WHICH LIES WITHIN YOUR CHEST.
THERE IS NOTHING YOU CAN OFFER US.
PERHAPS YOU MISUNDERSTAND.
WHAT LOKI WOULD CALL SERVANTS, OTHER GODS WOULD MORE CALL...SLAVES.
THE CURSE MEANS IF WE SLAY YOU, WE CANNOT EAT YOU.
BUT WE CAN STILL HOLD YOUR SWEET FLESH IN OUR MOUTHS A WHILE...

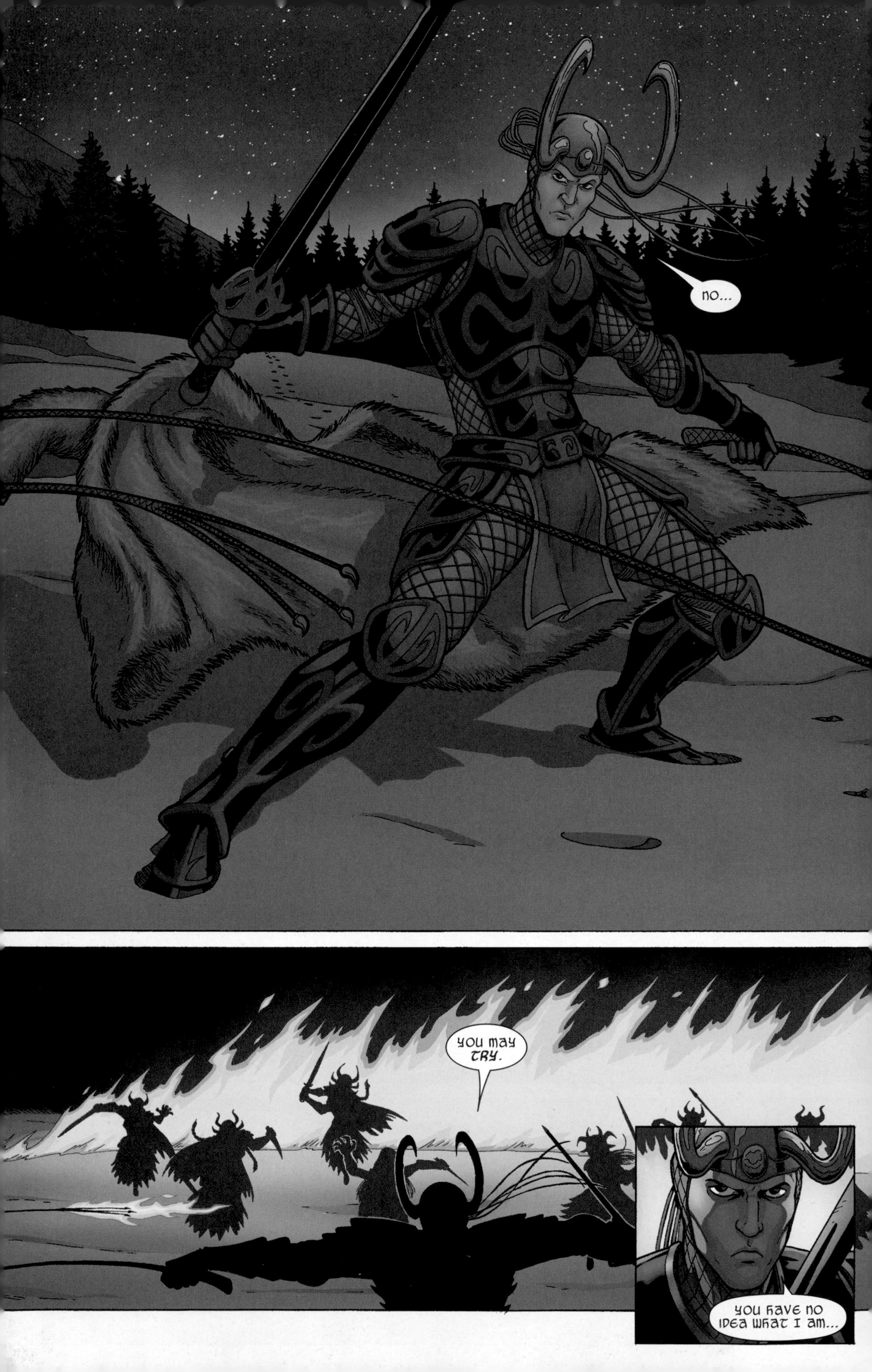
no...
YOU MAY TRY.
YOU HAVE NO IDEA WHAT I AM...

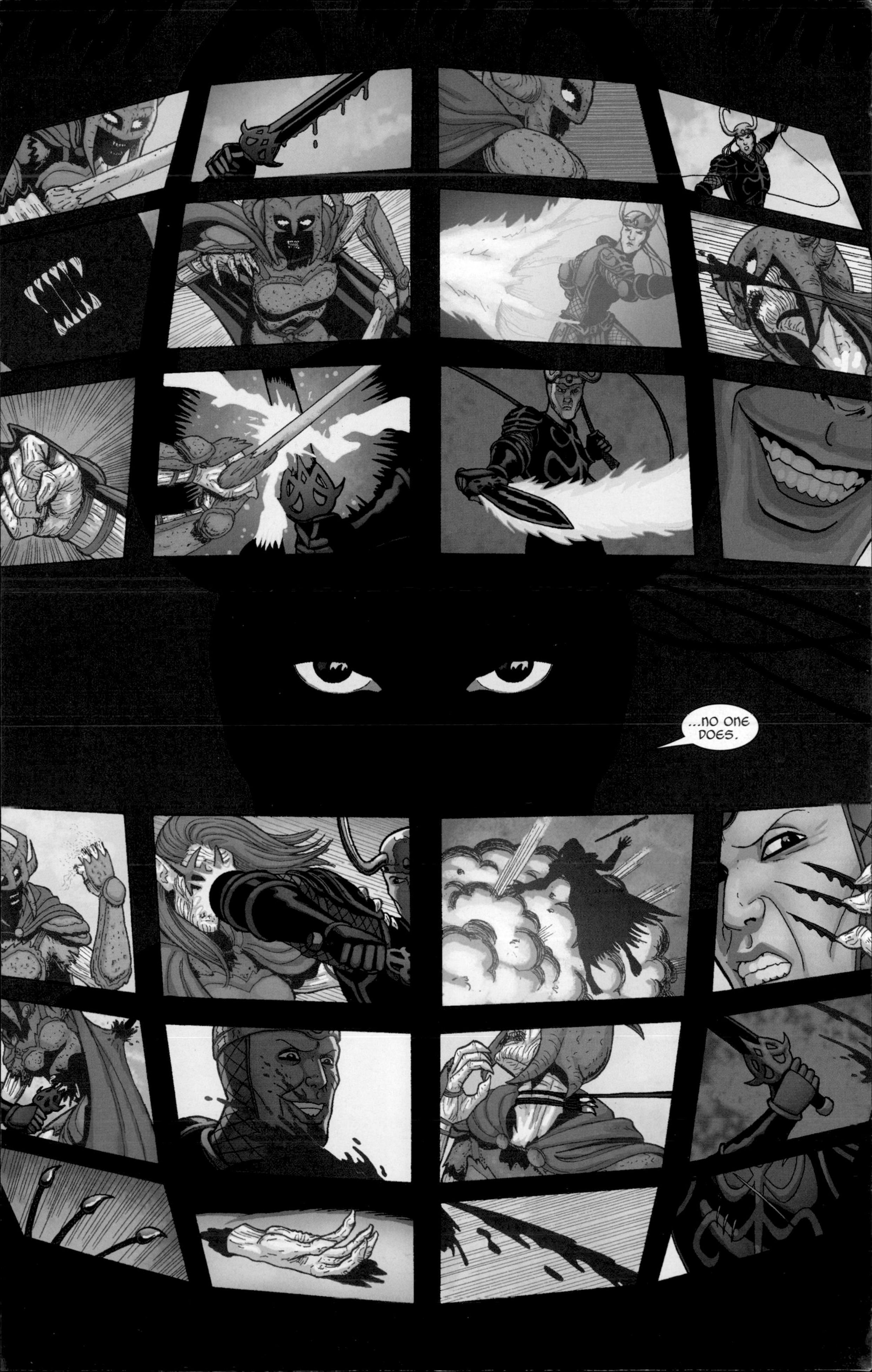
...NO ONE DOES.

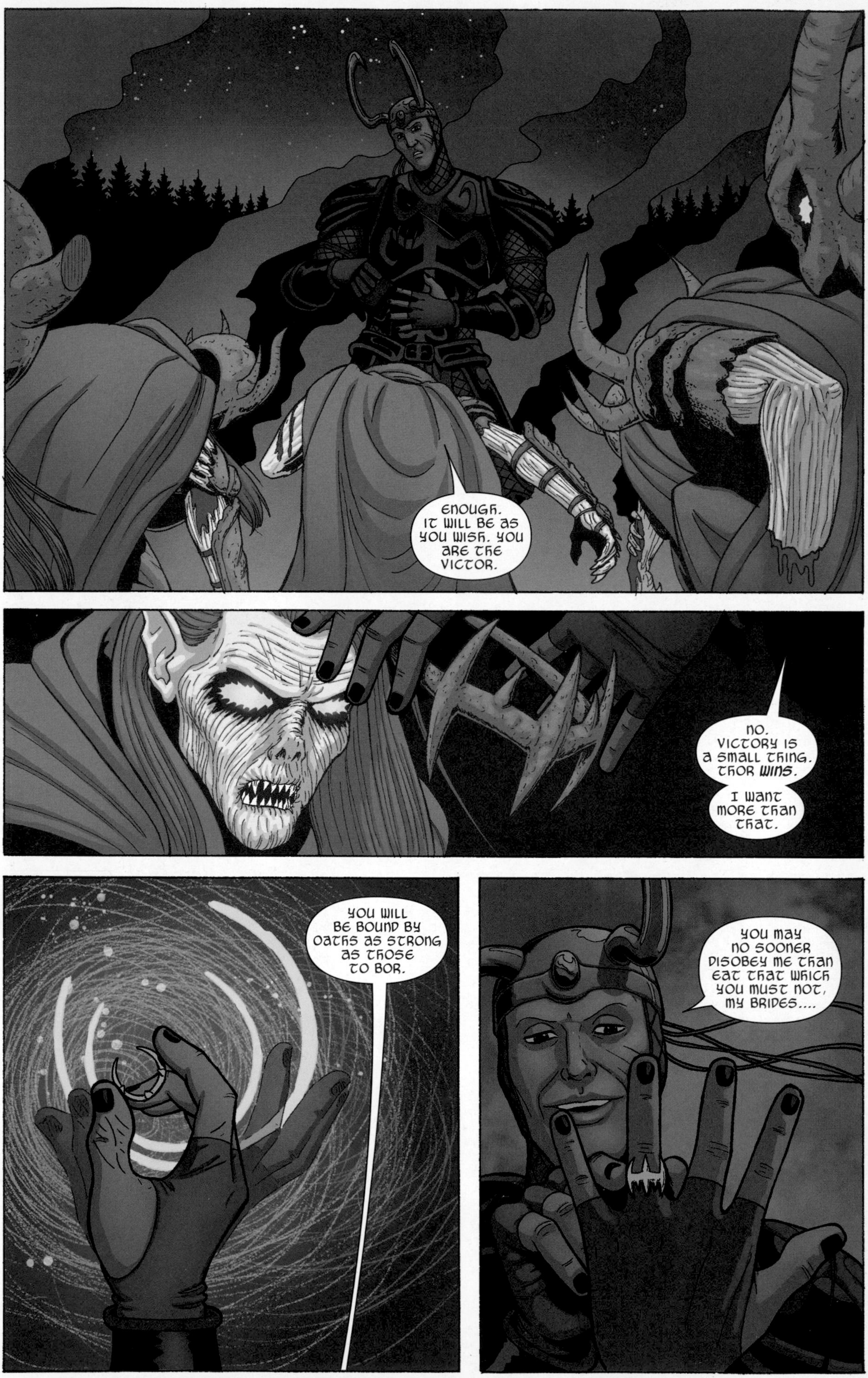
ENOUGH. IT WILL BE AS YOU WISH. YOU ARE THE VICTOR.
NO. VICTORY IS A SMALL THING. THOR WINS.
I WANT MORE THAN THAT.
YOU WILL BE BOUND BY OATHS AS STRONG AS THOSE TO BOR.
YOU MAY NO SOONER DISOBEY ME THAN EAT THAT WHICH YOU MUST NOT, MY BRIDES....

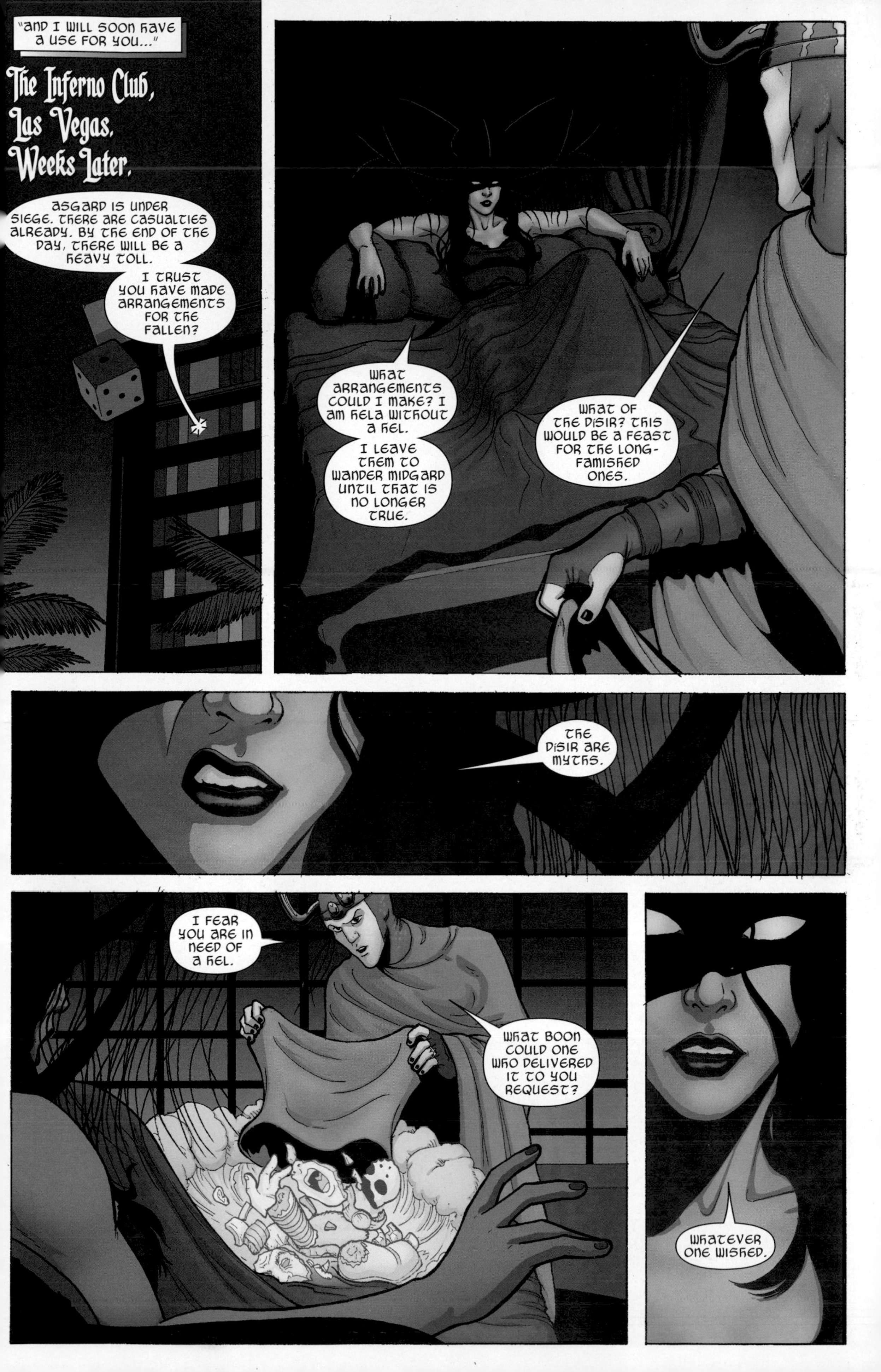
"AND I WILL SOON HAVE A USE FOR YOU..."
The Inferno Club, Las Vegas, Weeks Later.
ASGARD IS UNDER SIEGE. THERE ARE CASUALTIES ALREADY. BY THE END OF THE DAY, THERE WILL BE A HEAVY TOLL.
I TRUST YOU HAVE MADE ARRANGEMENTS FOR THE FALLEN?
WHAT ARRANGEMENTS COULD I MAKE? I AM HELA WITHOUT A HEL.
I LEAVE THEM TO WANDER MIDGARD UNTIL THAT IS NO LONGER TRUE.
WHAT OF THE DISIR? THIS WOULD BE A FEAST FOR THE LONG-FAMISHED ONES.
THE DISIR ARE MYTHS.
I FEAR YOU ARE IN NEED OF A HEL.
WHAT BOON COULD ONE WHO DELIVERED IT TO YOU REQUEST?
WHATEVER ONE WISHED.

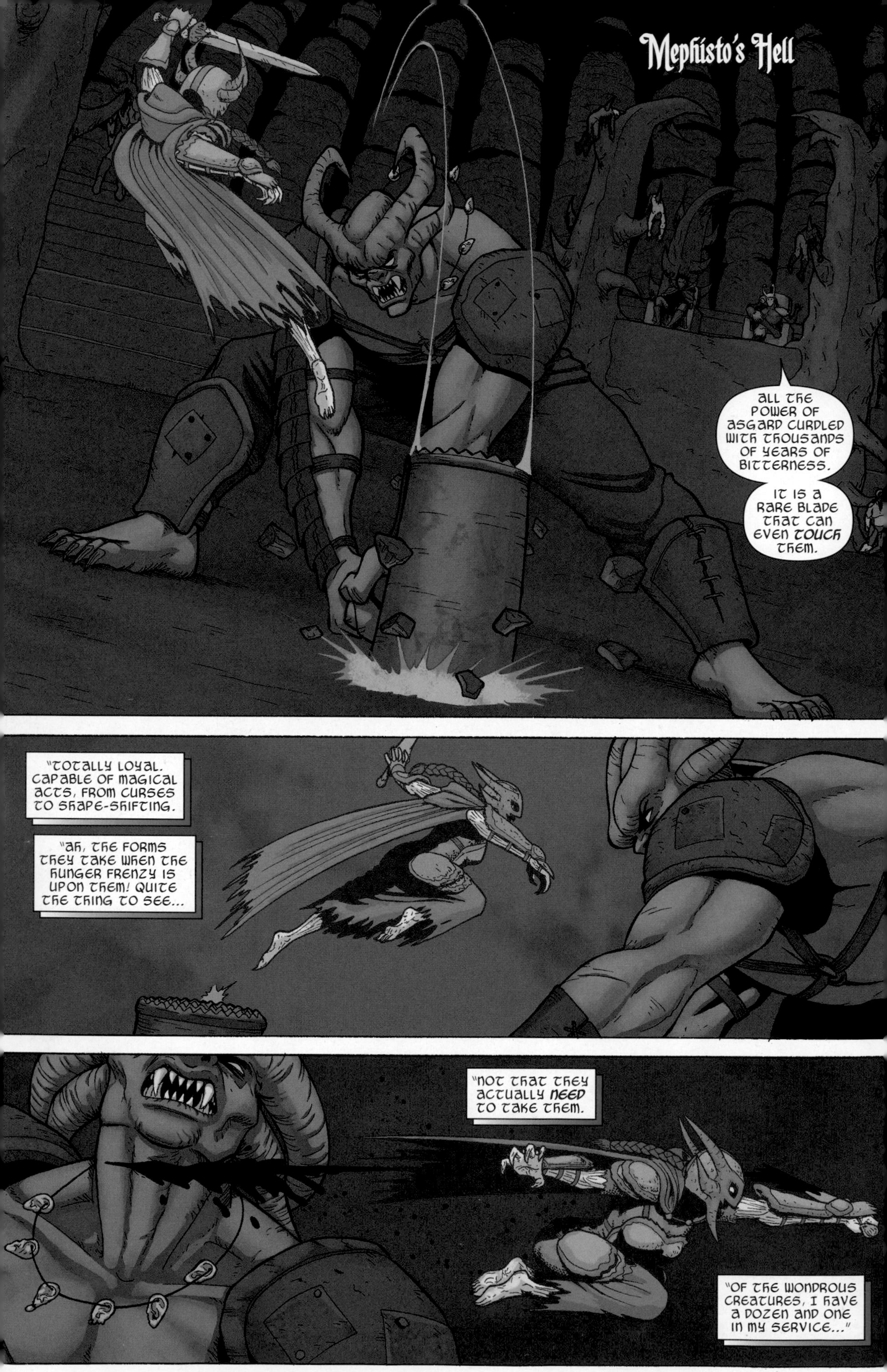
Mephisto's Hell
ALL THE POWER OF ASGARD CURDLED WITH THOUSANDS OF YEARS OF BITTERNESS.
IT IS A RARE BLADE THAT CAN EVEN TOUCH THEM.
"TOTALLY LOYAL. CAPABLE OF MAGICAL ACTS, FROM CURSES TO SHAPE-SHIFTING.
"AH, THE FORMS THEY TAKE WHEN THE HUNGER FRENZY IS UPON THEM! QUITE THE THING TO SEE...
"NOT THAT THEY ACTUALLY NEED TO TAKE THEM.
"OF THE WONDROUS CREATURES, I HAVE A DOZEN AND ONE IN MY SERVICE..."

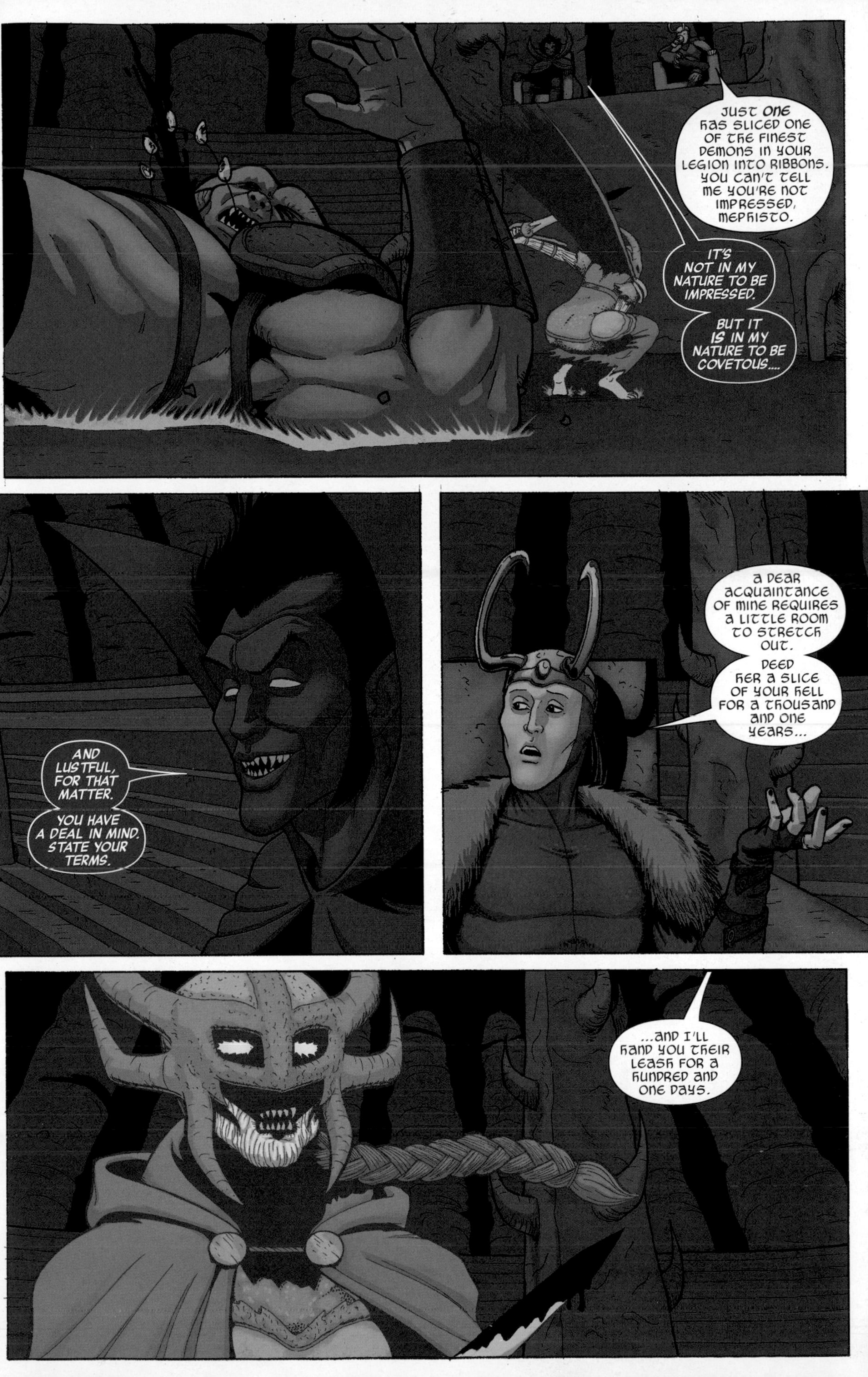
JUST ONE HAS SLICED ONE OF THE FINEST DEMONS IN YOUR LEGION INTO RIBBONS. YOU CAN'T TELL ME YOU'RE NOT IMPRESSED, MEPHISTO.
IT'S NOT IN MY NATURE TO BE IMPRESSED.
BUT IT IS IN MY NATURE TO BE COVETOUS....
AND LUSTFUL, FOR THAT MATTER.
YOU HAVE A DEAL IN MIND. STATE YOUR TERMS.
A DEAR ACQUAINTANCE OF MINE REQUIRES A LITTLE ROOM TO STRETCH OUT.
DEED HER A SLICE OF YOUR HELL FOR A THOUSAND AND ONE YEARS...
...AND I'LL HAND YOU THEIR LEASH FOR A HUNDRED AND ONE DAYS.

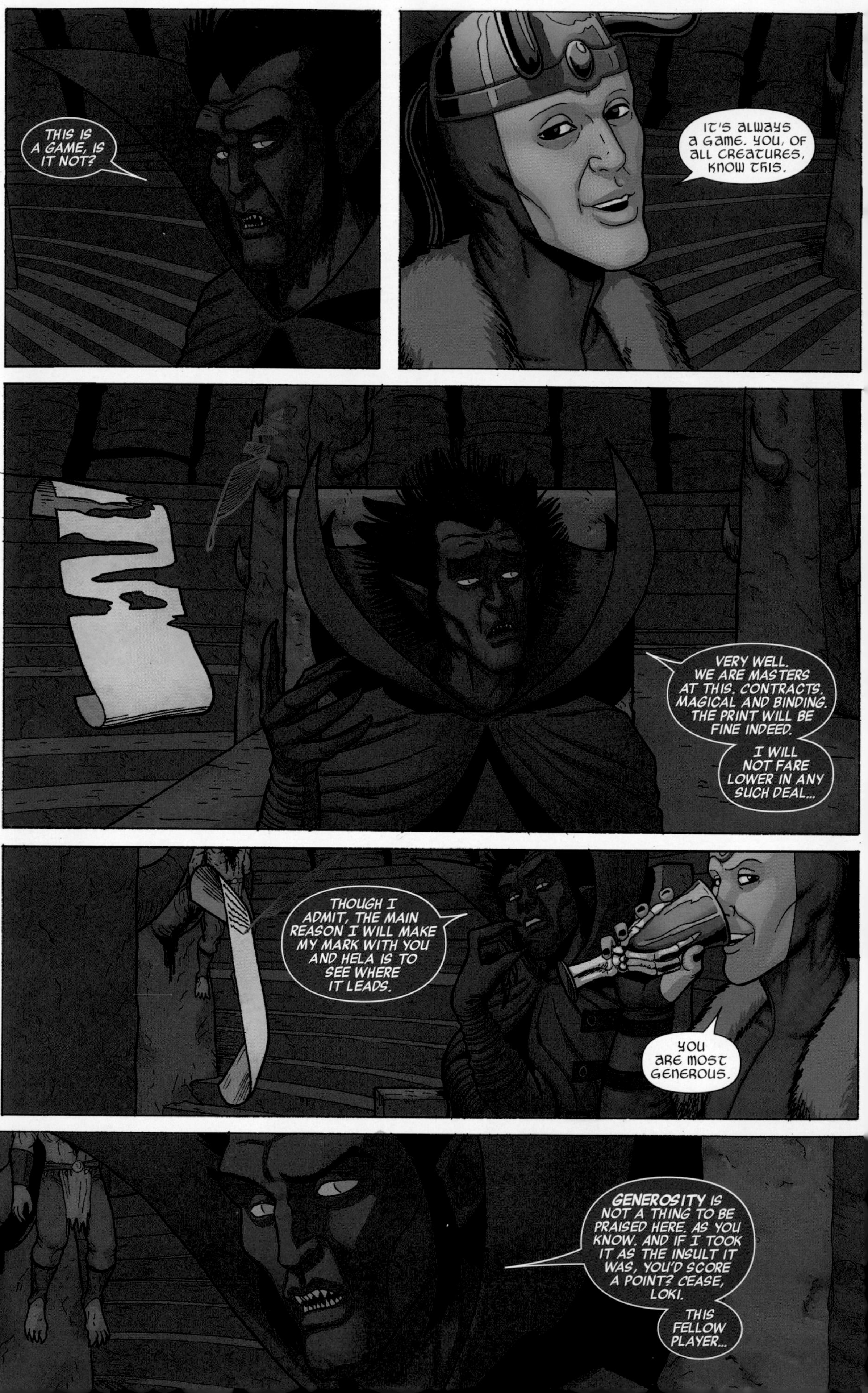
THIS IS A GAME, IS IT NOT?
IT'S ALWAYS A GAME. YOU, OF ALL CREATURES, KNOW THIS.
VERY WELL. WE ARE MASTERS AT THIS. CONTRACTS. MAGICAL AND BINDING. THE PRINT WILL BE FINE INDEED.
I WILL NOT FARE LOWER IN ANY SUCH DEAL...
THOUGH I ADMIT, THE MAIN REASON I WILL MAKE MY MARK WITH YOU AND HELA IS TO SEE WHERE IT LEADS.
YOU ARE MOST GENEROUS.
GENEROSITY IS NOT A THING TO BE PRAISED HERE. AS YOU KNOW. AND IF I TOOK IT AS THE INSULT IT WAS, YOU'D SCORE A POINT? CEASE, LOKI.
THIS FELLOW PLAYER...

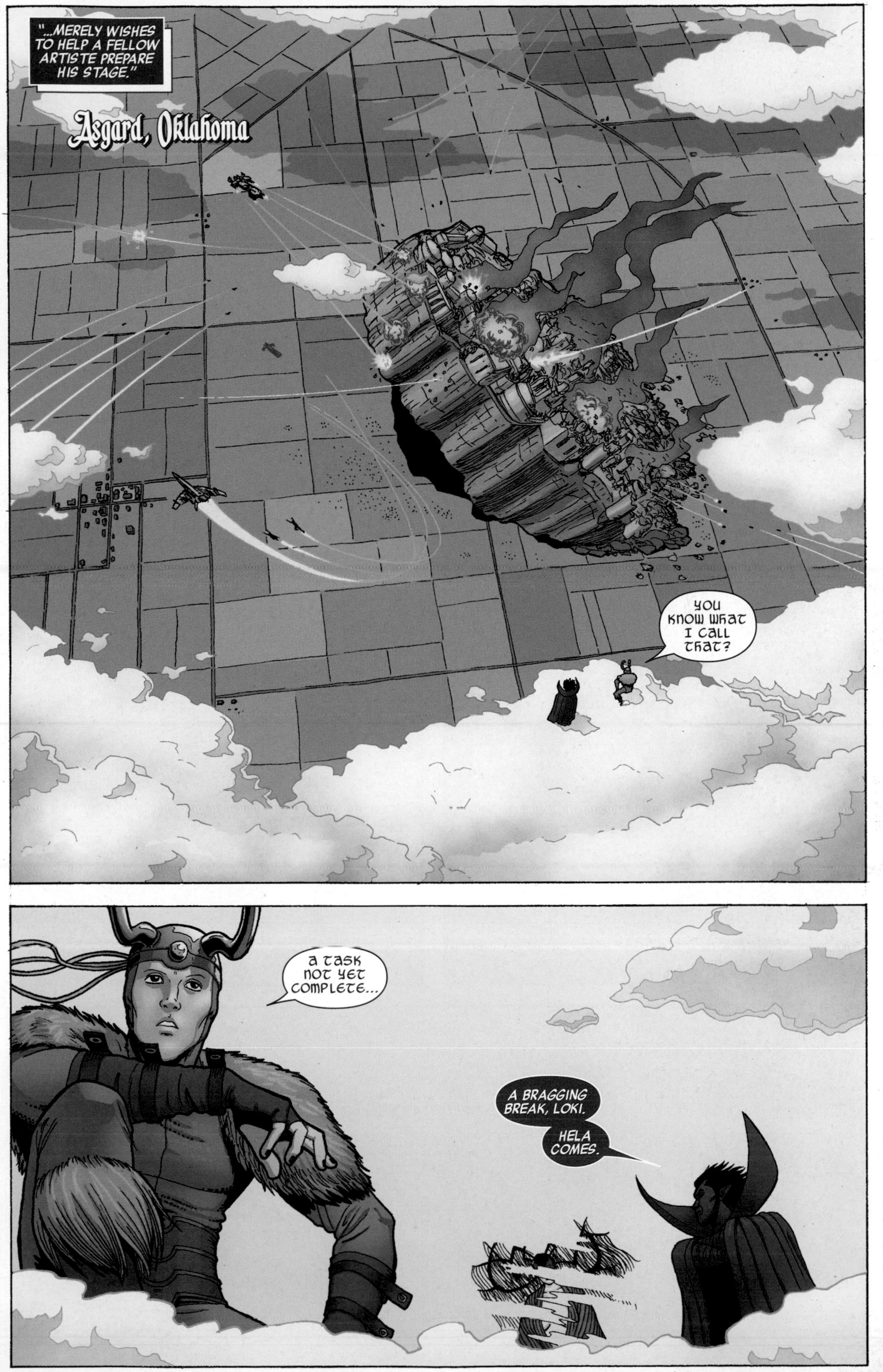
"...MERELY WISHES TO HELP A FELLOW ARTISTE PREPARE HIS STAGE."
Asgard, Oklahoma
YOU KNOW WHAT I CALL THAT?
A TASK NOT YET COMPLETE...
A BRAGGING BREAK, LOKI.
HELA COMES.

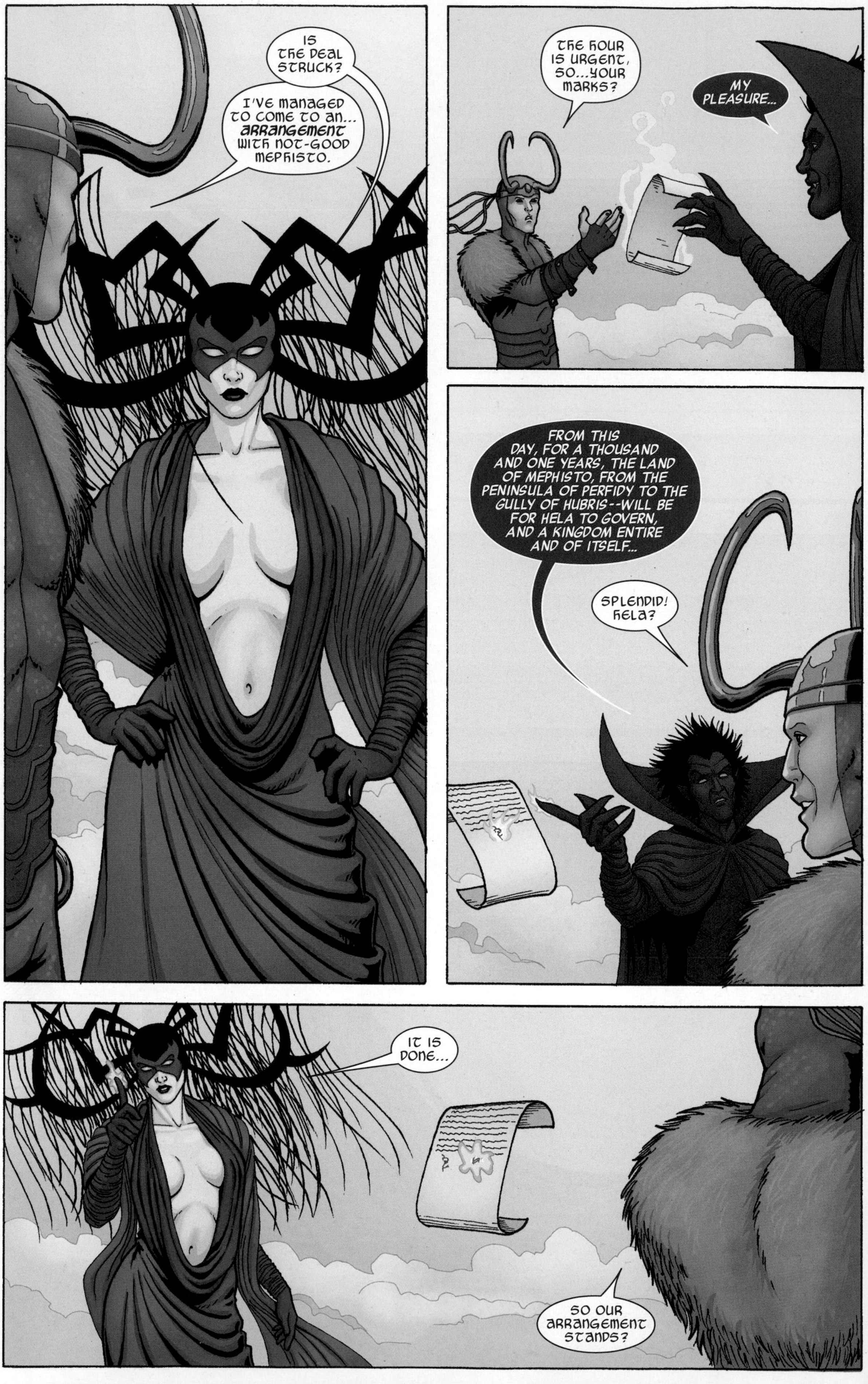
IS THE DEAL STRUCK?
I'VE MANAGED TO COME TO AN... ARRANGEMENT WITH NOT-GOOD MEPHISTO.
THE HOUR IS URGENT, SO...YOUR MARKS?
MY PLEASURE...
FROM THIS DAY, FOR A THOUSAND AND ONE YEARS, THE LAND OF MEPHISTO, FROM THE PENINSULA OF PERFIDY TO THE GULLY OF HUBRIS--WILL BE FOR HELA TO GOVERN, AND A KINGDOM ENTIRE AND OF ITSELF...
SPLENDID! HELA?
IT IS DONE...
SO OUR ARRANGEMENT STANDS?

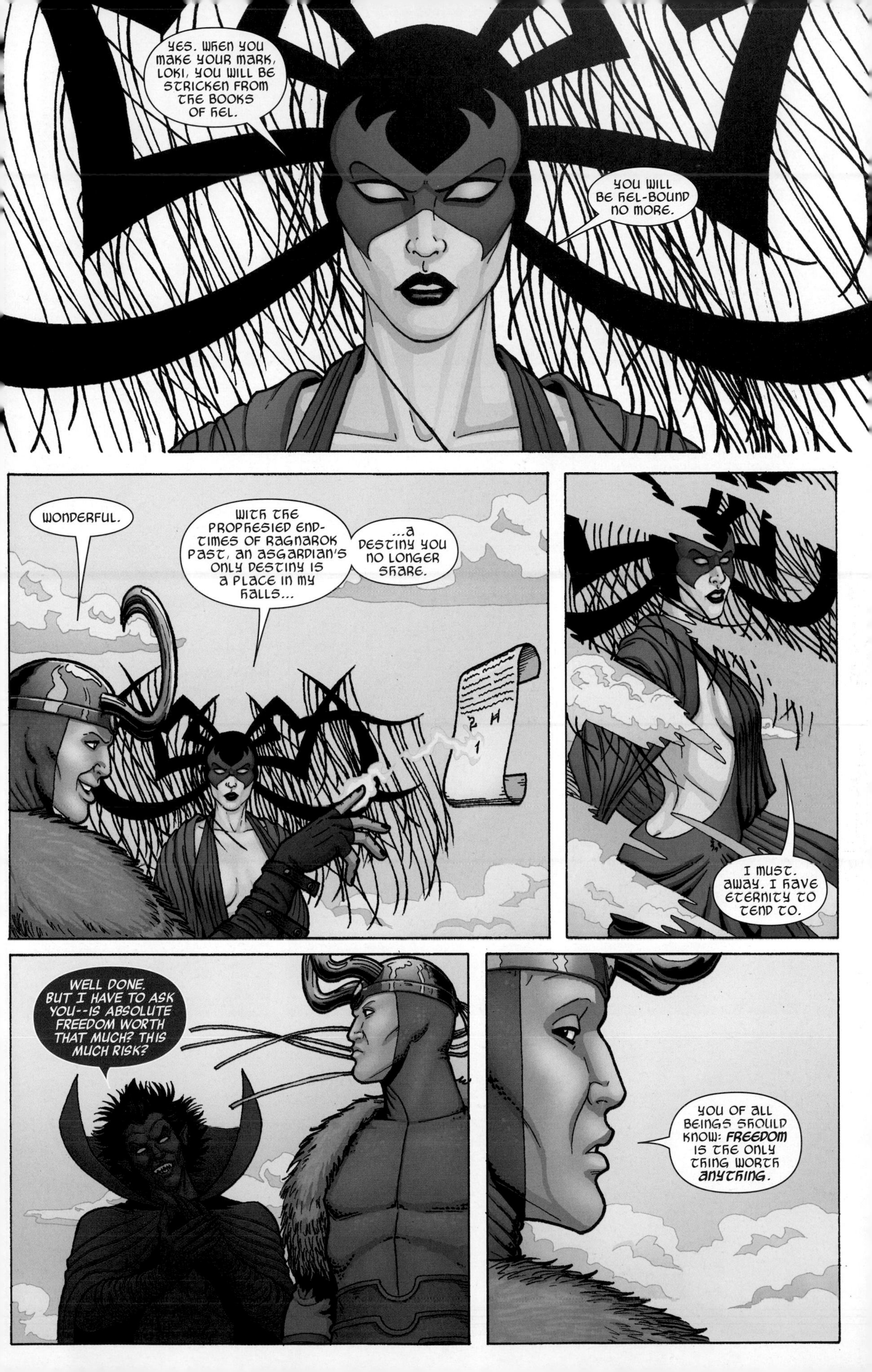
YES. WHEN YOU MAKE YOUR MARK, LOKI, YOU WILL BE STRICKEN FROM THE BOOKS OF HEL.
YOU WILL BE HEL-BOUND NO MORE.
WONDERFUL.
WITH THE PROPHESIED END-TIMES OF RAGNAROK PAST, AN ASGARDIAN'S ONLY DESTINY IS A PLACE IN MY HALLS...
...A DESTINY YOU NO LONGER SHARE.
I MUST. AWAY. I HAVE ETERNITY TO TEND TO.
WELL DONE. BUT I HAVE TO ASK YOU--IS ABSOLUTE FREEDOM WORTH THAT MUCH? THIS MUCH RISK?
YOU OF ALL BEINGS SHOULD KNOW: FREEDOM IS THE ONLY THING WORTH ANYTHING.

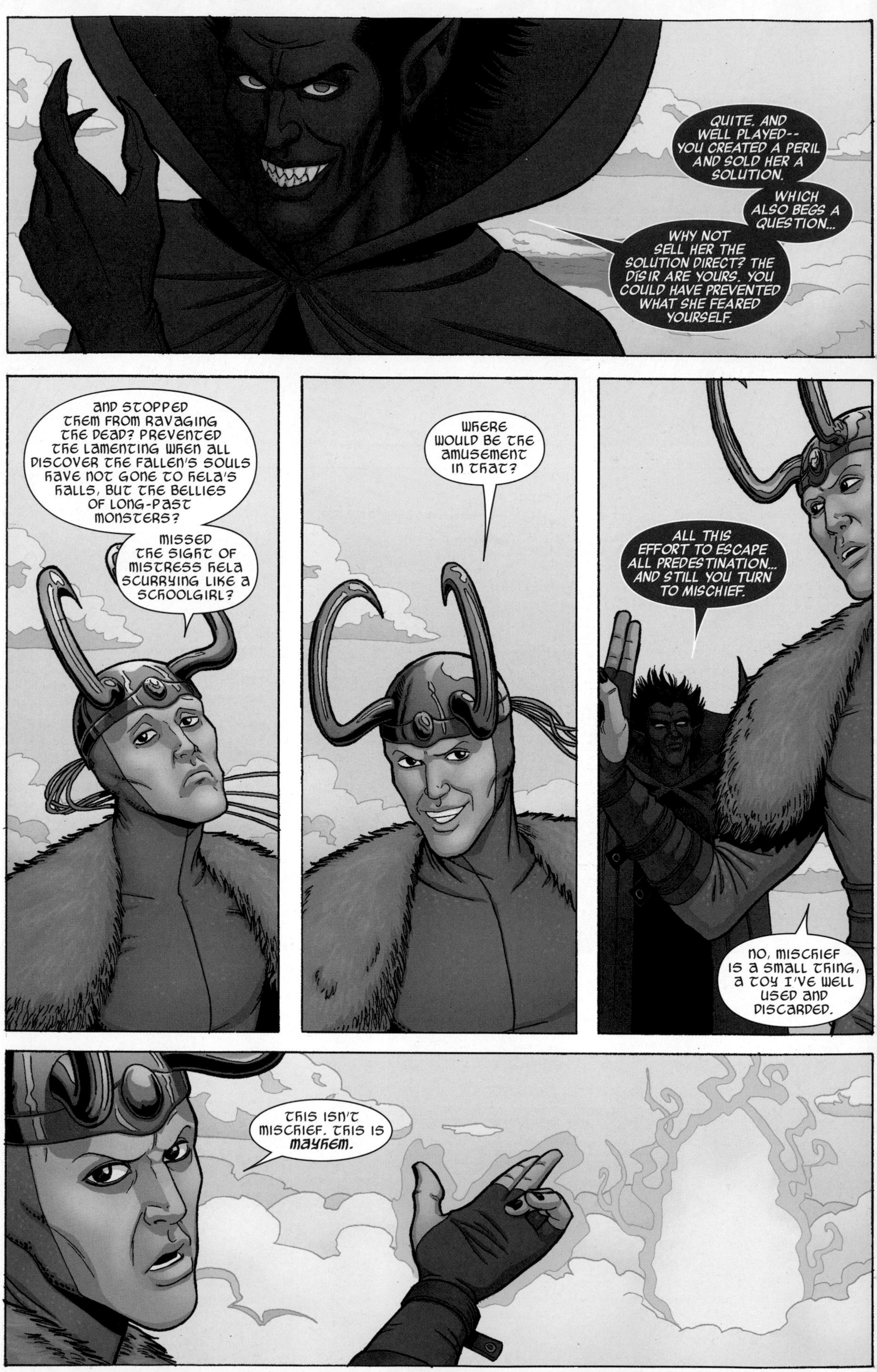
QUITE. AND WELL PLAYED-- YOU CREATED A PERIL AND SOLD HER A SOLUTION.
WHICH ALSO BEGS A QUESTION...
WHY NOT SELL HER THE SOLUTION DIRECT? THE DISIR ARE YOURS. YOU COULD HAVE PREVENTED WHAT SHE FEARED YOURSELF.
AND STOPPED THEM FROM RAVAGING THE DEAD? PREVENTED THE LAMENTING WHEN ALL DISCOVER THE FALLEN'S SOULS HAVE NOT GONE TO HELA'S HALLS, BUT THE BELLIES OF LONG-PAST MONSTERS?
MISSED THE SIGHT OF MISTRESS HELA SCURRYING LIKE A SCHOOLGIRL?
WHERE WOULD BE THE AMUSEMENT IN THAT?
ALL THIS EFFORT TO ESCAPE ALL PREDESTINATION... AND STILL YOU TURN TO MISCHIEF.
NO, MISCHIEF IS A SMALL THING, A TOY I'VE WELL USED AND DISCARDED.
THIS ISN'T MISCHIEF. THIS IS *MAYHEM.*

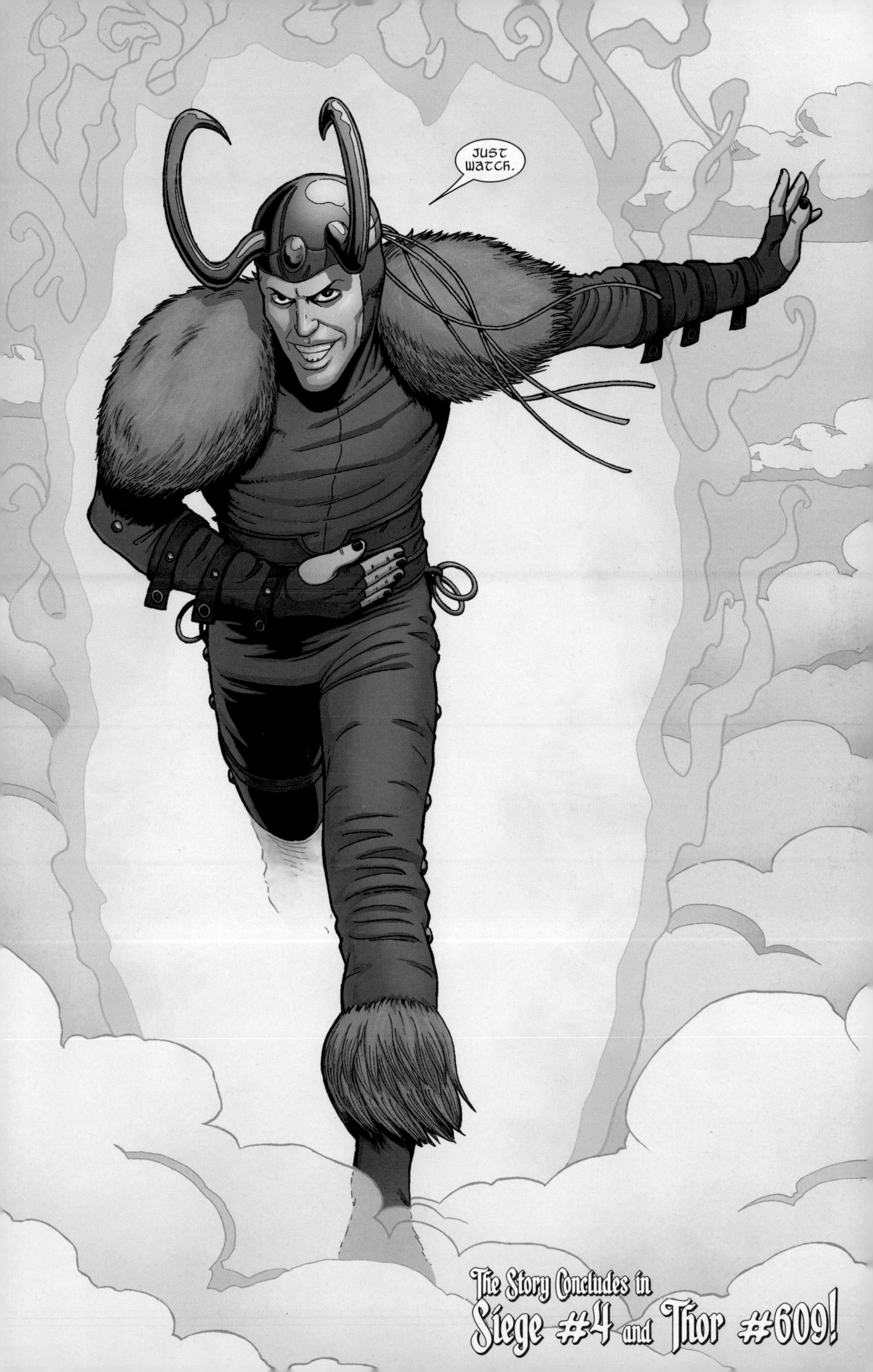
JUST WATCH.
The Story Concludes in
Siege #4 and Thor #609!

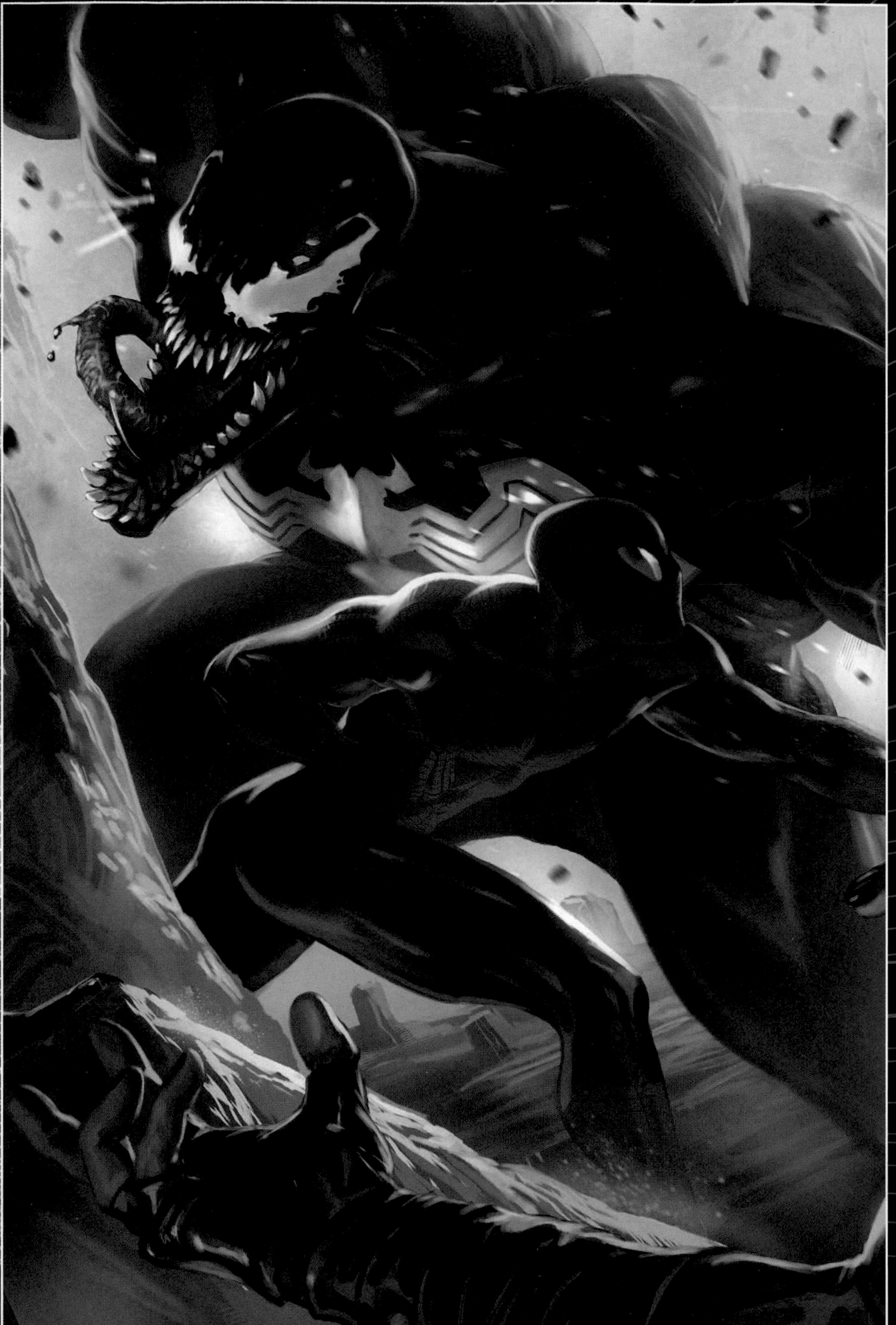

SIEGE: SPIDER-MAN

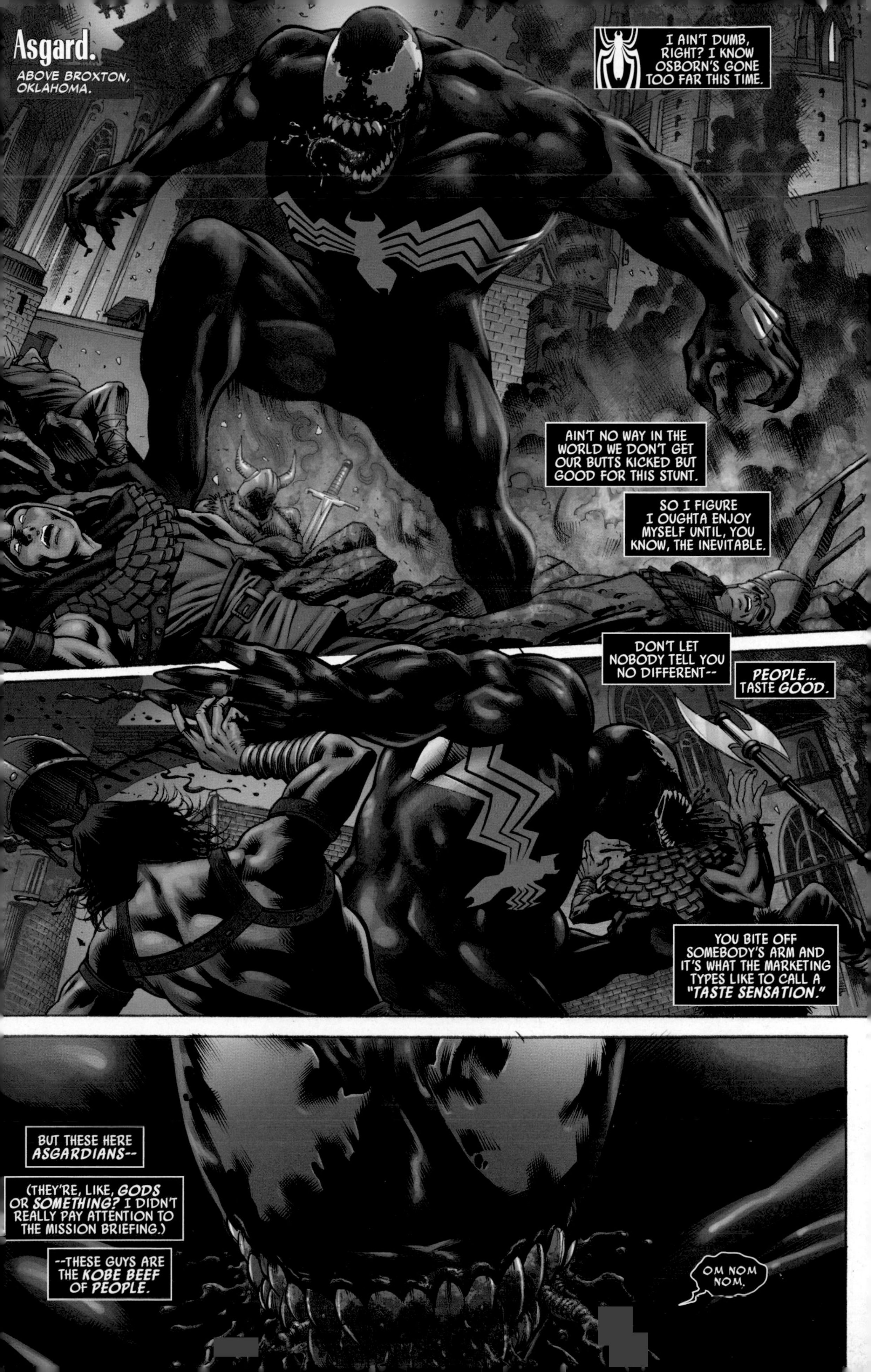
Asgard.
ABOVE BROXTON, OKLAHOMA.
I AIN'T DUMB, RIGHT? I KNOW OSBORN'S GONE TOO FAR THIS TIME.
AIN'T NO WAY IN THE WORLD WE DON'T GET OUR BUTTS KICKED BUT GOOD FOR THIS STUNT.
SO I FIGURE I OUGHTA ENJOY MYSELF UNTIL, YOU KNOW, THE INEVITABLE.
DON'T LET NOBODY TELL YOU NO DIFFERENT--
PEOPLE... TASTE GOOD.
YOU BITE OFF SOMEBODY'S ARM AND IT'S WHAT THE MARKETING TYPES LIKE TO CALL A "TASTE SENSATION."
BUT THESE HERE ASGARDIANS--
(THEY'RE, LIKE, GODS OR SOMETHING? I DIDN'T REALLY PAY ATTENTION TO THE MISSION BRIEFING.)
--THESE GUYS ARE THE KOBE BEEF OF PEOPLE.
OM NOM NOM.

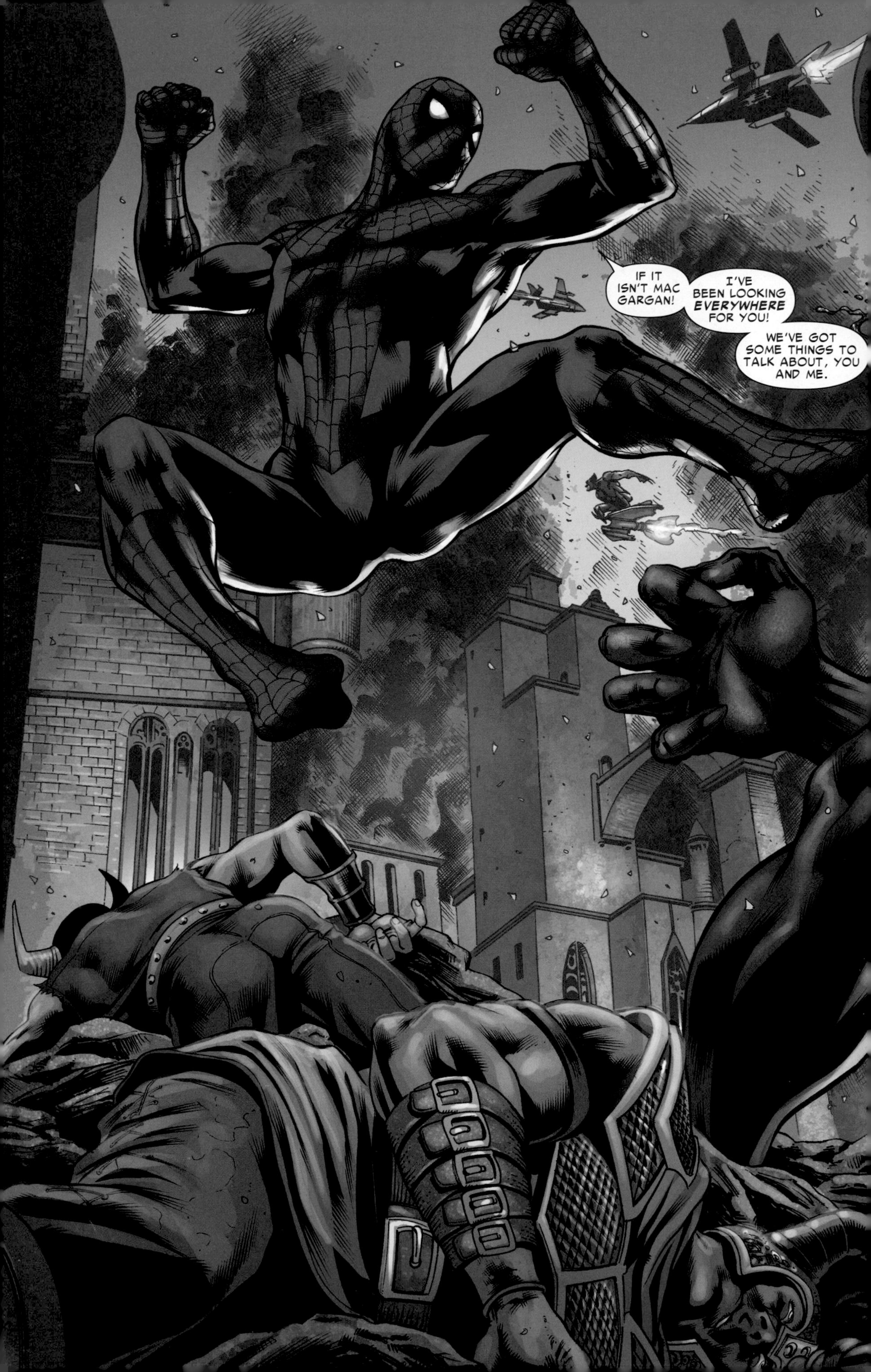
IF IT ISN'T MAC GARGAN!
I'VE BEEN LOOKING EVERYWHERE FOR YOU!
WE'VE GOT SOME THINGS TO TALK ABOUT, YOU AND ME.

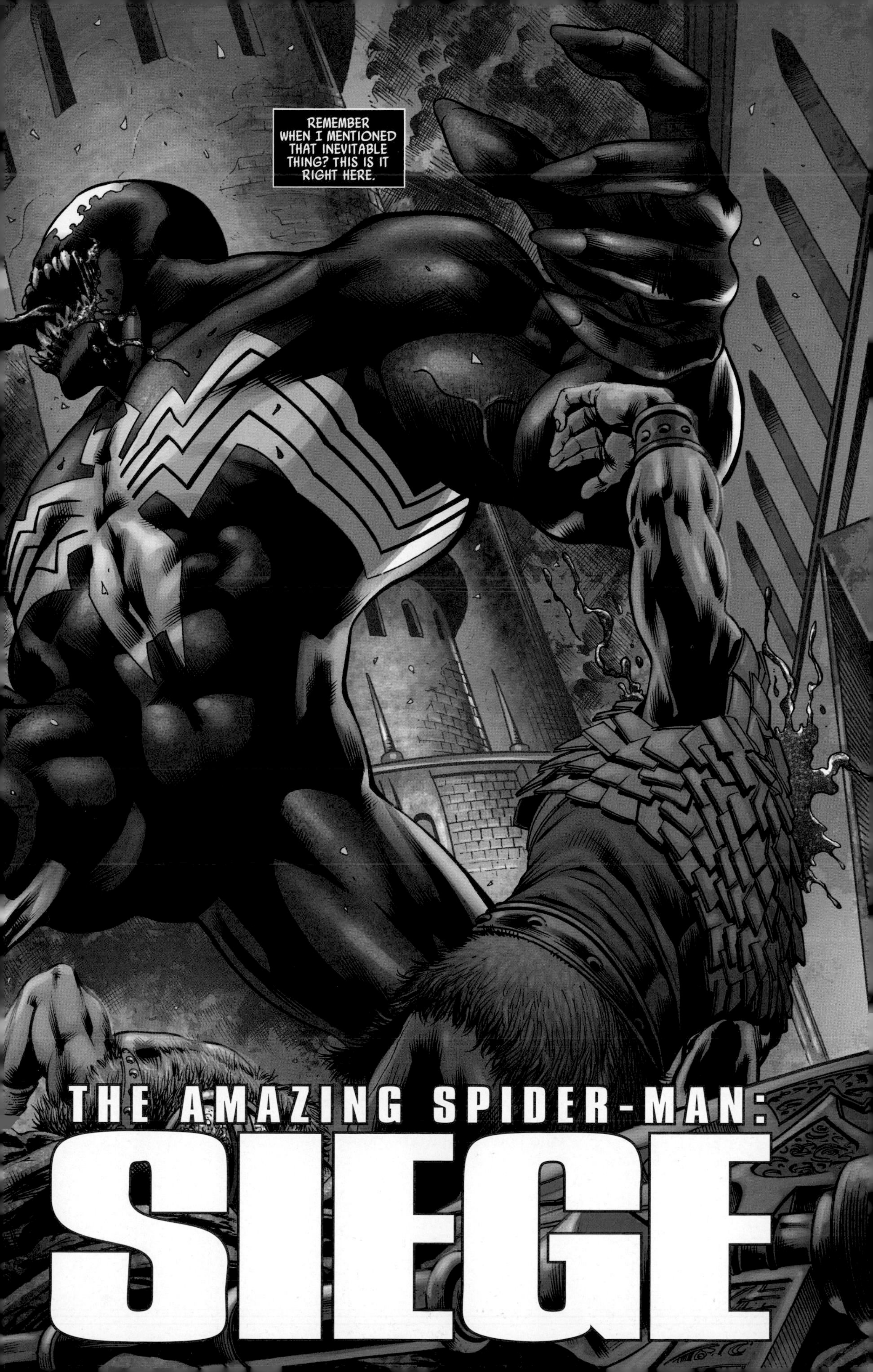
REMEMBER WHEN I MENTIONED THAT INEVITABLE THING? THIS IS IT RIGHT HERE.
THE AMAZING SPIDER-MAN:
SIEGE

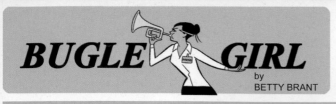

BUGLE GIRL
by BETTY BRANT

RSS | ARCHIVE | ABOUT | CONTACT | ADVERTISE

NEW USER? CREATE AN ACCOUNT!

SEARCH GO

Brian Reed – Writer
Marco Santucci – Artist
Chris Sotomayor – Color Artist
VC's Joe Caramagna – Letterer
Marko Djurdjevic – Cover
Tom Brennan – Editor
Stephen Wacker – Supervising Editor
Tom Brevoort – Executive Editor
Joe Quesada – Editor in Chief
Dan Buckley – Publisher
Alan Fine – Executive Producer

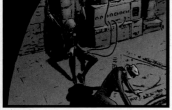

DISAPPEARING ACT? Mayor Jameson has authorized the police department to create a special task force on kidnapping in the wake of a rash of disappearances amongst New York women. Cassandra Webb & Mattie Franklin have been missing since last... more...

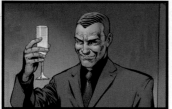

STORMIN' NORMAN STRIKES AGAIN! Stormin' Norman Strikes Again! Norman Osborn, director of H.A.M.M.E.R. and the U.S. Government's defacto leader on all things Superhuman, has turned the full force of his Avengers and Camp Hammond's Initiative forces on Asgard after Asgardian Volstagg accidentally destroyed Chicago's Soldier Field... more...

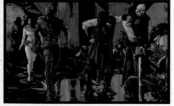

CAN'T STAND THE HEAT? Witnesses say the Hell's Kitchen neighborhood, site of an "epic" firefight between H.A.M.M.E.R. agents and Daredevil, has been cordoned off by mysterious interests. No one will talk on the record, but one source says "something big is brewing in Hell's Kitchen." more...

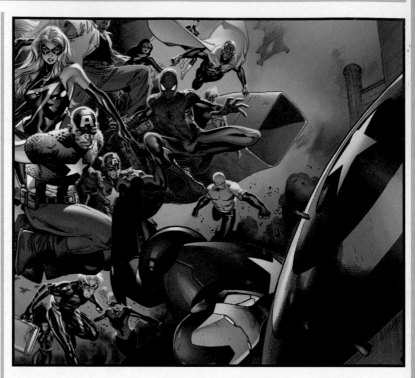

When Norman Osborn, the former Green Goblin, became the public face of heroism after the Skrull Invasion, he was handed the keys to national and superhuman security. He installed his own Avengers team, made up of super villains in the guise of true heroes, including Mac Gargan, the former Venom, disguised as Spider-Man. His team took control of S.H.I.E.L.D.'s old operation and were beloved across the country as Earth's Mightiest Heroes.

Needless to say, Spider-Man and the other Avengers, living in hiding and on the run from their now-empowered deadliest foes, weren't thrilled. For the better part of a year, they've been publicly torn down and pushed to their limits by Osborn and his cronies.

But when Osborn teamed with the evil Norse god Loki to lay siege to Asgard – and took down the Mighty Thor in the process – a line was crossed. Led by the original Captain America, Steve Rogers, a group of Avengers came to Asgard to take their world back.

Included in this group of Avengers are Spider-Man and Ms. Marvel, who have grown close over the past year. But any interest Spidey has in Ms. Marvel will have to wait – 'cuz there's a slobbering psycho who's been eating people and calling himself Spider-Man who needs a thwomping.

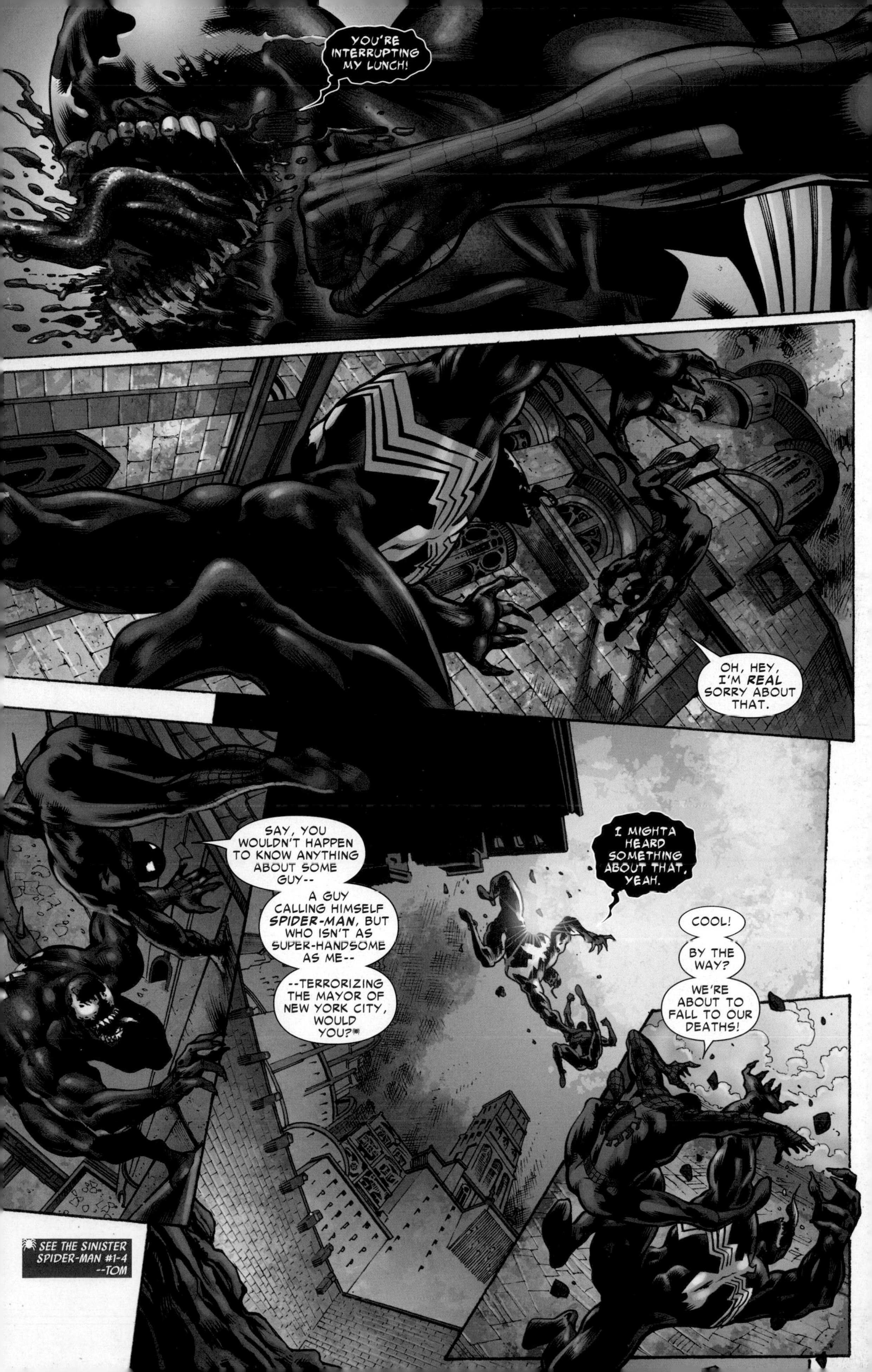

YOU'RE INTERRUPTING MY LUNCH!
OH, HEY, I'M REAL SORRY ABOUT THAT.
SAY, YOU WOULDN'T HAPPEN TO KNOW ANYTHING ABOUT SOME GUY--
A GUY CALLING HIMSELF SPIDER-MAN, BUT WHO ISN'T AS SUPER-HANDSOME AS ME--
--TERRORIZING THE MAYOR OF NEW YORK CITY, WOULD YOU?*
I MIGHTA HEARD SOMETHING ABOUT THAT, YEAH.
COOL!
BY THE WAY?
WE'RE ABOUT TO FALL TO OUR DEATHS!
*SEE THE SINISTER SPIDER-MAN #1-4 --TOM

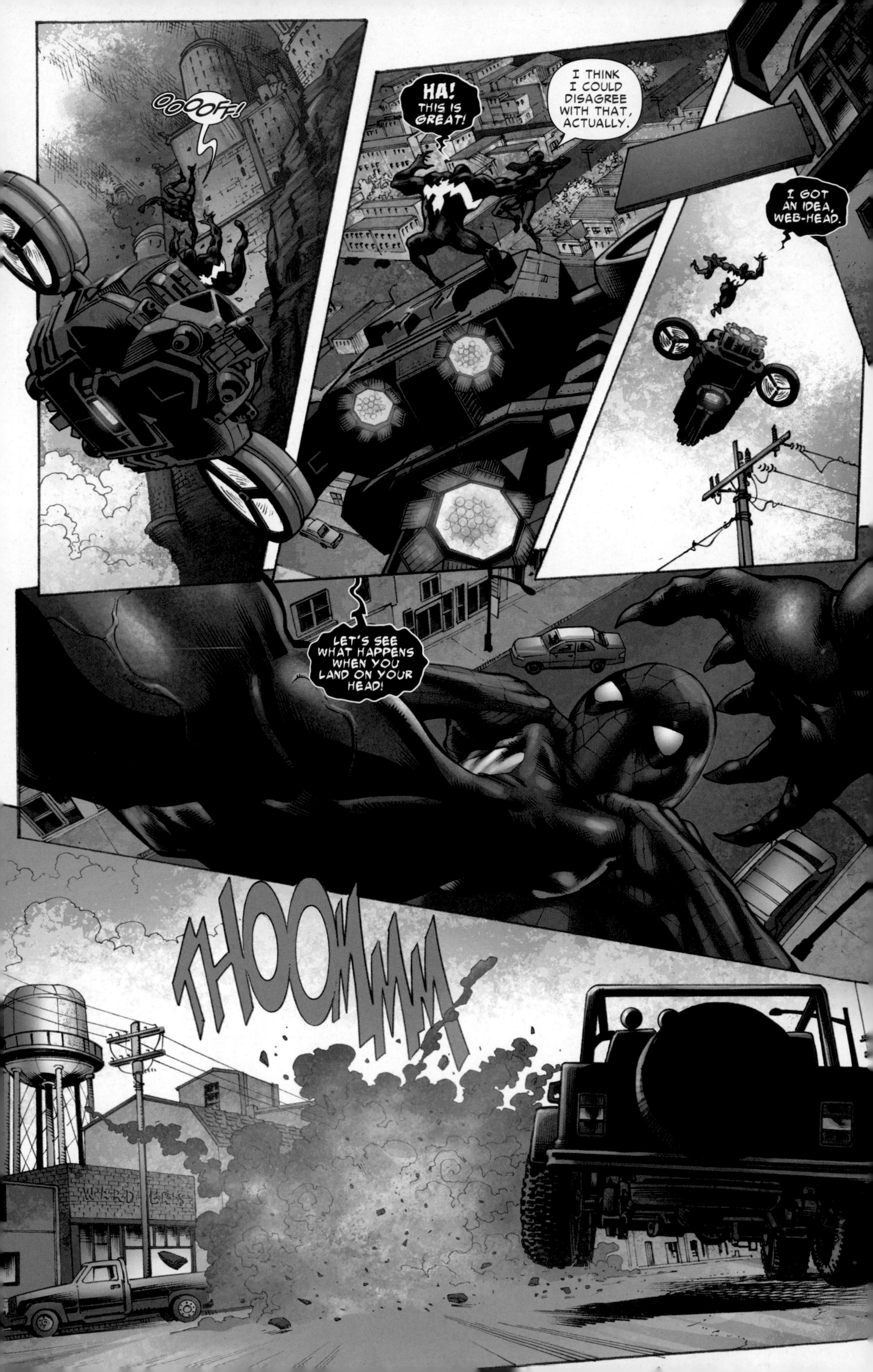
OOOOFF!
HA! THIS IS GREAT!
I THINK I COULD DISAGREE WITH THAT, ACTUALLY.
I GOT AN IDEA, WEB-HEAD.
LET'S SEE WHAT HAPPENS WHEN YOU LAND ON YOUR HEAD!
THOOMMM

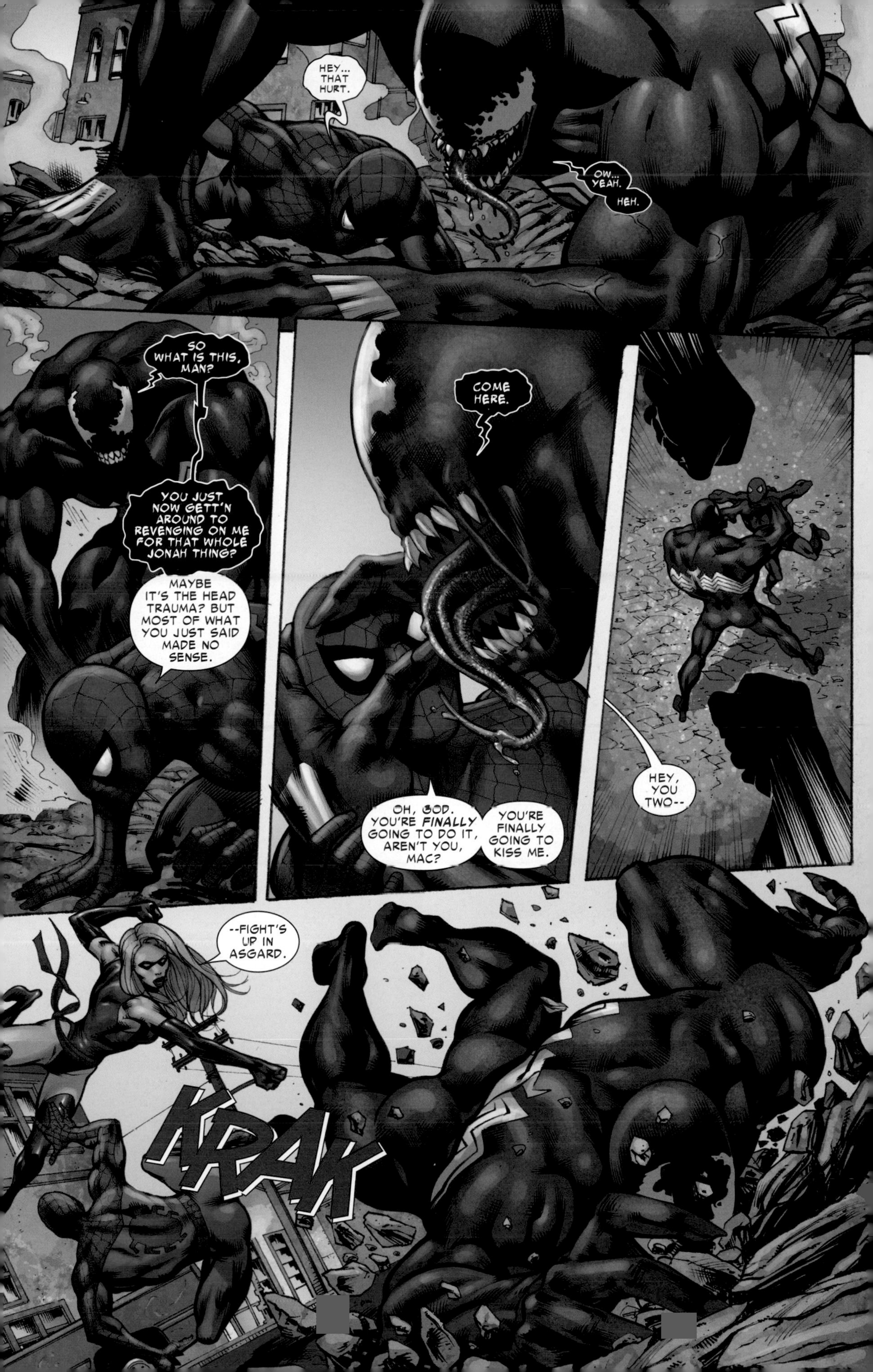
HEY... THAT HURT.
OW... YEAH.
HEH.
SO WHAT IS THIS, MAN?
YOU JUST NOW GETT'N AROUND TO REVENGING ON ME FOR THAT WHOLE JONAH THING?
MAYBE IT'S THE HEAD TRAUMA? BUT MOST OF WHAT YOU JUST SAID MADE NO SENSE.
COME HERE.
OH, GOD. YOU'RE FINALLY GOING TO DO IT, AREN'T YOU, MAC?
YOU'RE FINALLY GOING TO KISS ME.
HEY, YOU TWO--
--FIGHT'S UP IN ASGARD.
KRAK

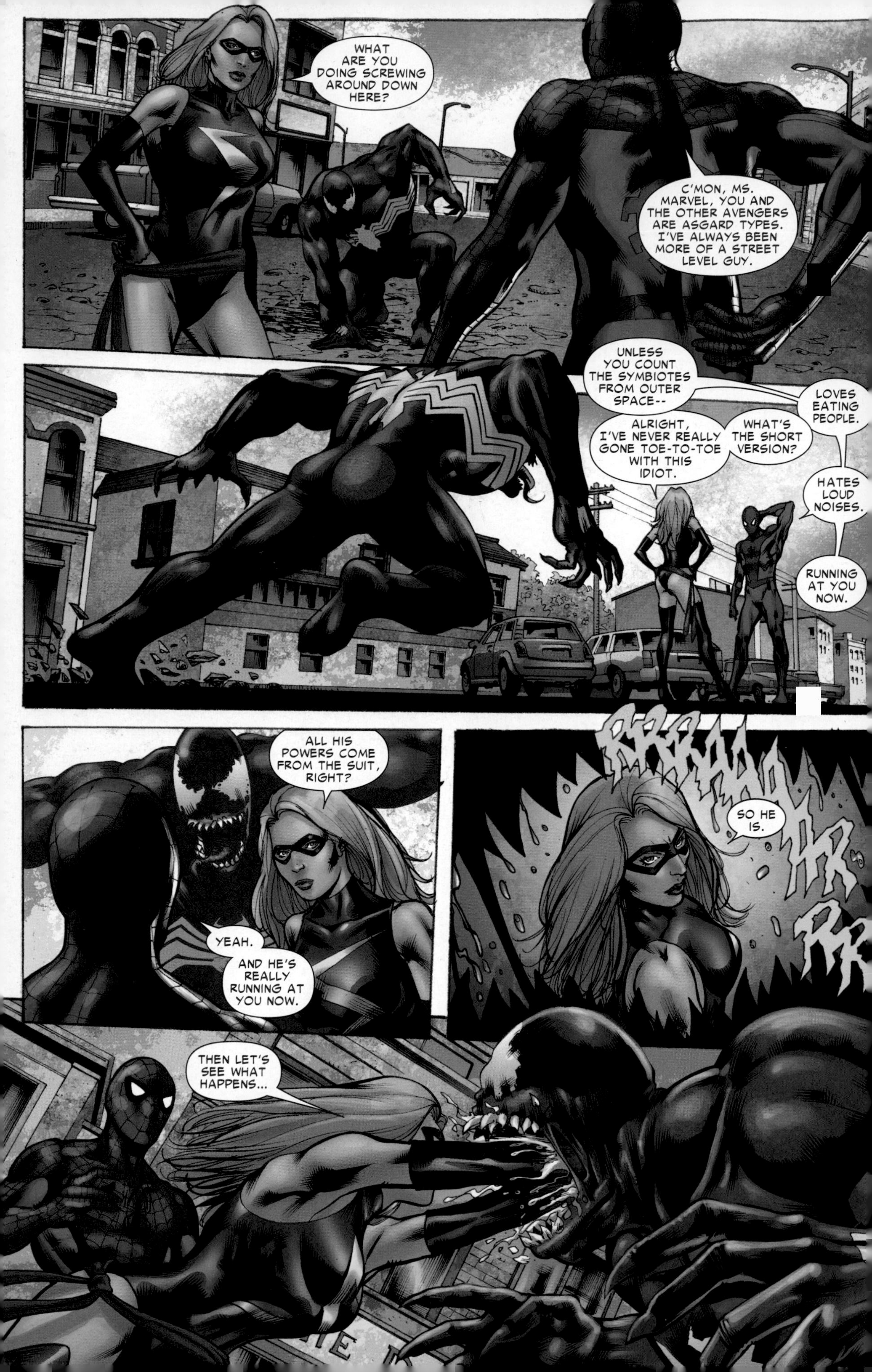
WHAT ARE YOU DOING SCREWING AROUND DOWN HERE?
C'MON, MS. MARVEL, YOU AND THE OTHER AVENGERS ARE ASGARD TYPES. I'VE ALWAYS BEEN MORE OF A STREET LEVEL GUY.
UNLESS YOU COUNT THE SYMBIOTES FROM OUTER SPACE--
ALRIGHT, I'VE NEVER REALLY GONE TOE-TO-TOE WITH THIS IDIOT.
WHAT'S THE SHORT VERSION?
LOVES EATING PEOPLE.
HATES LOUD NOISES.
RUNNING AT YOU NOW.
ALL HIS POWERS COME FROM THE SUIT, RIGHT?
YEAH.
AND HE'S REALLY RUNNING AT YOU NOW.
RRRAAAHR RR
SO HE IS.
THEN LET'S SEE WHAT HAPPENS...

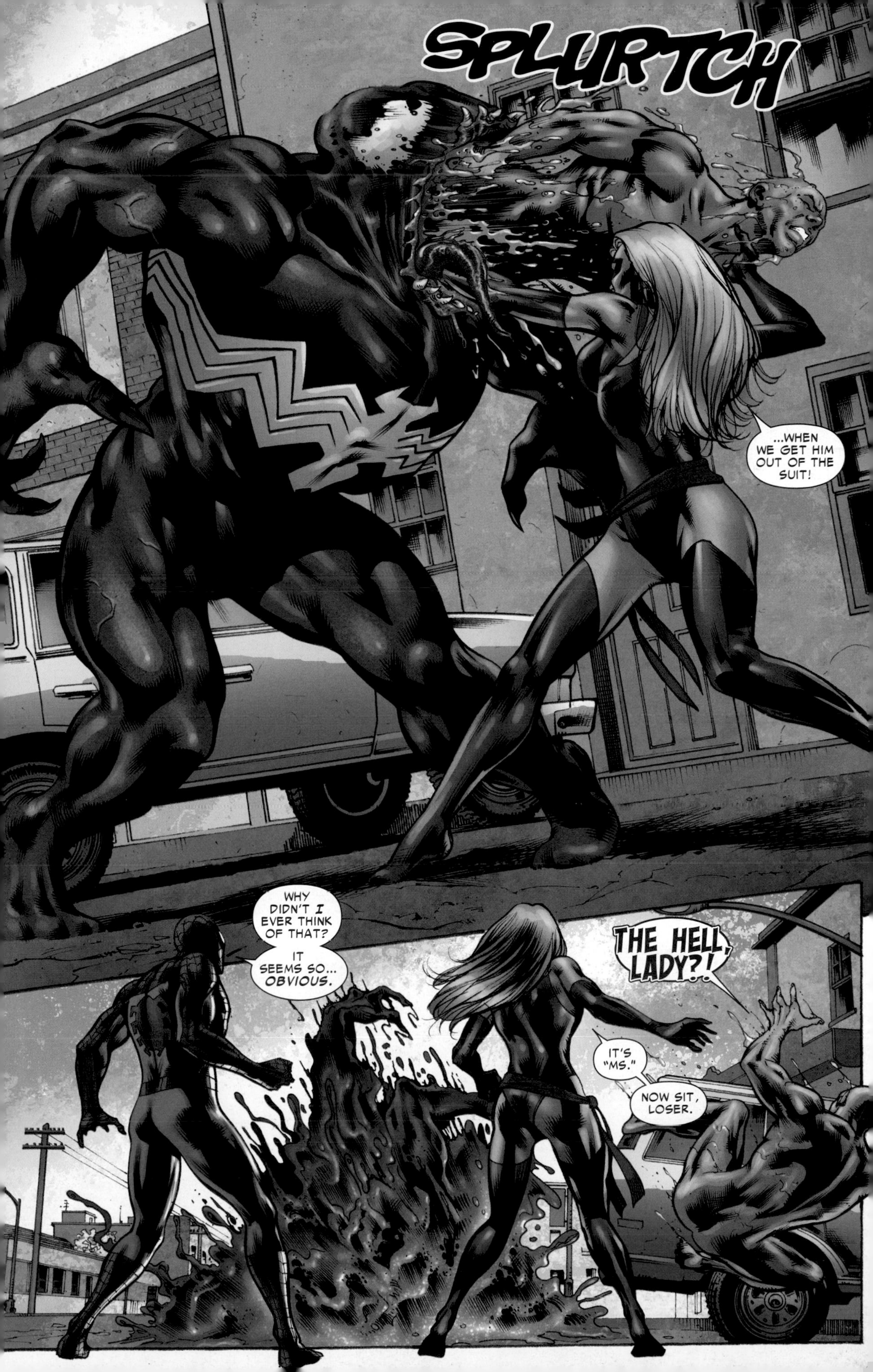
SPLURTCH
...WHEN WE GET HIM OUT OF THE SUIT!
WHY DIDN'T I EVER THINK OF THAT?
IT SEEMS SO... OBVIOUS.
THE HELL, LADY?!
IT'S "MS."
NOW SIT, LOSER.

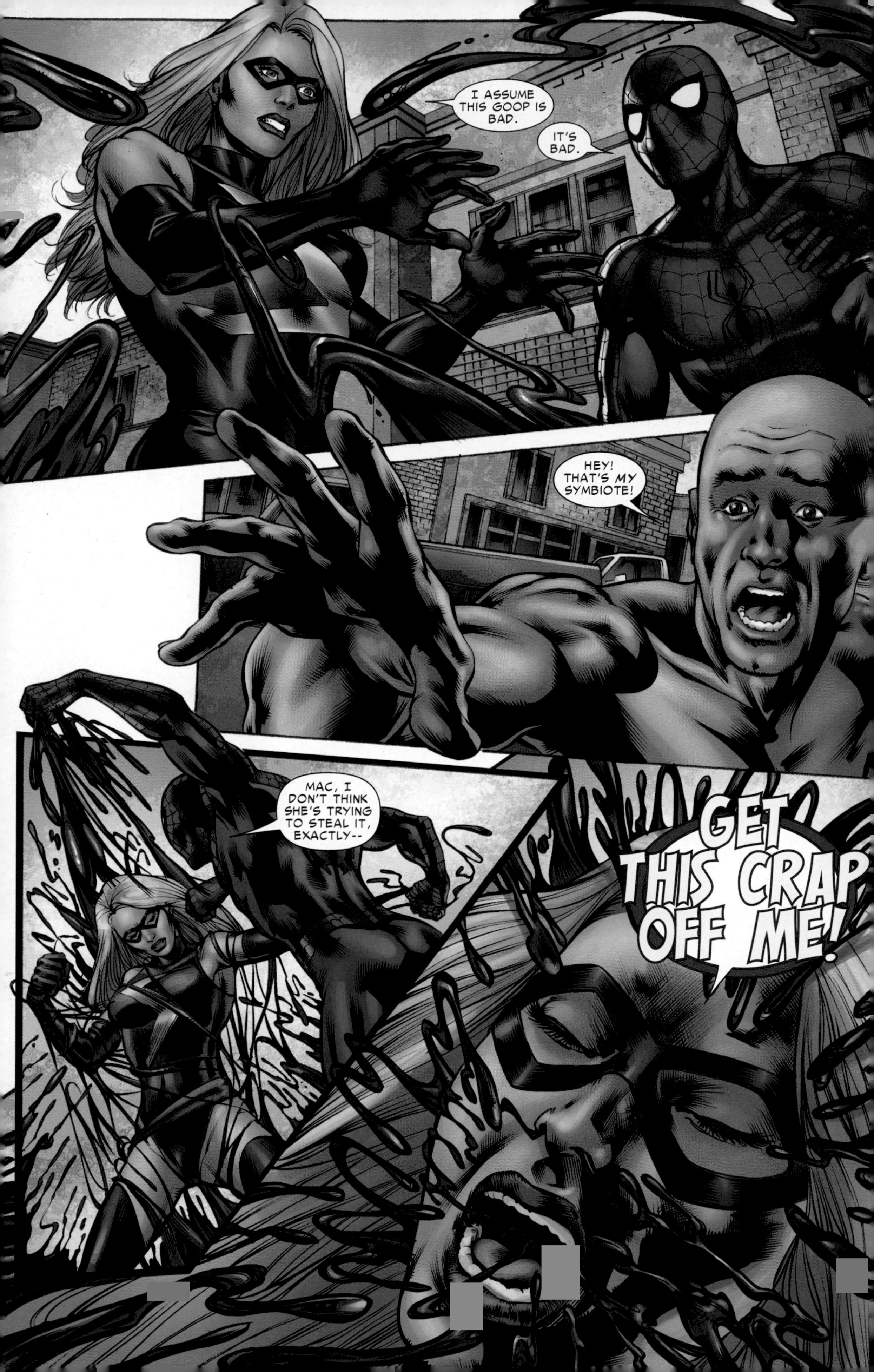
I ASSUME THIS GOOP IS BAD.
IT'S BAD.
HEY! THAT'S MY SYMBIOTE!
MAC, I DON'T THINK SHE'S TRYING TO STEAL IT, EXACTLY--
GET THIS CRAP OFF ME!

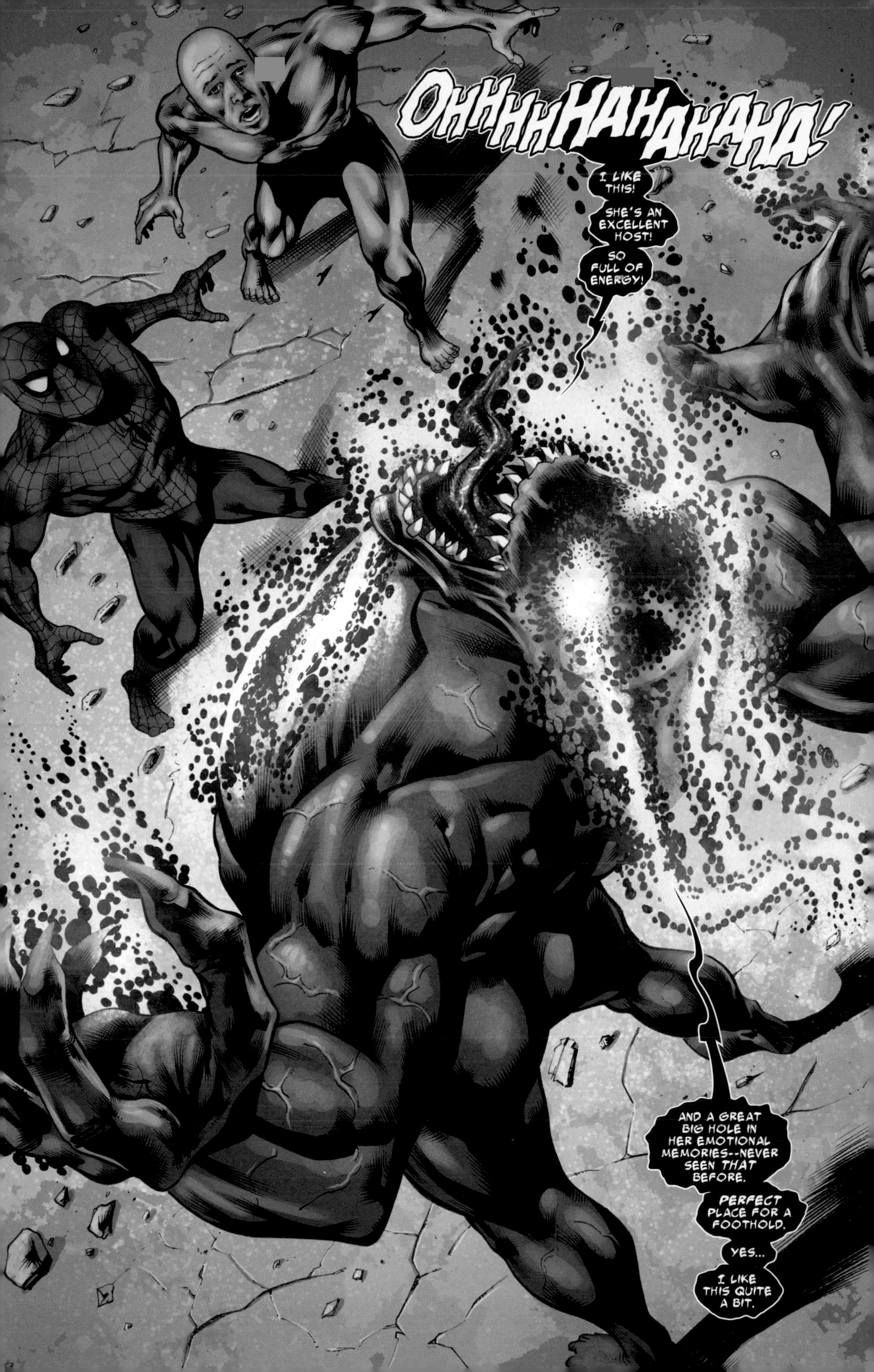
OHHHHHAHAHAHAHA!
I LIKE THIS!
SHE'S AN EXCELLENT HOST!
SO FULL OF ENERGY!
AND A GREAT BIG HOLE IN HER EMOTIONAL MEMORIES--NEVER SEEN THAT BEFORE.
PERFECT PLACE FOR A FOOTHOLD.
YES...
I LIKE THIS QUITE A BIT.

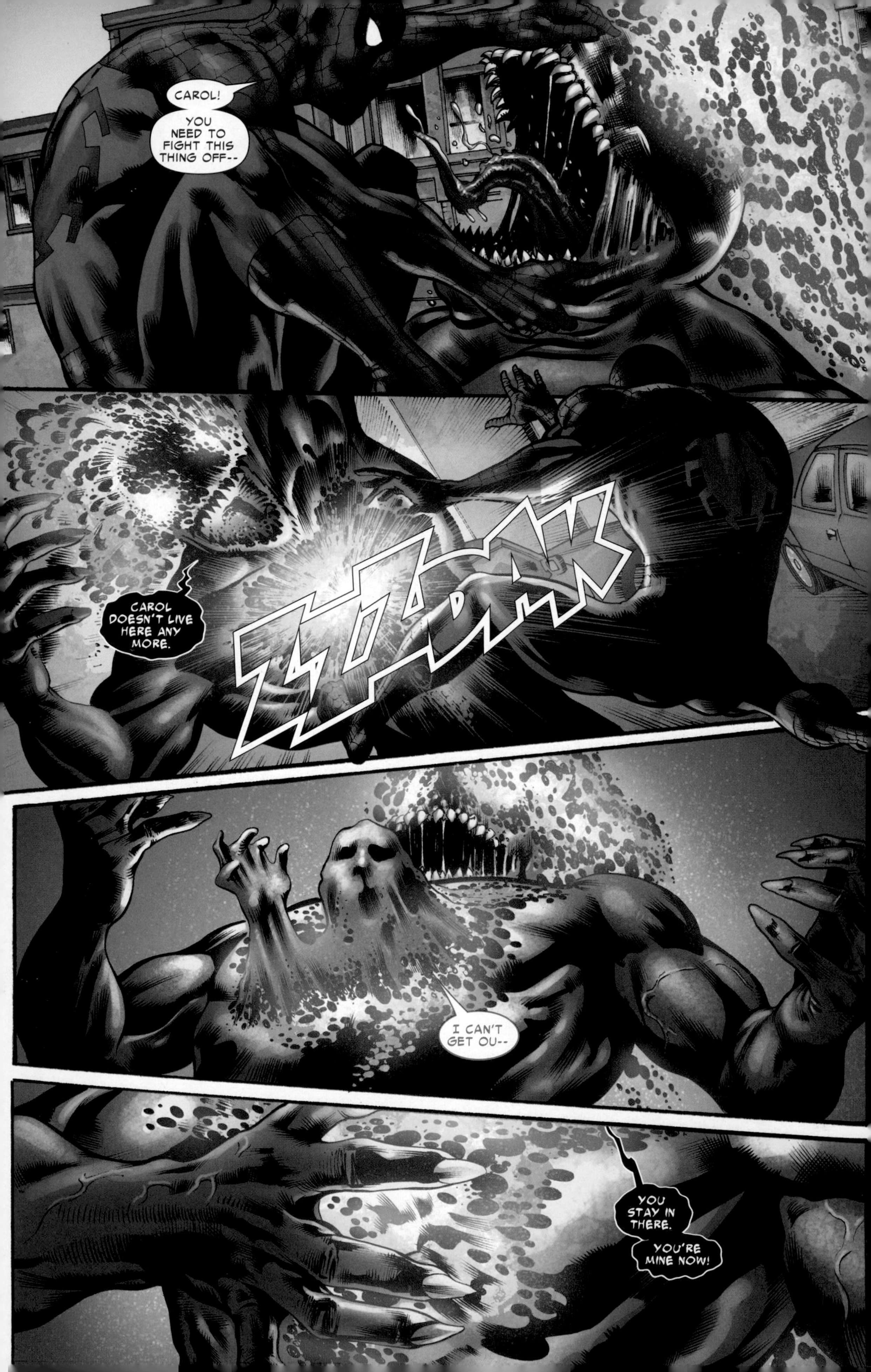
CAROL!
YOU NEED TO FIGHT THIS THING OFF--
CAROL DOESN'T LIVE HERE ANY MORE.
ZZDAK
I CAN'T GET OU--
YOU STAY IN THERE.
YOU'RE MINE NOW!

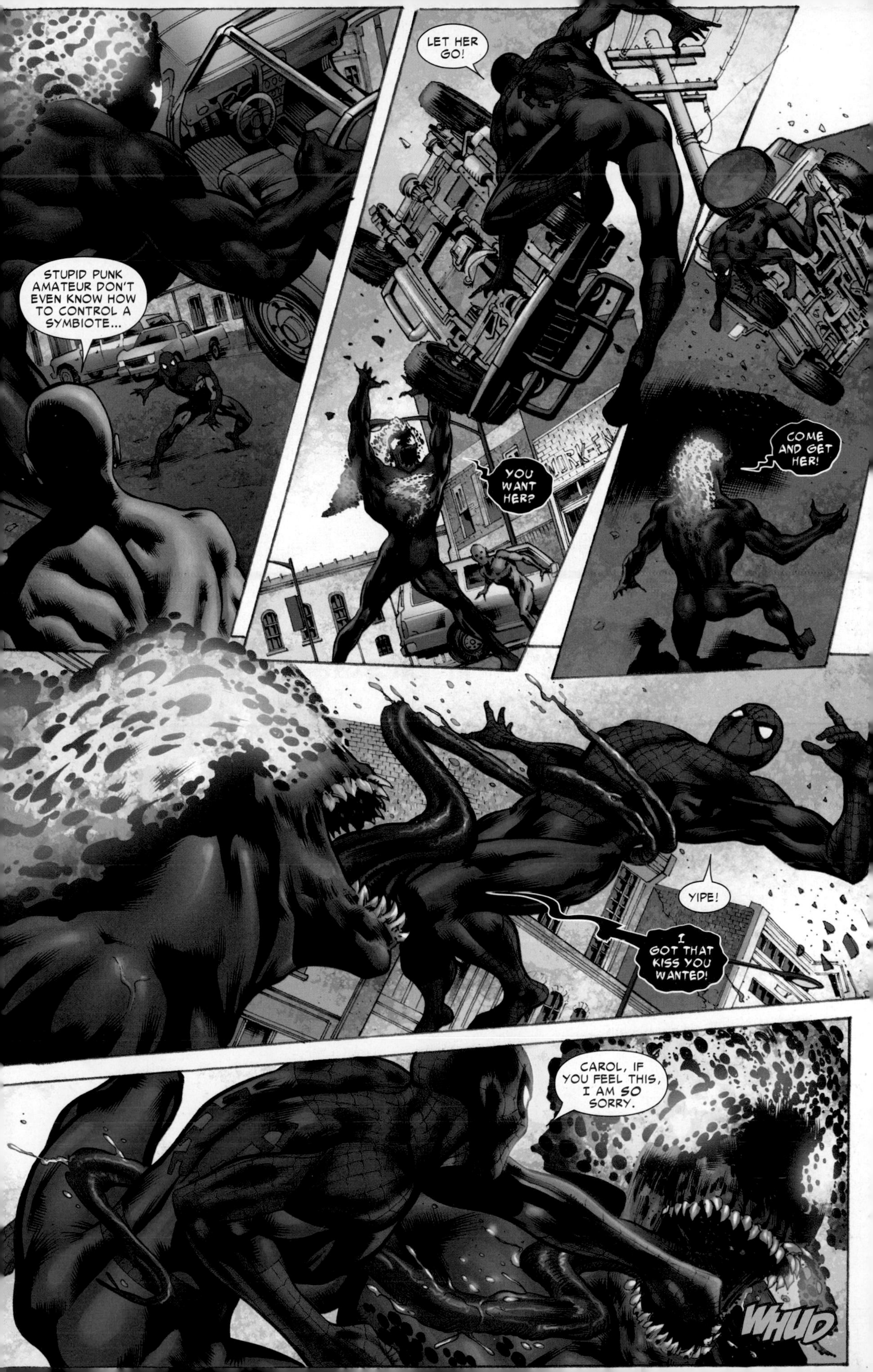

STUPID PUNK AMATEUR DON'T EVEN KNOW HOW TO CONTROL A SYMBIOTE...
LET HER GO!
YOU WANT HER?
COME AND GET HER!
YIPE!
I GOT THAT KISS YOU WANTED!
CAROL, IF YOU FEEL THIS, I AM SO SORRY.
WHUD

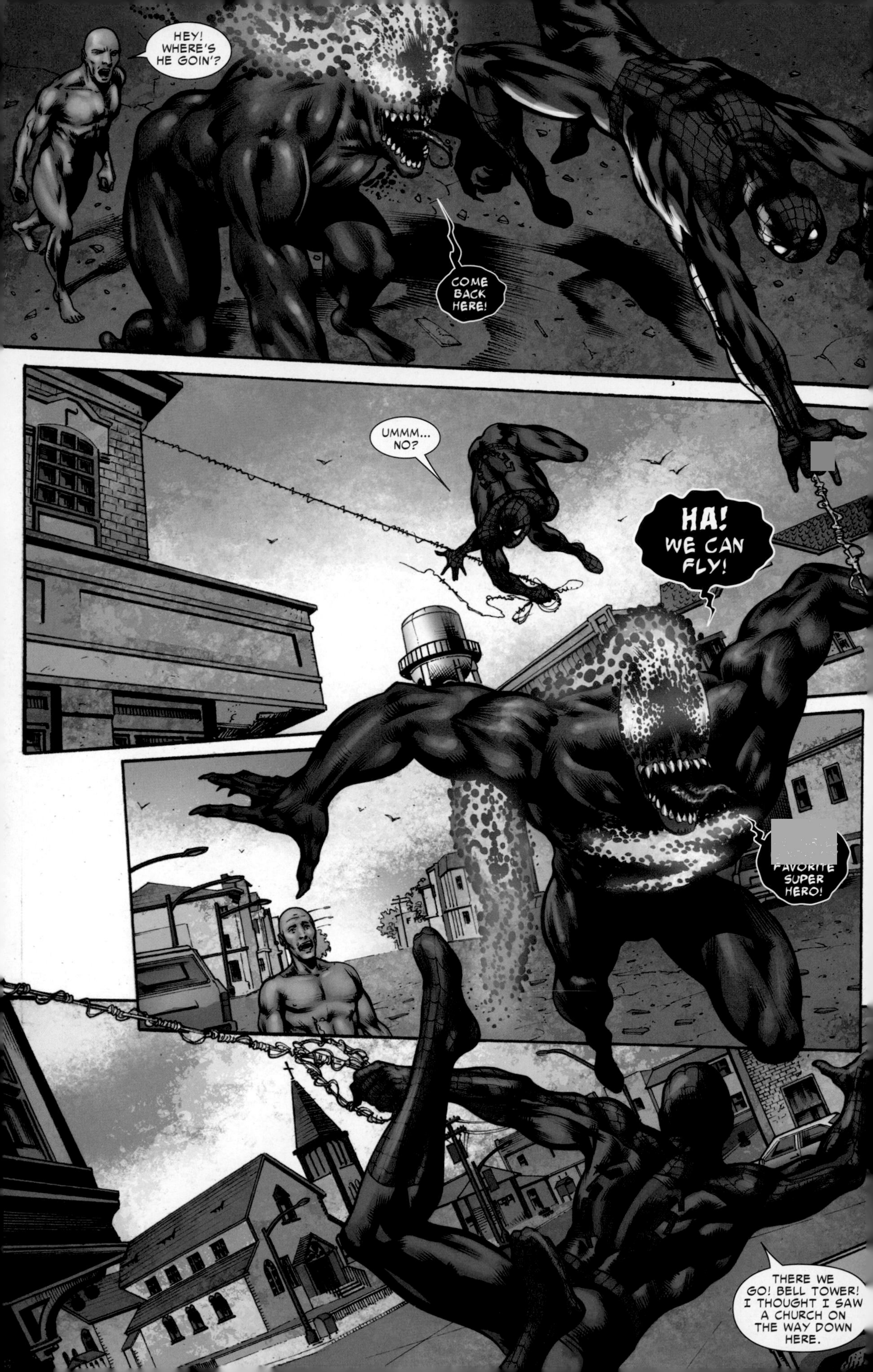
HEY! WHERE'S HE GOIN'?
COME BACK HERE!
UMMM... NO?
HA! WE CAN FLY!
FAVORITE SUPER HERO!
THERE WE GO! BELL TOWER! I THOUGHT I SAW A CHURCH ON THE WAY DOWN HERE.

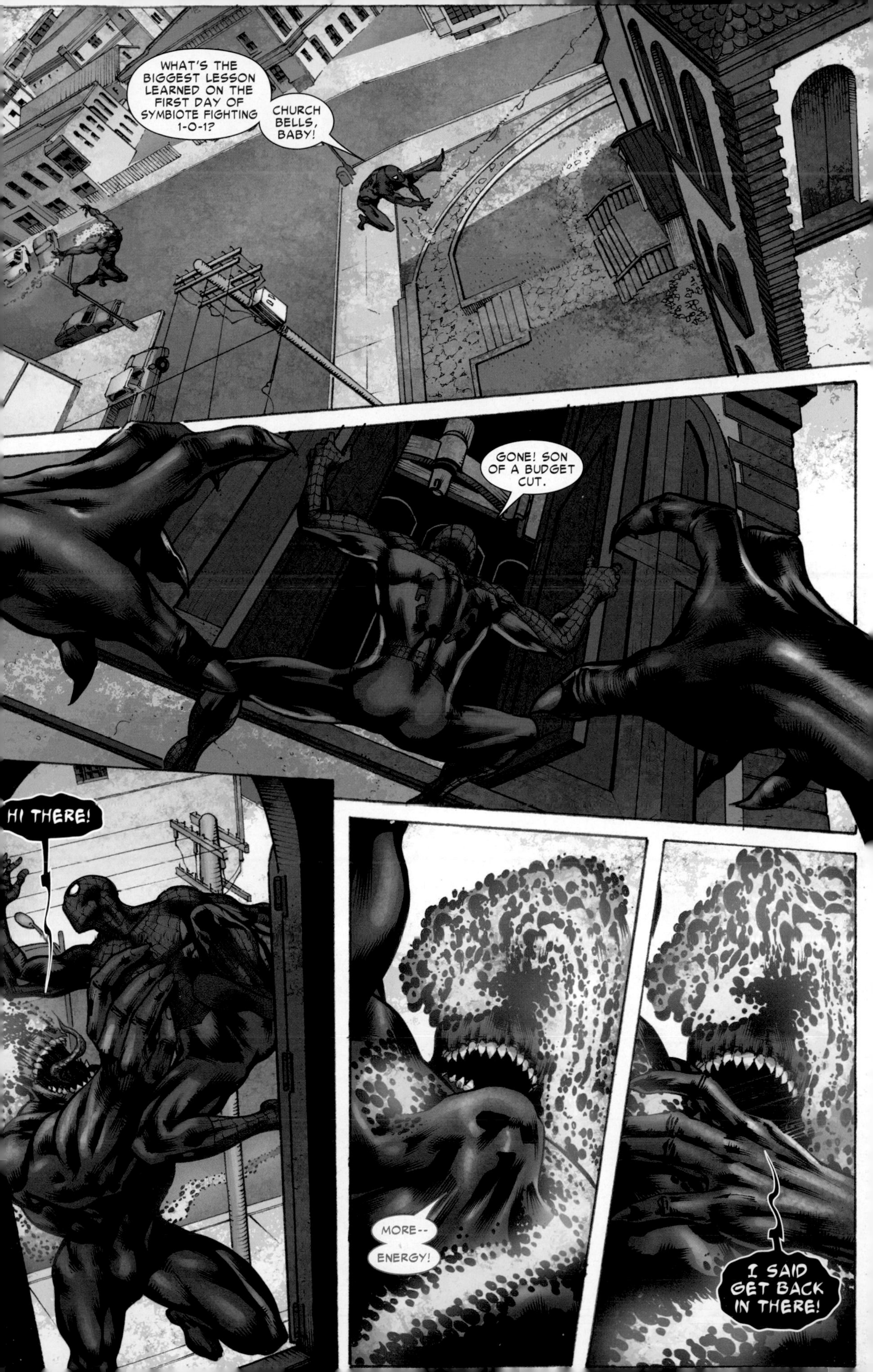
WHAT'S THE BIGGEST LESSON LEARNED ON THE FIRST DAY OF SYMBIOTE FIGHTING 1-0-1?
CHURCH BELLS, BABY!
GONE! SON OF A BUDGET CUT.
HI THERE!
MORE--
ENERGY!
I SAID GET BACK IN THERE!

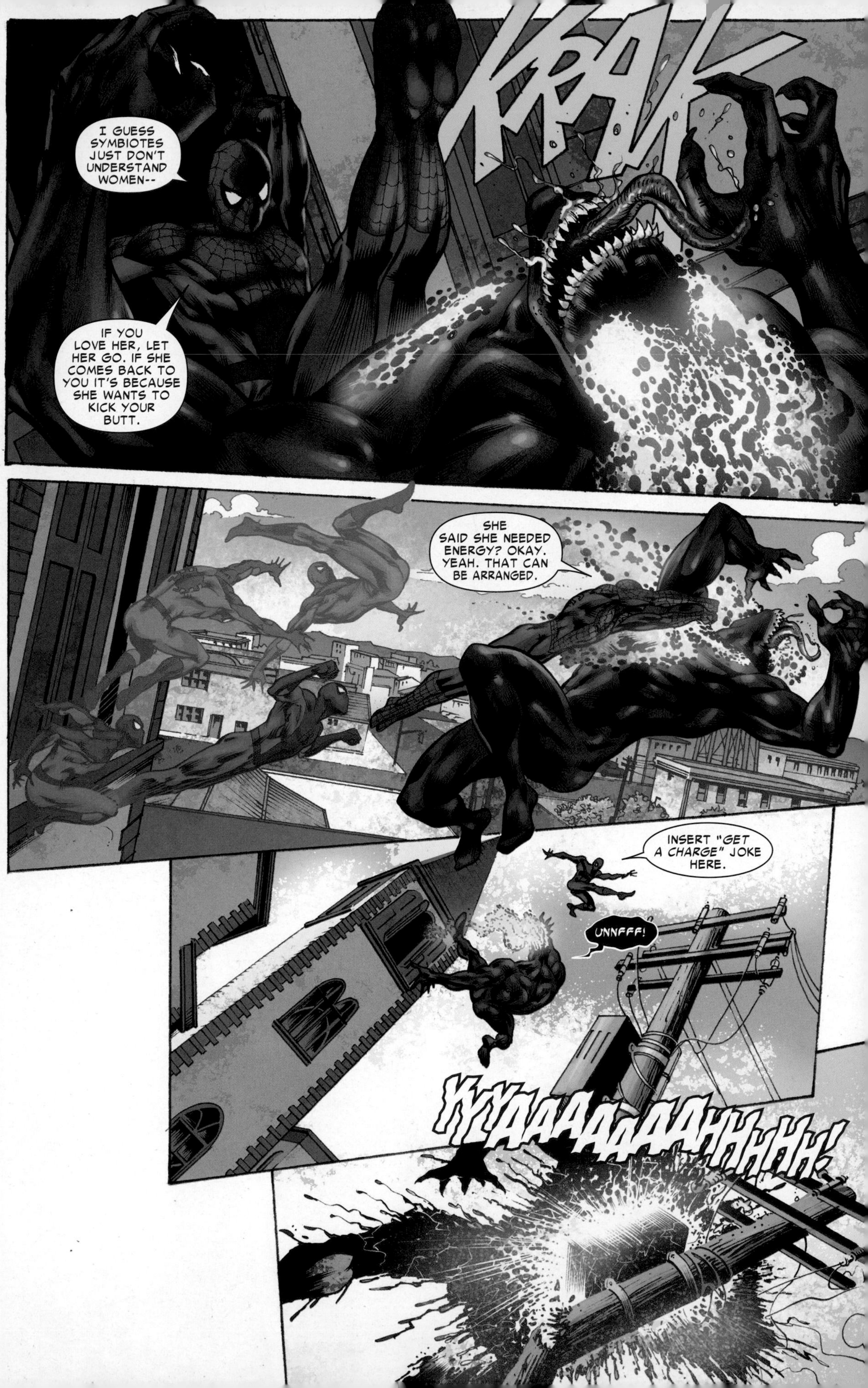

KRAAK
I GUESS SYMBIOTES JUST DON'T UNDERSTAND WOMEN--
IF YOU LOVE HER, LET HER GO. IF SHE COMES BACK TO YOU IT'S BECAUSE SHE WANTS TO KICK YOUR BUTT.
SHE SAID SHE NEEDED ENERGY? OKAY. YEAH. THAT CAN BE ARRANGED.
INSERT "GET A CHARGE" JOKE HERE.
UNNFFF!
YYAAAAAAAHHHHH!

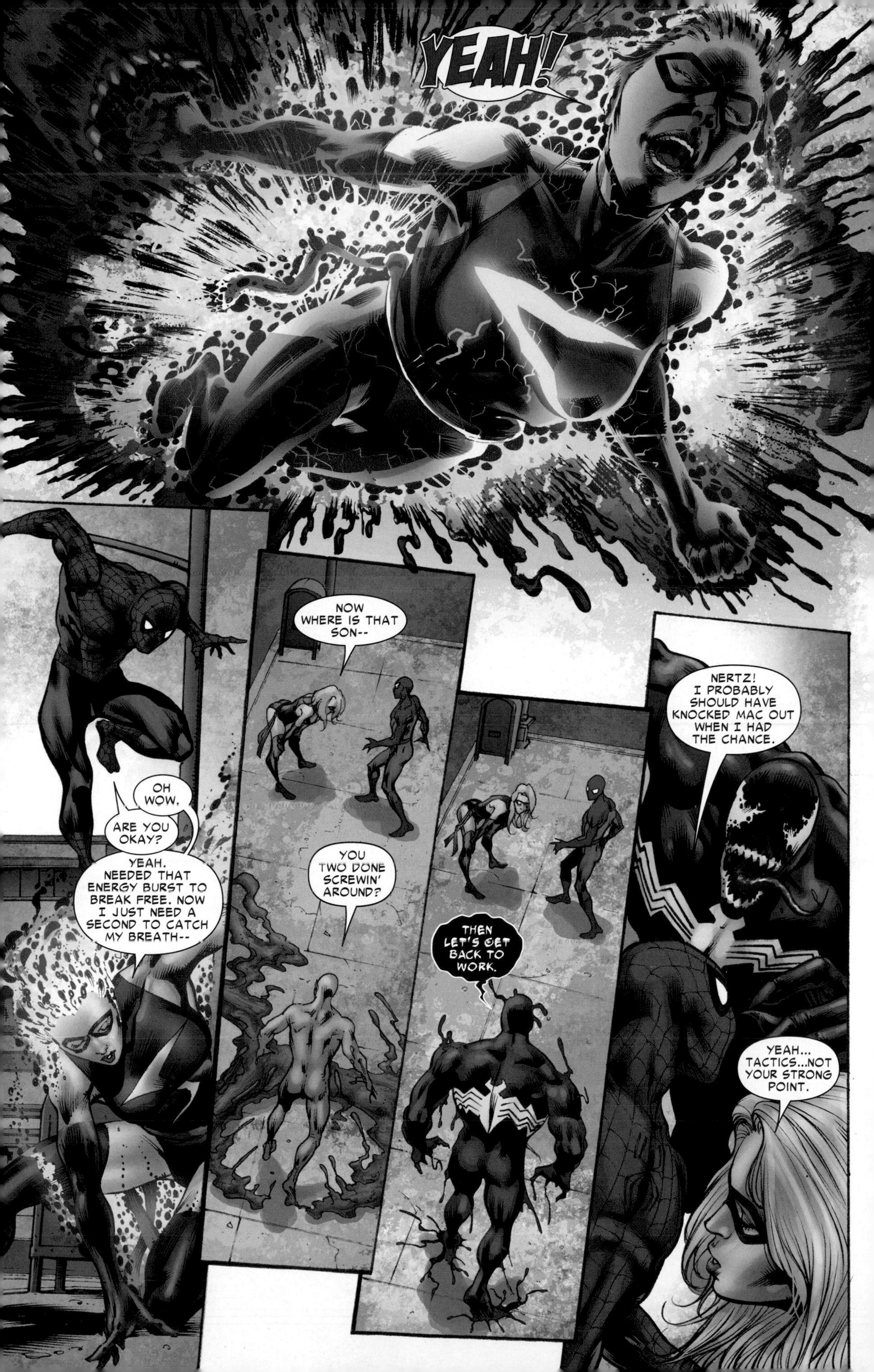
YEAH!
OH WOW,
ARE YOU OKAY?
YEAH. NEEDED THAT ENERGY BURST TO BREAK FREE. NOW I JUST NEED A SECOND TO CATCH MY BREATH--
NOW WHERE IS THAT SON--
YOU TWO DONE SCREWIN' AROUND?
THEN LET'S GET BACK TO WORK.
NERTZ! I PROBABLY SHOULD HAVE KNOCKED MAC OUT WHEN I HAD THE CHANCE.
YEAH... TACTICS...NOT YOUR STRONG POINT.

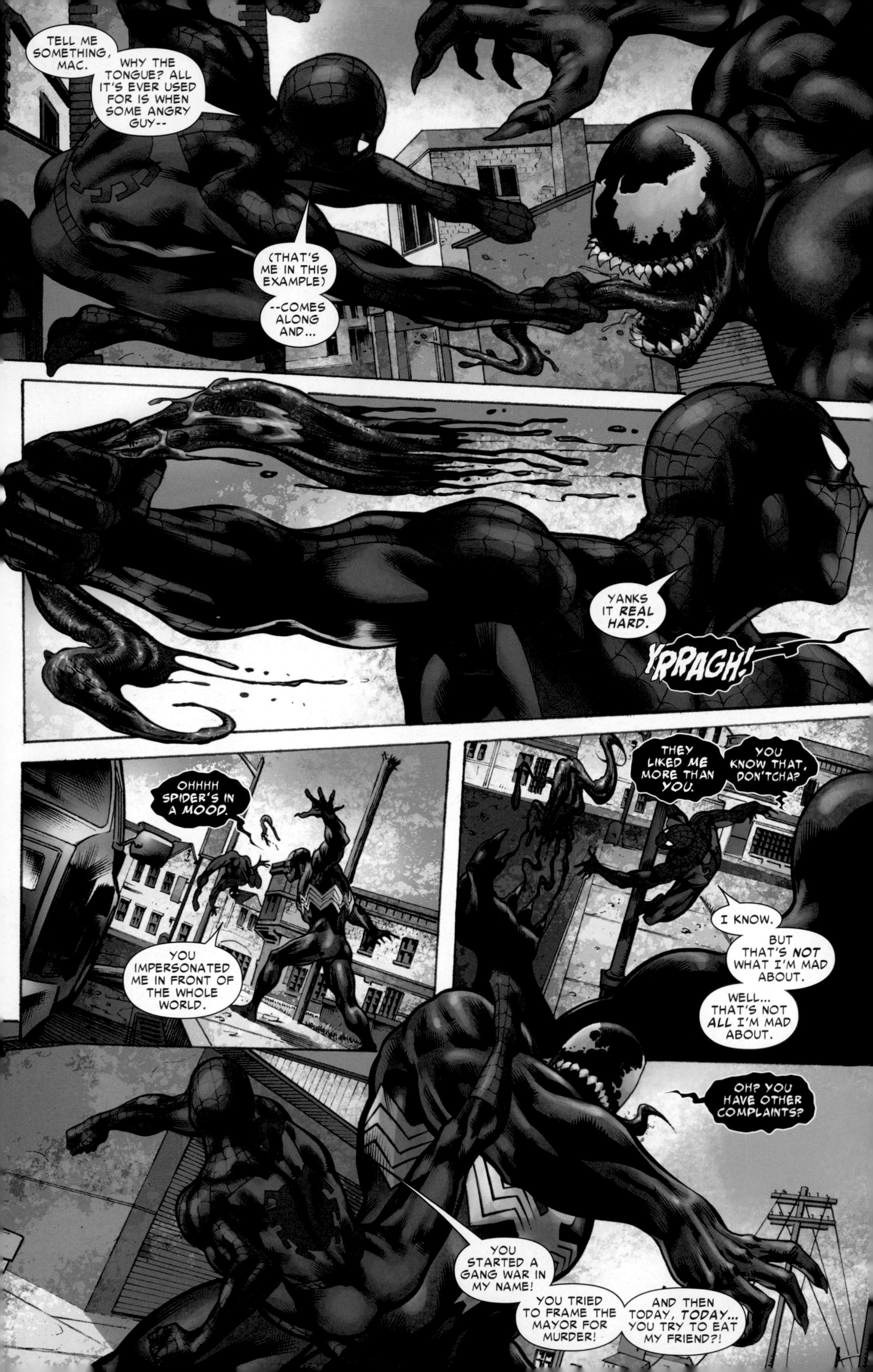
TELL ME SOMETHING, MAC.
WHY THE TONGUE? ALL IT'S EVER USED FOR IS WHEN SOME ANGRY GUY--
(THAT'S ME IN THIS EXAMPLE)
--COMES ALONG AND...
YANKS IT REAL HARD.
YRRAGH!
OHHHH SPIDER'S IN A MOOD.
YOU IMPERSONATED ME IN FRONT OF THE WHOLE WORLD.
THEY LIKED ME MORE THAN YOU.
YOU KNOW THAT, DON'TCHA?
I KNOW.
BUT THAT'S NOT WHAT I'M MAD ABOUT.
WELL... THAT'S NOT ALL I'M MAD ABOUT.
OH? YOU HAVE OTHER COMPLAINTS?
YOU STARTED A GANG WAR IN MY NAME!
YOU TRIED TO FRAME THE MAYOR FOR MURDER!
AND THEN TODAY, TODAY... YOU TRY TO EAT MY FRIEND?!

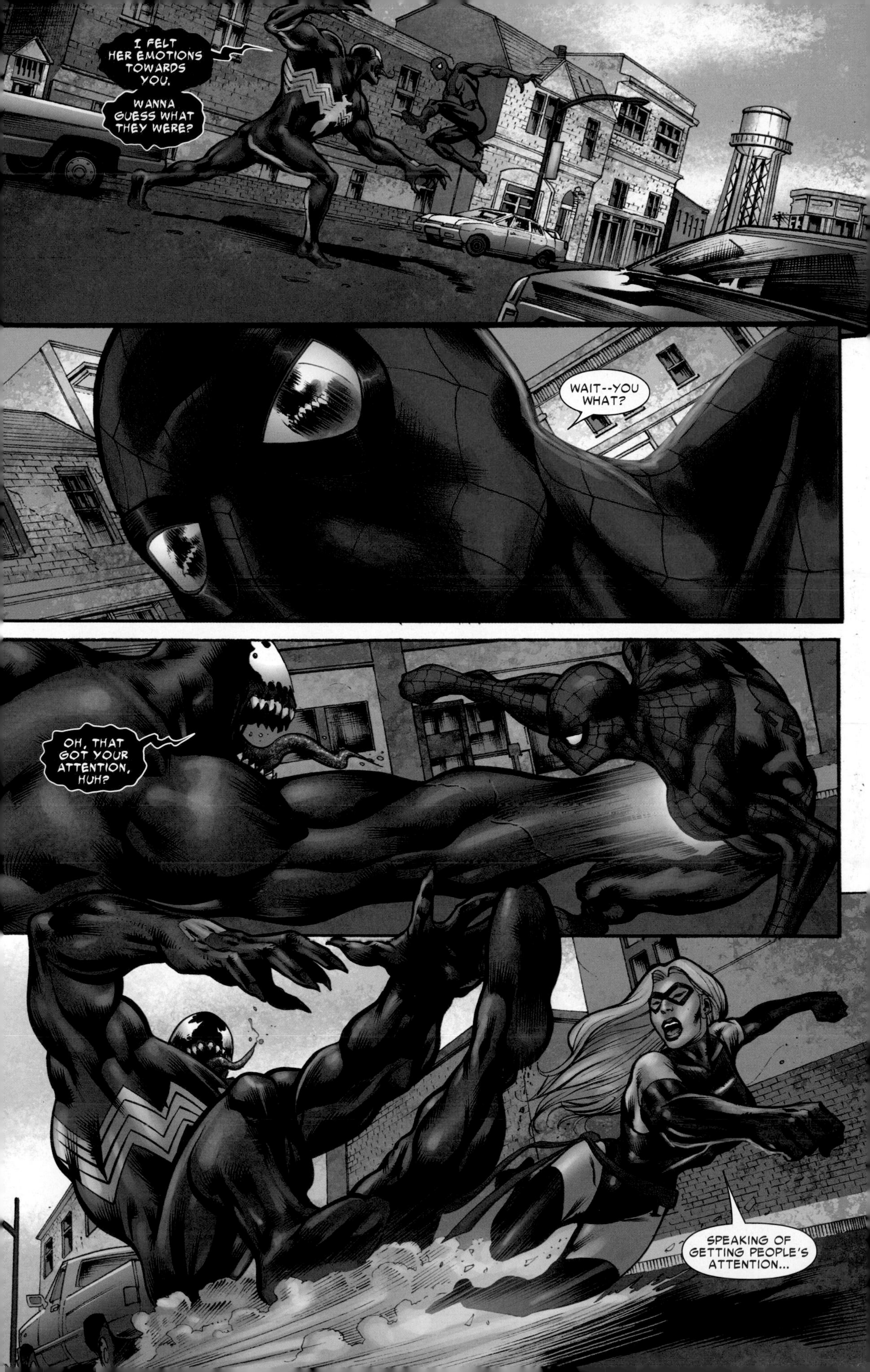
I FELT HER EMOTIONS TOWARDS YOU.
WANNA GUESS WHAT THEY WERE?
WAIT--YOU WHAT?
OH, THAT GOT YOUR ATTENTION, HUH?
SPEAKING OF GETTING PEOPLE'S ATTENTION...

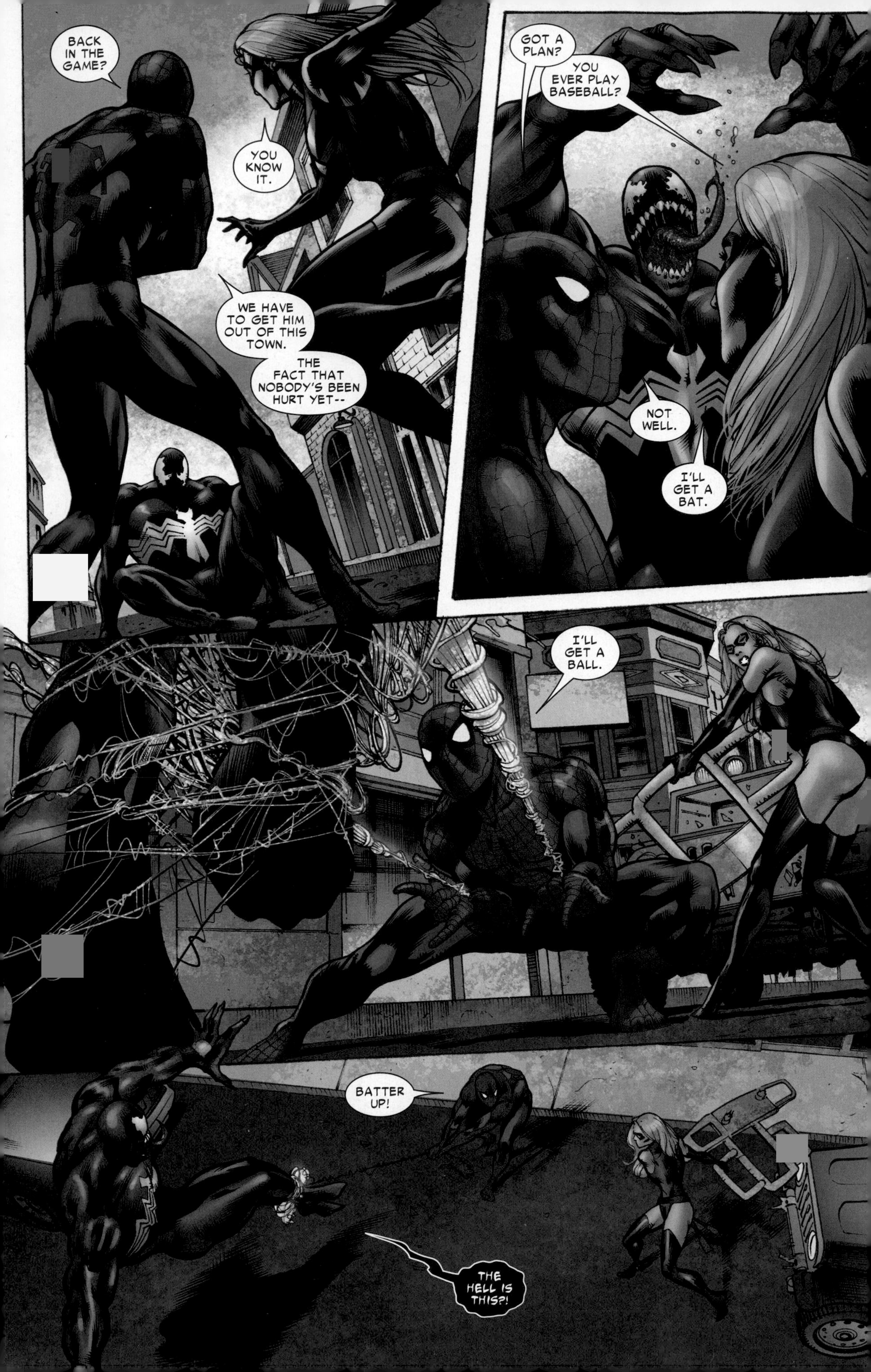
BACK IN THE GAME?
YOU KNOW IT.
WE HAVE TO GET HIM OUT OF THIS TOWN.
THE FACT THAT NOBODY'S BEEN HURT YET--
GOT A PLAN?
YOU EVER PLAY BASEBALL?
NOT WELL.
I'LL GET A BAT.
I'LL GET A BALL.
BATTER UP!
THE HELL IS THIS?!

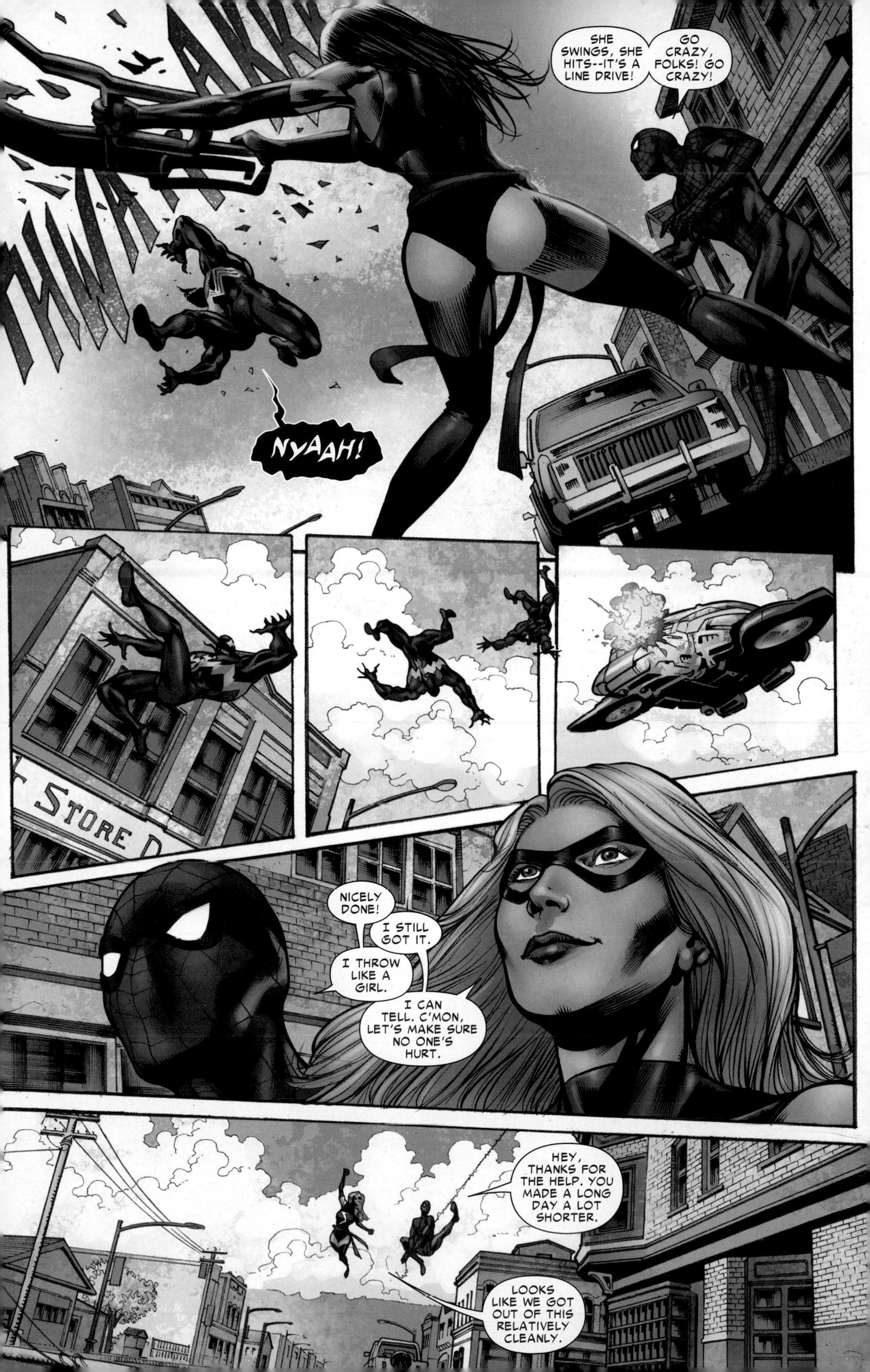
THWAKK
SHE SWINGS, SHE HITS--IT'S A LINE DRIVE!
GO CRAZY, FOLKS! GO CRAZY!
NYAAH!
STORE D
NICELY DONE!
I STILL GOT IT.
I THROW LIKE A GIRL.
I CAN TELL. C'MON, LET'S MAKE SURE NO ONE'S HURT.
HEY, THANKS FOR THE HELP. YOU MADE A LONG DAY A LOT SHORTER.
LOOKS LIKE WE GOT OUT OF THIS RELATIVELY CLEANLY.

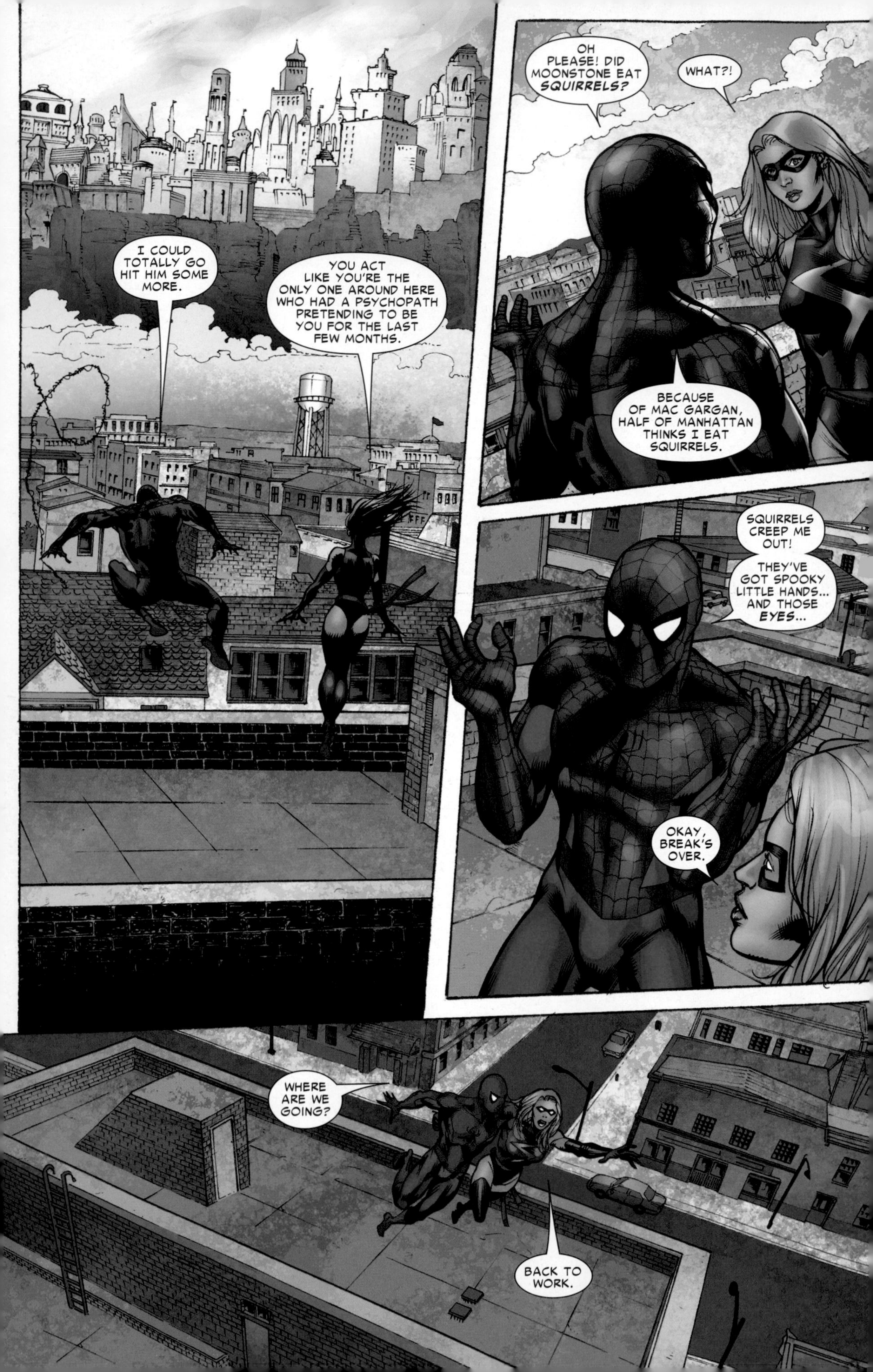
I COULD TOTALLY GO HIT HIM SOME MORE.
YOU ACT LIKE YOU'RE THE ONLY ONE AROUND HERE WHO HAD A PSYCHOPATH PRETENDING TO BE YOU FOR THE LAST FEW MONTHS.
OH PLEASE! DID MOONSTONE EAT SQUIRRELS?
WHAT?!
BECAUSE OF MAC GARGAN, HALF OF MANHATTAN THINKS I EAT SQUIRRELS.
SQUIRRELS CREEP ME OUT!
THEY'VE GOT SPOOKY LITTLE HANDS... AND THOSE EYES...
OKAY, BREAK'S OVER.
WHERE ARE WE GOING?
BACK TO WORK.

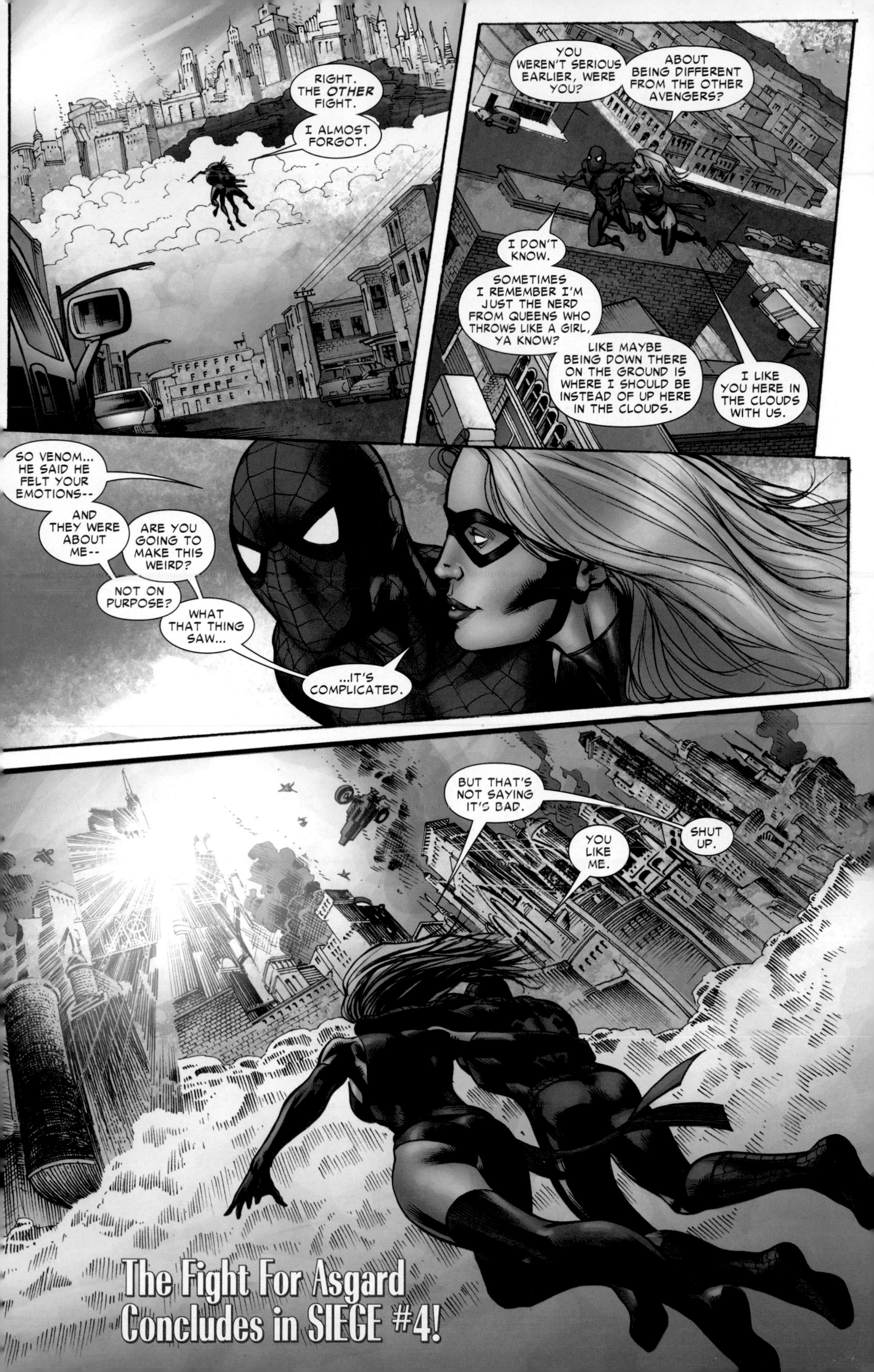
RIGHT. THE OTHER FIGHT.
I ALMOST FORGOT.
YOU WEREN'T SERIOUS EARLIER, WERE YOU?
ABOUT BEING DIFFERENT FROM THE OTHER AVENGERS?
I DON'T KNOW.
SOMETIMES I REMEMBER I'M JUST THE NERD FROM QUEENS WHO THROWS LIKE A GIRL, YA KNOW?
LIKE MAYBE BEING DOWN THERE ON THE GROUND IS WHERE I SHOULD BE INSTEAD OF UP HERE IN THE CLOUDS.
I LIKE YOU HERE IN THE CLOUDS WITH US.
SO VENOM... HE SAID HE FELT YOUR EMOTIONS--
AND THEY WERE ABOUT ME--
ARE YOU GOING TO MAKE THIS WEIRD?
NOT ON PURPOSE?
WHAT THAT THING SAW...
...IT'S COMPLICATED.
BUT THAT'S NOT SAYING IT'S BAD.
YOU LIKE ME.
SHUT UP.
The Fight For Asgard Concludes in SIEGE #4!

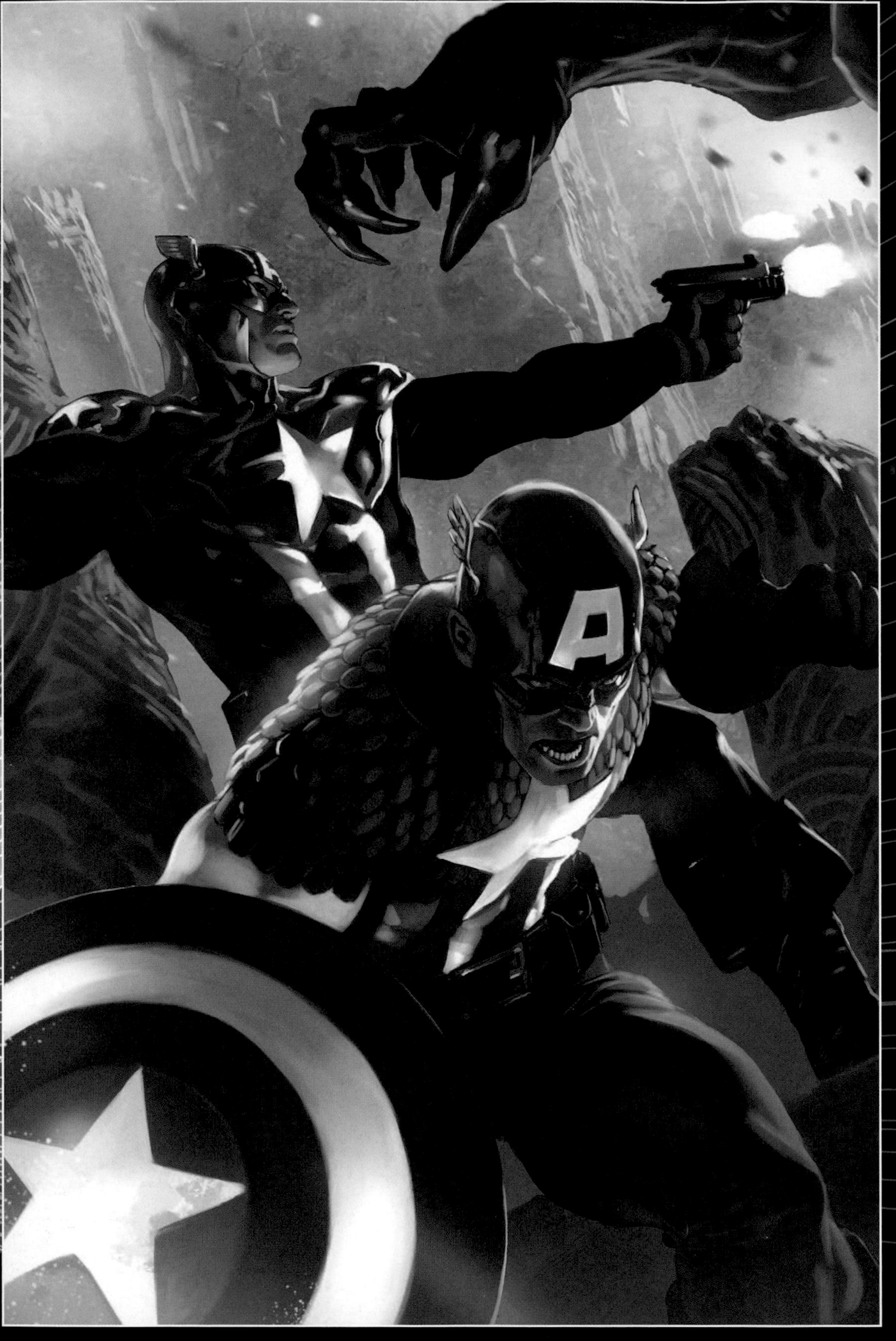

SIEGE: CAPTAIN AMERICA

SIEGE
CAPTAIN AMERICA

AT THE END OF WORLD WAR II, STEVE ROGERS–A.K.A. CAPTAIN AMERICA––AND HIS DEDICATED SIDEKICK BUCKY BARNES FOUGHT VALIANTLY TO DISARM AN EXPLOSIVE DRONE FLYING OVER THE NORTH ATLANTIC OCEAN. WHILE THEY SUCCESSFULLY PREVENTED IT FROM REACHING ITS INTENDED TARGET, THE TWO HEROES WERE THOUGHT LOST FOREVER TO AN ICY GRAVE. EXTRAORDINARILY, HOWEVER, BOTH HEROES SURVIVED.

DECADES LATER, IN THE CIVIL WAR CAUSED BY THE SUPERHUMAN REGISTRATION ACT, STEVE ROGERS WAS ASSASSINATED, LEAVING BUCKY––RETURNED FROM HIS DAYS AS THE COMMUNIST CONTROLLED WINTER SOLDIER–TO PICK UP HIS FALLEN FRIEND'S MANTLE OF CAPTAIN AMERICA. STEVE HAS ALSO RETURNED AMIDST THE DARK REIGN OF NORMAN OSBORN, ONCE AGAIN DONNING THE STARS AND STRIPES.

NOW NORMAN OSBORN, THE FORMER GREEN GOBLIN PRESENTLY OPERATING UNDER THE ALIAS OF IRON PATRIOT WITH AN AVENGERS TEAM OF HIS OWN, HAS LAID SIEGE TO ASGARD. BUCKY AND STEVE HAVE ONCE AGAIN COME TOGETHER AS FRIENDS AND ALLIES TO STAND AGAINST OSBORN AND HIS INSANE AMBITIONS.

CHRISTOS N. GAGE WRITER

FEDERICO DALLOCCHIO ARTIST

GIULIA BRUSCO ROB SCHWAGER COLORISTS

DAVE SHARPE LETTERER

MARKO DJURDJEVIC COVER ART

RACHEL PINNELAS ASSISTANT EDITOR

BILL ROSEMANN EDITOR

JOE QUESADA EDITOR IN CHIEF

DAN BUCKLEY PUBLISHER

ALAN FINE EXECUTIVE PRODUCER

CAPTAIN AMERICA CREATED BY **JOE SIMON** and **JACK KIRBY**

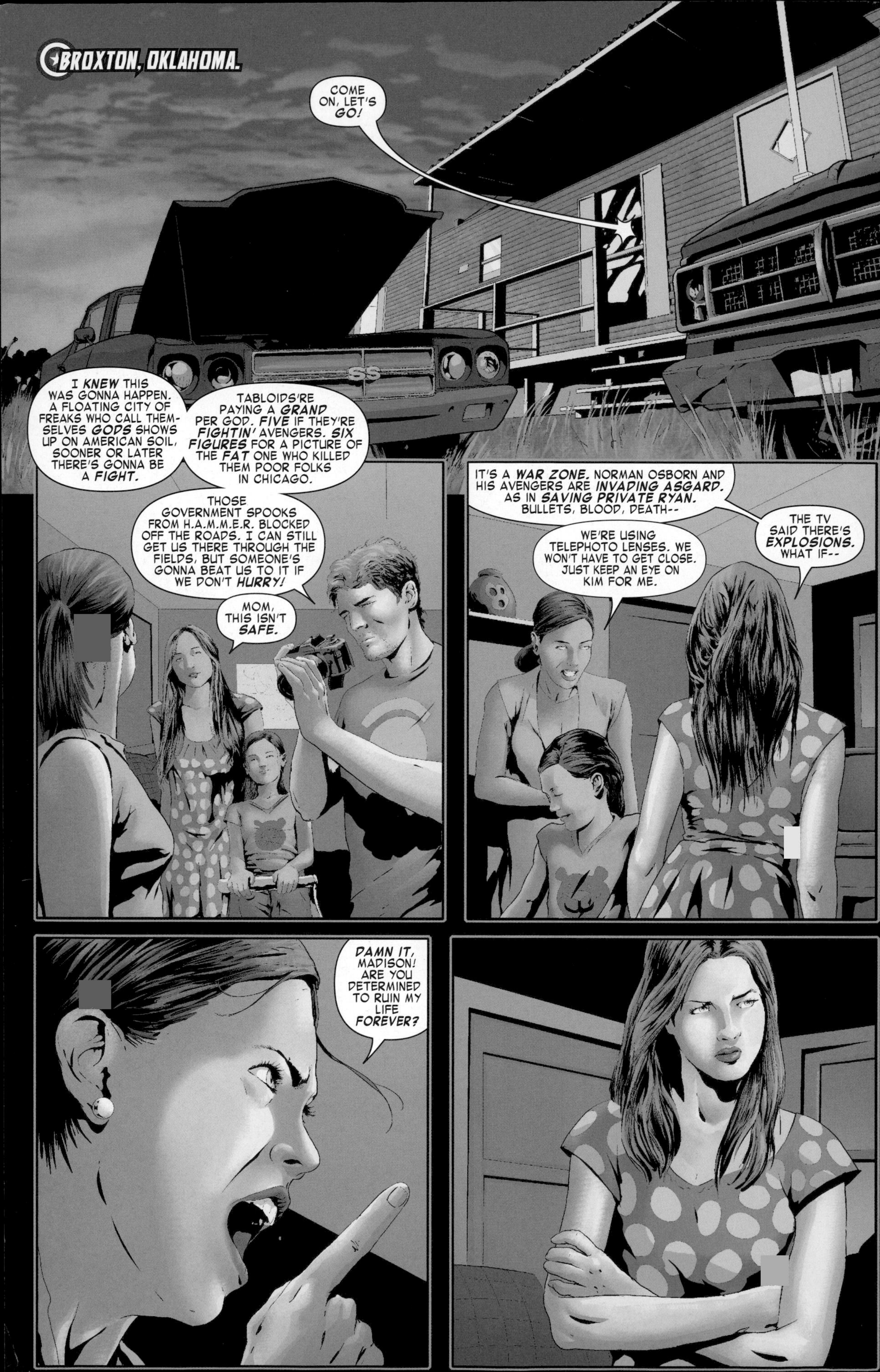
BROXTON, OKLAHOMA.
COME ON, LET'S GO!
I KNEW THIS WAS GONNA HAPPEN. A FLOATING CITY OF FREAKS WHO CALL THEMSELVES GODS SHOWS UP ON AMERICAN SOIL, SOONER OR LATER THERE'S GONNA BE A FIGHT.
TABLOIDS'RE PAYING A GRAND PER GOD. FIVE IF THEY'RE FIGHTIN' AVENGERS. SIX FIGURES FOR A PICTURE OF THE FAT ONE WHO KILLED THEM POOR FOLKS IN CHICAGO.
THOSE GOVERNMENT SPOOKS FROM H.A.M.M.E.R. BLOCKED OFF THE ROADS. I CAN STILL GET US THERE THROUGH THE FIELDS, BUT SOMEONE'S GONNA BEAT US TO IT IF WE DON'T HURRY!
MOM, THIS ISN'T SAFE.
IT'S A WAR ZONE. NORMAN OSBORN AND HIS AVENGERS ARE INVADING ASGARD. AS IN SAVING PRIVATE RYAN. BULLETS, BLOOD, DEATH--
THE TV SAID THERE'S EXPLOSIONS. WHAT IF--
WE'RE USING TELEPHOTO LENSES. WE WON'T HAVE TO GET CLOSE. JUST KEEP AN EYE ON KIM FOR ME.
DAMN IT, MADISON! ARE YOU DETERMINED TO RUIN MY LIFE FOREVER?

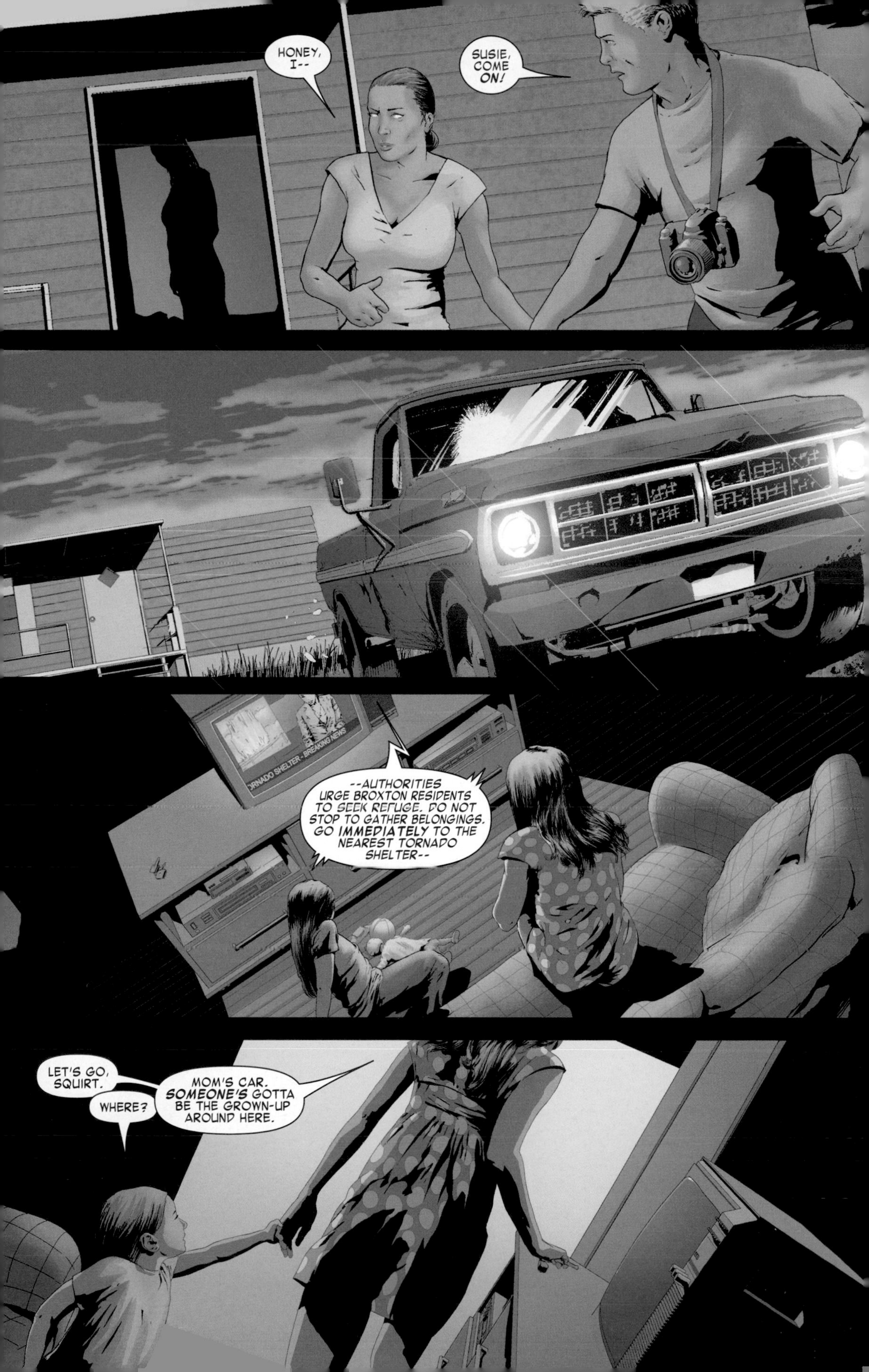
HONEY, I--
SUSIE, COME ON!
--AUTHORITIES URGE BROXTON RESIDENTS TO SEEK REFUGE. DO NOT STOP TO GATHER BELONGINGS. GO IMMEDIATELY TO THE NEAREST TORNADO SHELTER--
TORNADO SHELTER - BREAKING NEWS
LET'S GO, SQUIRT.
WHERE?
MOM'S CAR. SOMEONE'S GOTTA BE THE GROWN-UP AROUND HERE.

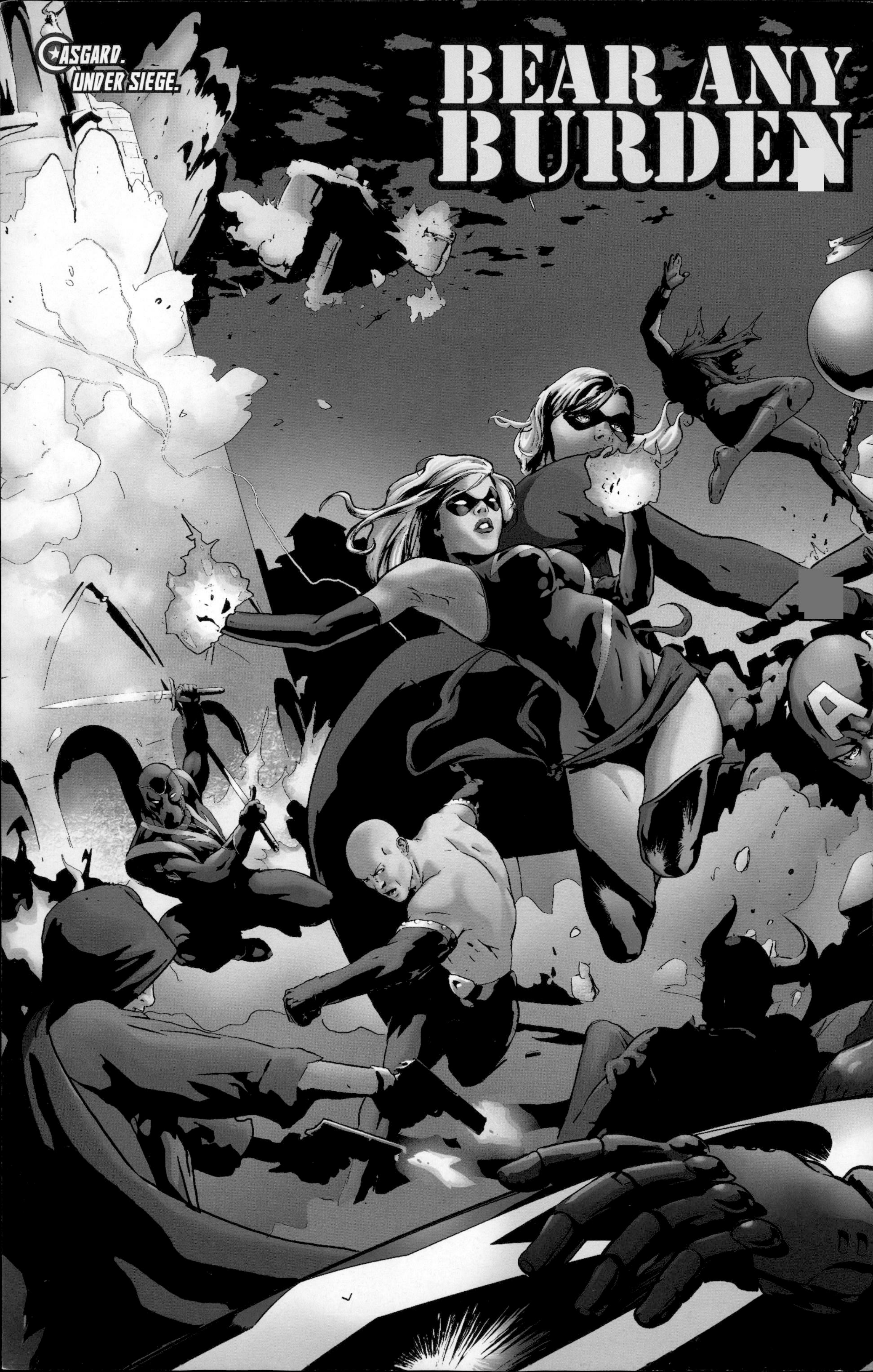
ASGARD. UNDER SIEGE.
BEAR ANY BURDEN

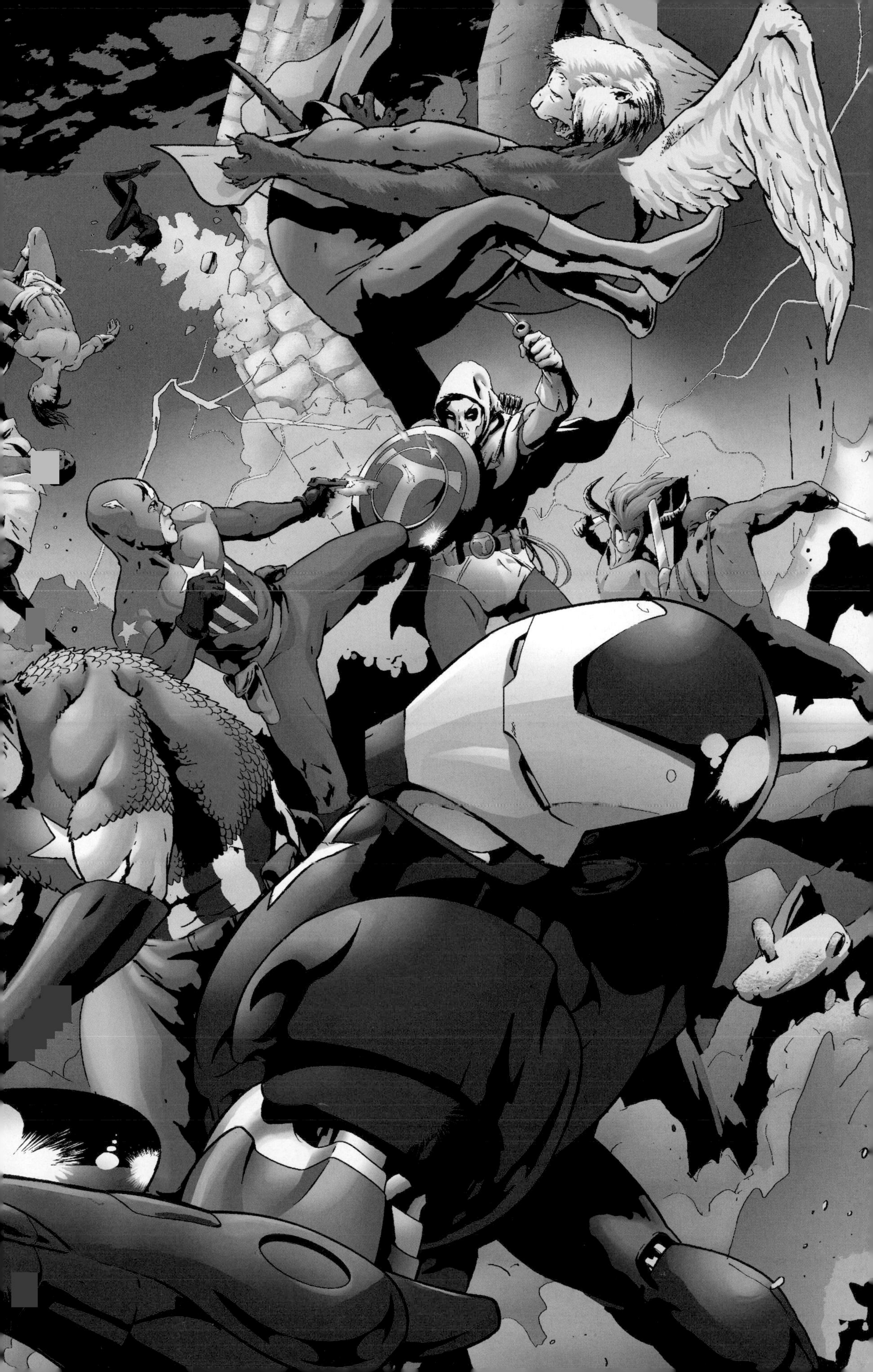

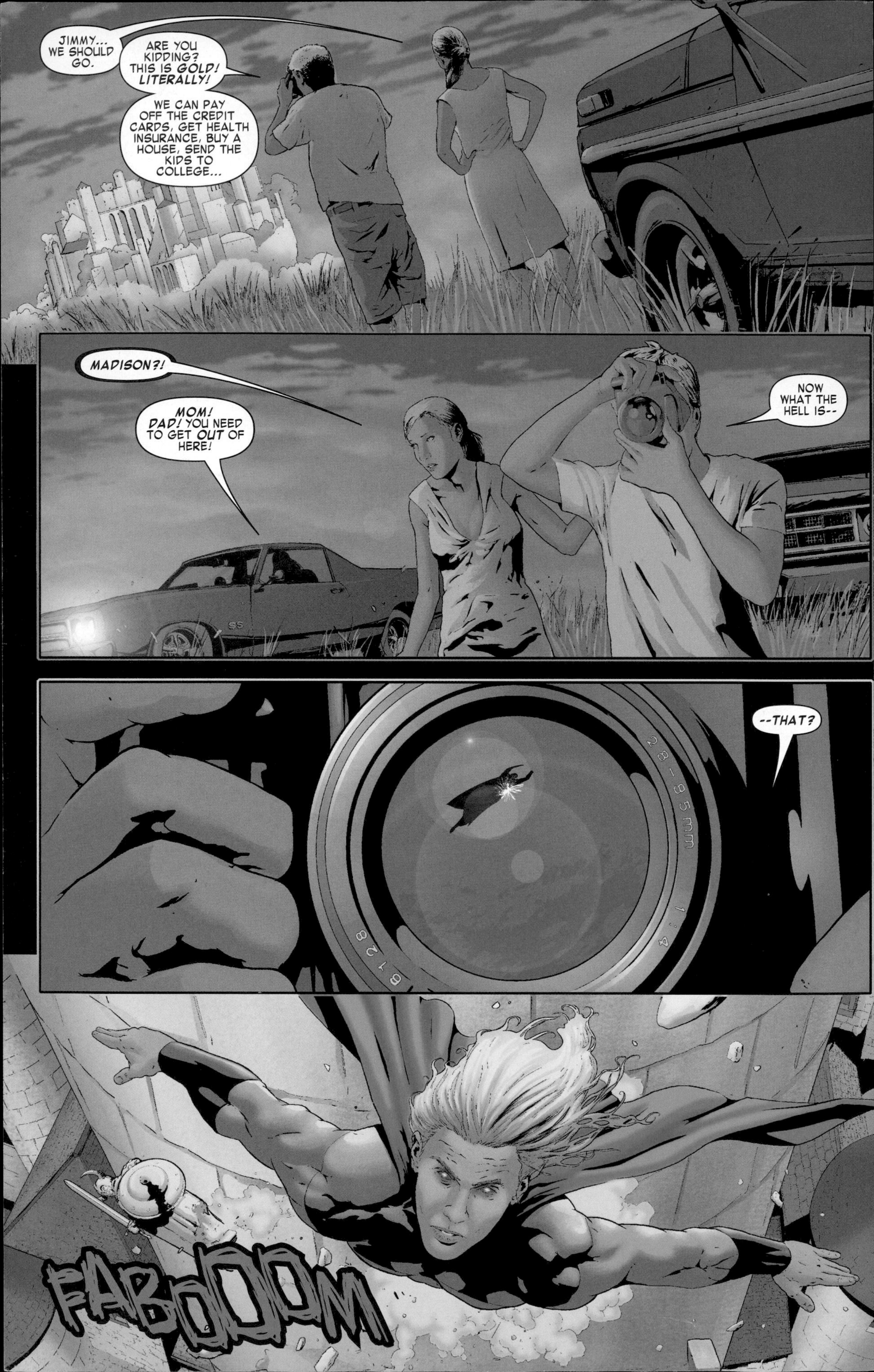

JIMMY... WE SHOULD GO.
ARE YOU KIDDING? THIS IS GOLD! LITERALLY!
WE CAN PAY OFF THE CREDIT CARDS, GET HEALTH INSURANCE, BUY A HOUSE, SEND THE KIDS TO COLLEGE...
MADISON?!
MOM! DAD! YOU NEED TO GET OUT OF HERE!
NOW WHAT THE HELL IS--
--THAT?
28-95mm
1:4
FABDOOM

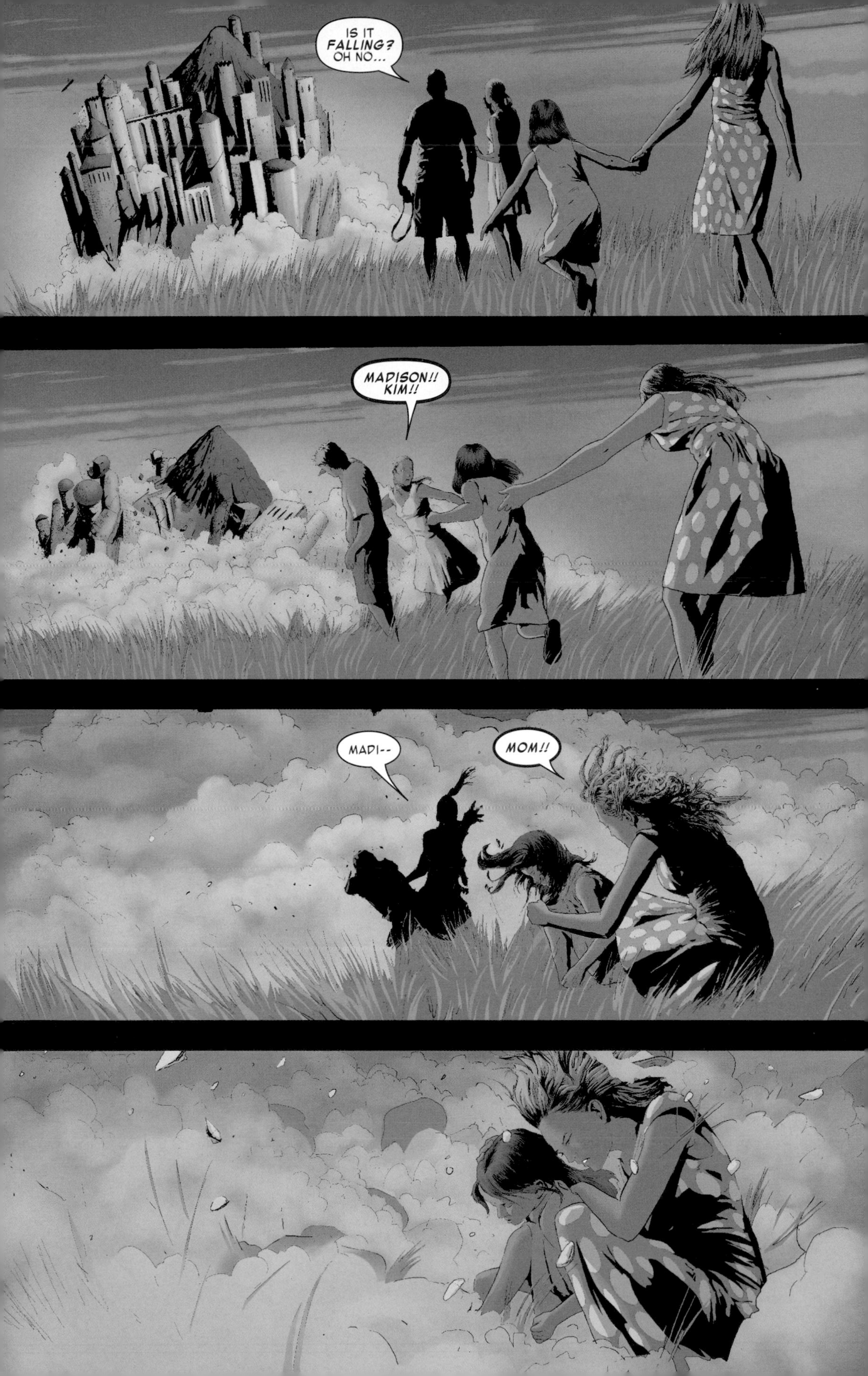
IS IT FALLING? OH NO...
MADISON!! KIM!!
MADI--
MOM!!

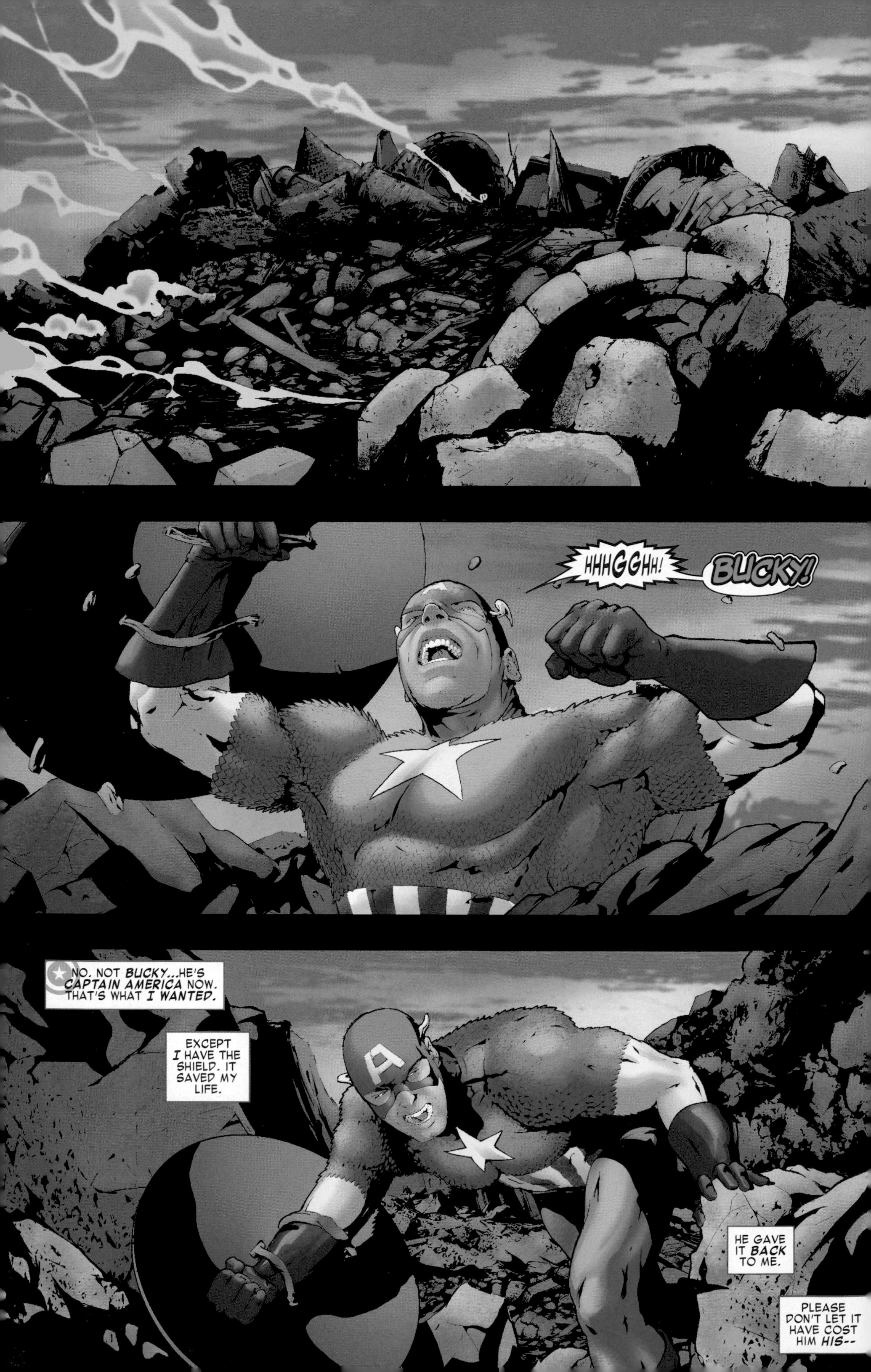
HHHGGHH!
BUCKY!
NO. NOT BUCKY...HE'S CAPTAIN AMERICA NOW. THAT'S WHAT I WANTED.
EXCEPT I HAVE THE SHIELD. IT SAVED MY LIFE.
HE GAVE IT BACK TO ME.
PLEASE DON'T LET IT HAVE COST HIM HIS--

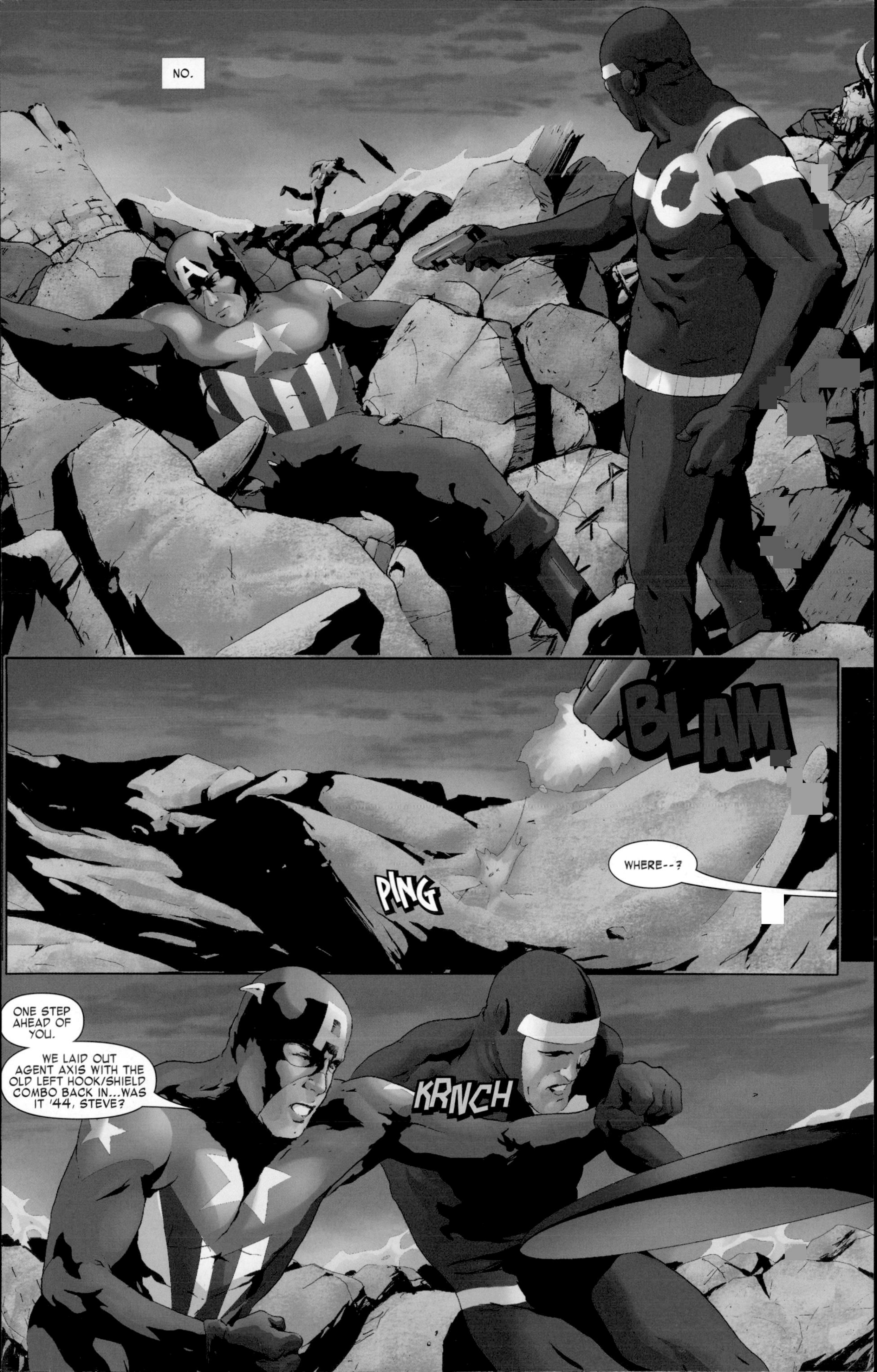
NO.
BLAM
WHERE--?
PING
ONE STEP AHEAD OF YOU.
WE LAID OUT AGENT AXIS WITH THE OLD LEFT HOOK/SHIELD COMBO BACK IN...WAS IT '44, STEVE?
KRNCH

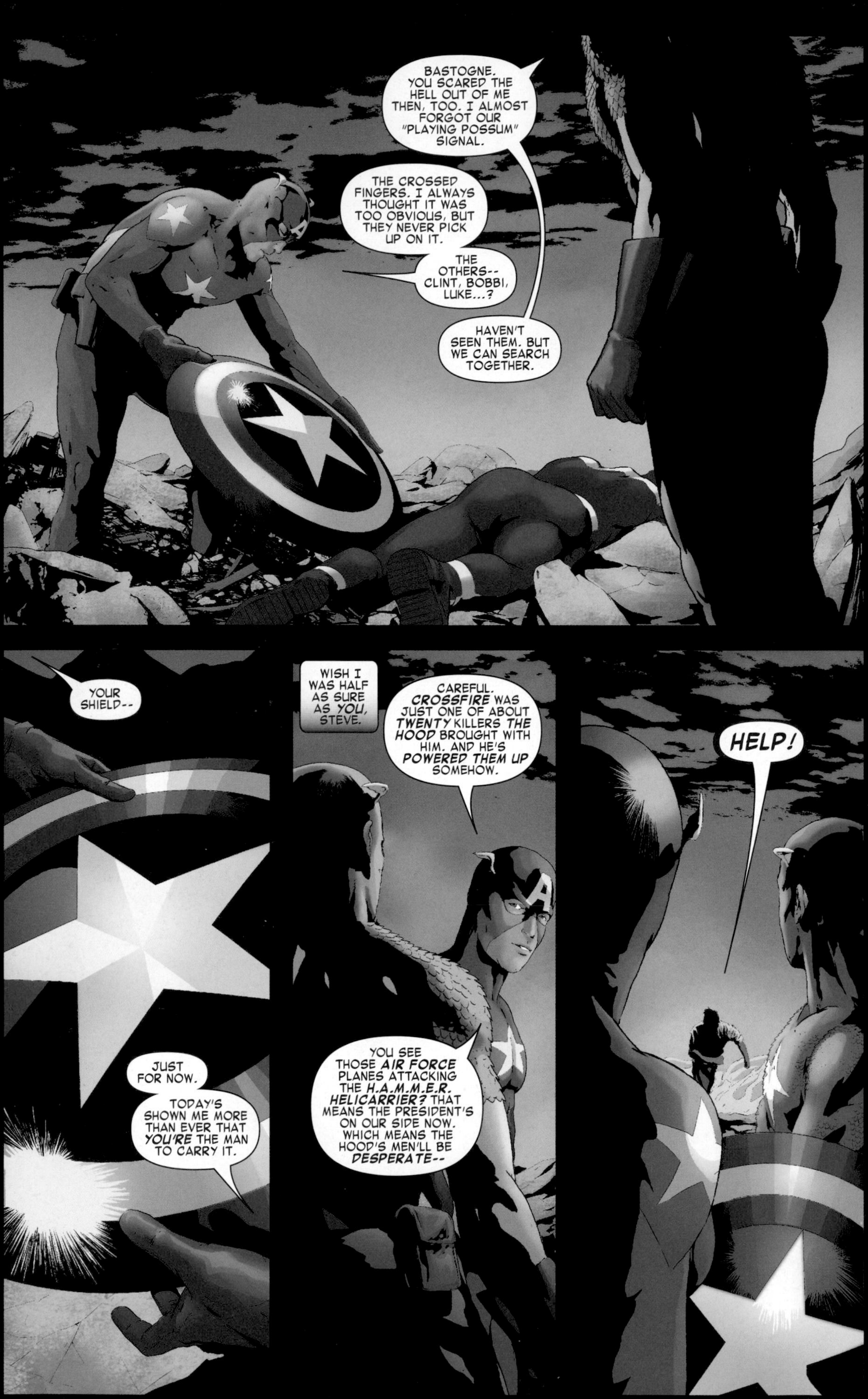
BASTOGNE. YOU SCARED THE HELL OUT OF ME THEN, TOO. I ALMOST FORGOT OUR "PLAYING POSSUM" SIGNAL.
THE CROSSED FINGERS. I ALWAYS THOUGHT IT WAS TOO OBVIOUS, BUT THEY NEVER PICK UP ON IT.
THE OTHERS-- CLINT, BOBBI, LUKE...?
HAVEN'T SEEN THEM. BUT WE CAN SEARCH TOGETHER.
YOUR SHIELD--
JUST FOR NOW.
TODAY'S SHOWN ME MORE THAN EVER THAT YOU'RE THE MAN TO CARRY IT.
WISH I WAS HALF AS SURE AS YOU, STEVE.
CAREFUL. CROSSFIRE WAS JUST ONE OF ABOUT TWENTY KILLERS THE HOOD BROUGHT WITH HIM. AND HE'S POWERED THEM UP SOMEHOW.
YOU SEE THOSE AIR FORCE PLANES ATTACKING THE H.A.M.M.E.R. HELICARRIER? THAT MEANS THE PRESIDENT'S ON OUR SIDE NOW. WHICH MEANS THE HOOD'S MEN'LL BE DESPERATE--
HELP!

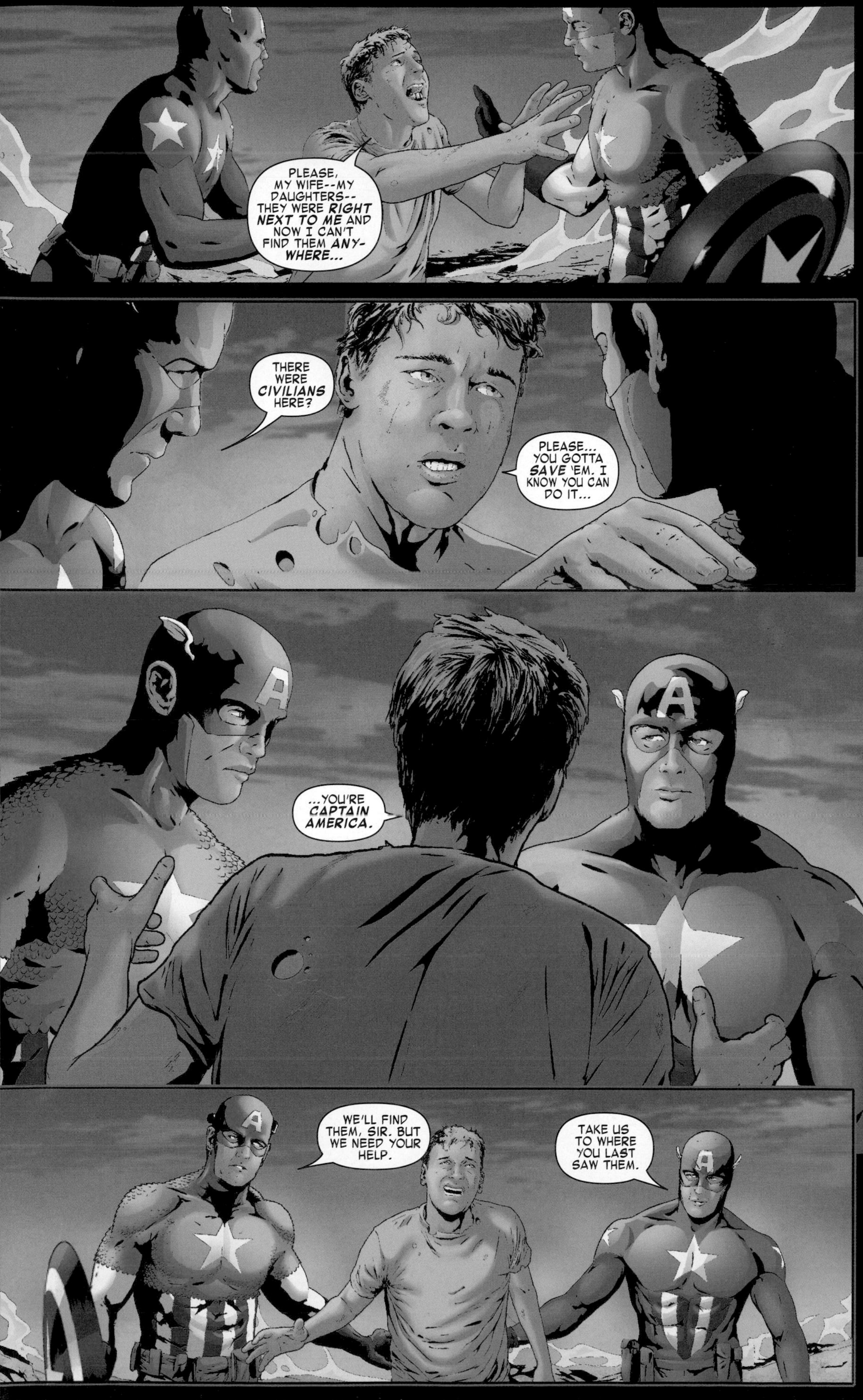
PLEASE, MY WIFE--MY DAUGHTERS-- THEY WERE RIGHT NEXT TO ME AND NOW I CAN'T FIND THEM ANY-WHERE...
THERE WERE CIVILIANS HERE?
PLEASE... YOU GOTTA SAVE 'EM. I KNOW YOU CAN DO IT...
...YOU'RE CAPTAIN AMERICA.
WE'LL FIND THEM, SIR. BUT WE NEED YOUR HELP.
TAKE US TO WHERE YOU LAST SAW THEM.

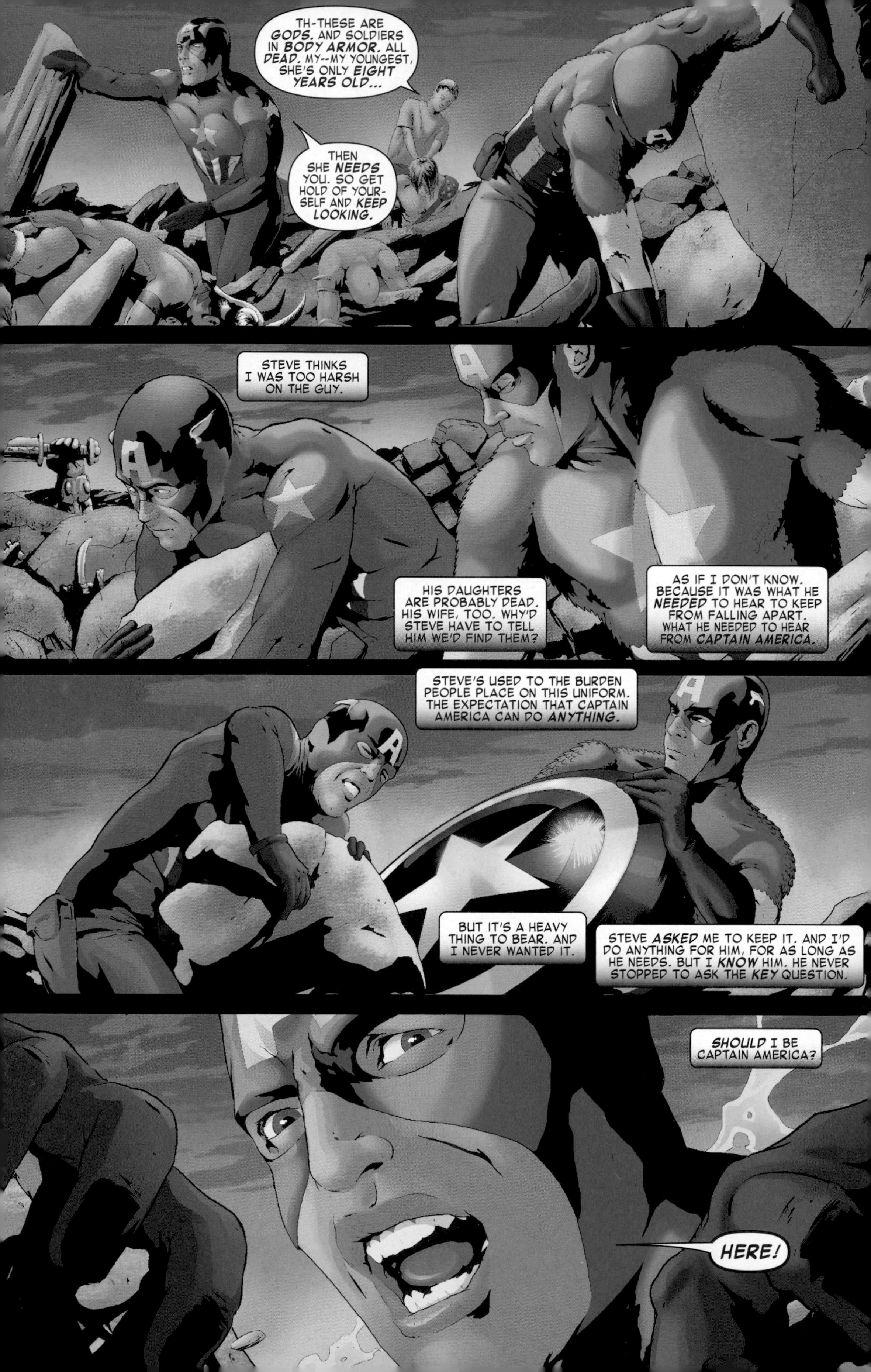
TH-THESE ARE GODS. AND SOLDIERS IN BODY ARMOR. ALL DEAD. MY--MY YOUNGEST, SHE'S ONLY EIGHT YEARS OLD...
THEN SHE NEEDS YOU. SO GET HOLD OF YOURSELF AND KEEP LOOKING.
STEVE THINKS I WAS TOO HARSH ON THE GUY.
HIS DAUGHTERS ARE PROBABLY DEAD. HIS WIFE, TOO. WHY'D STEVE HAVE TO TELL HIM WE'D FIND THEM?
AS IF I DON'T KNOW. BECAUSE IT WAS WHAT HE NEEDED TO HEAR TO KEEP FROM FALLING APART. WHAT HE NEEDED TO HEAR FROM CAPTAIN AMERICA.
STEVE'S USED TO THE BURDEN PEOPLE PLACE ON THIS UNIFORM. THE EXPECTATION THAT CAPTAIN AMERICA CAN DO ANYTHING.
BUT IT'S A HEAVY THING TO BEAR. AND I NEVER WANTED IT.
STEVE ASKED ME TO KEEP IT. AND I'D DO ANYTHING FOR HIM, FOR AS LONG AS HE NEEDS. BUT I KNOW HIM. HE NEVER STOPPED TO ASK THE KEY QUESTION.
SHOULD I BE CAPTAIN AMERICA?
HERE!

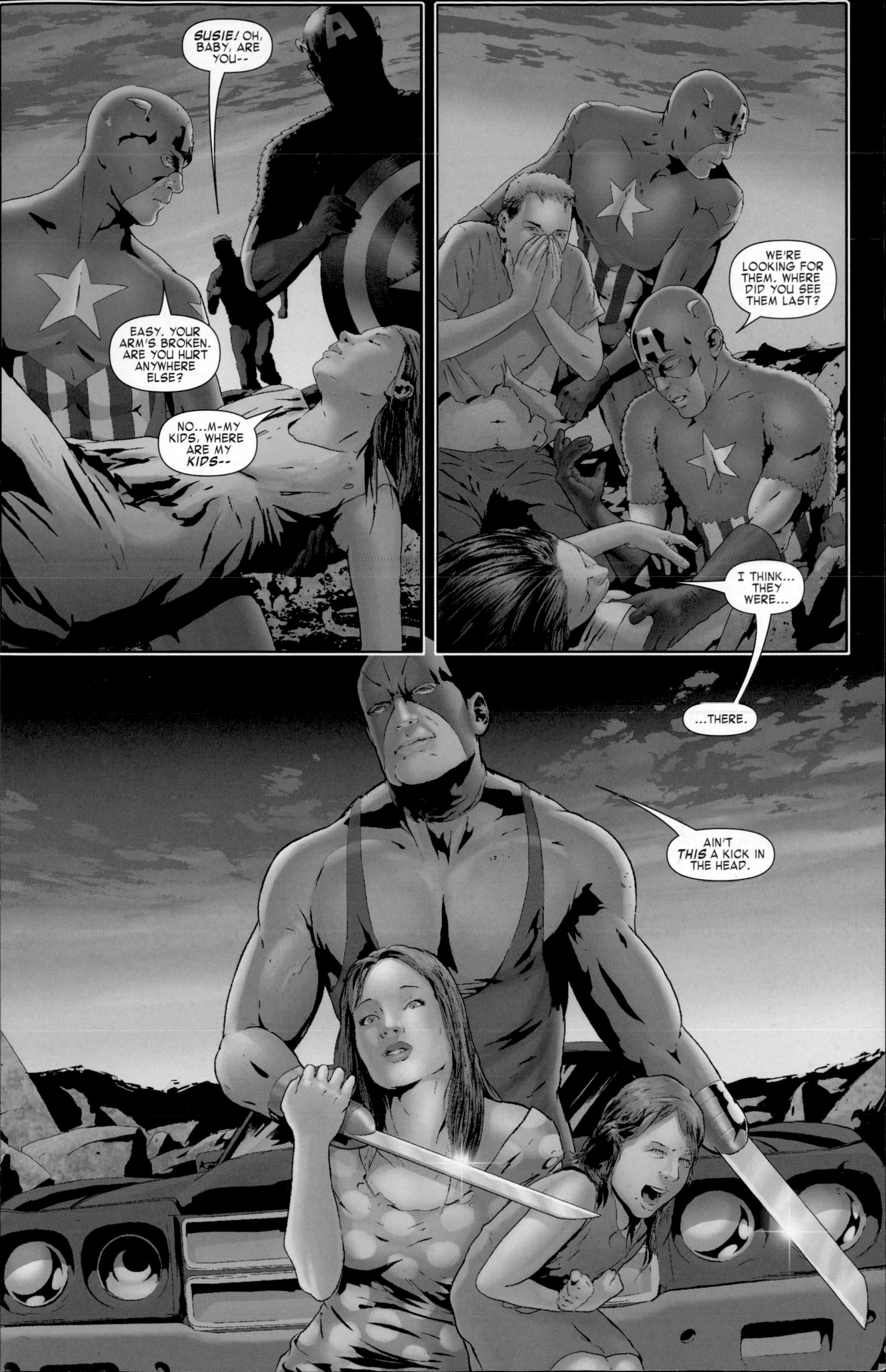
SUSIE! OH, BABY, ARE YOU--
EASY. YOUR ARM'S BROKEN. ARE YOU HURT ANYWHERE ELSE?
NO...M-MY KIDS, WHERE ARE MY KIDS--
WE'RE LOOKING FOR THEM. WHERE DID YOU SEE THEM LAST?
I THINK... THEY WERE...
...THERE.
AIN'T THIS A KICK IN THE HEAD.

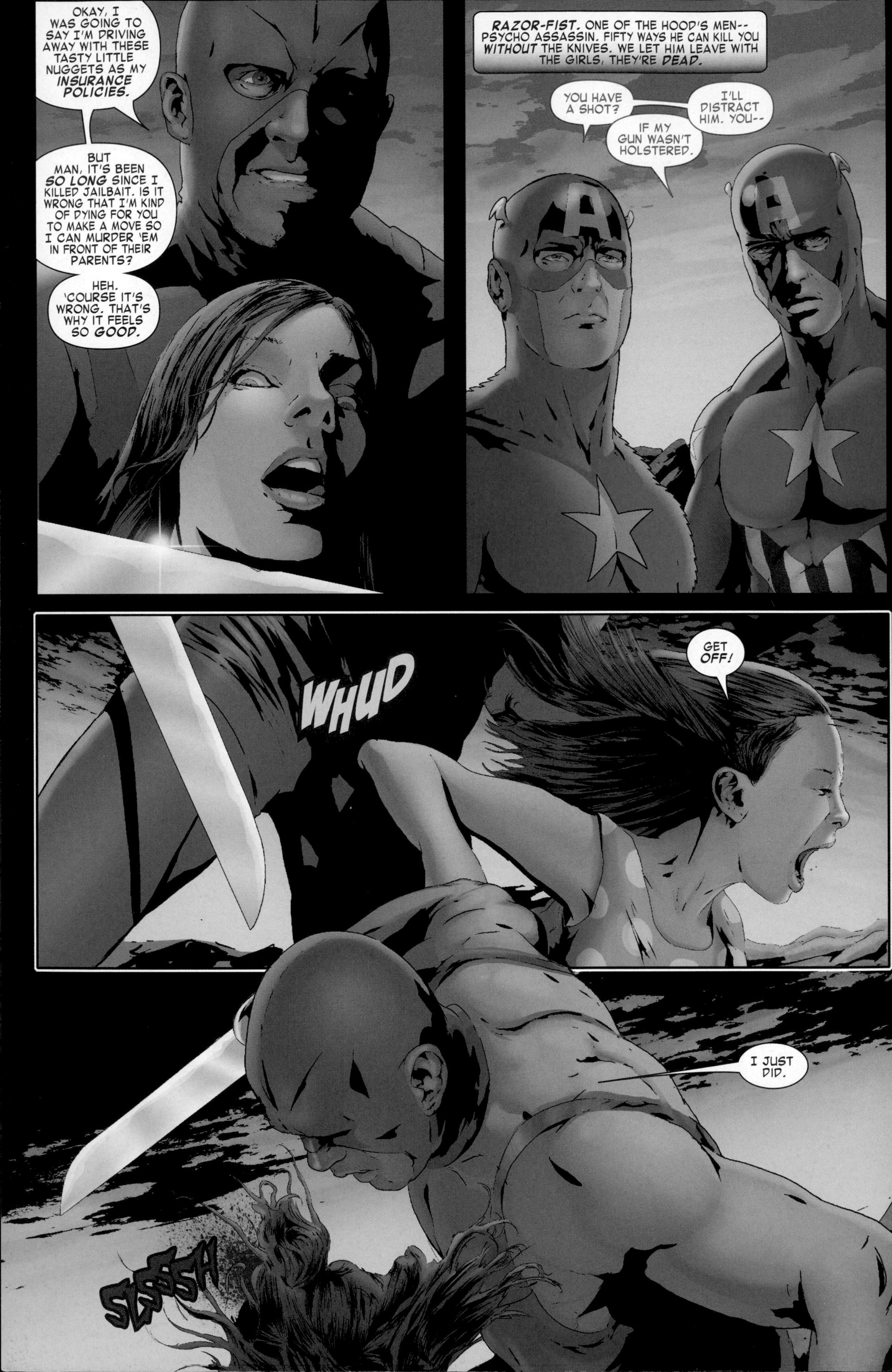
OKAY, I WAS GOING TO SAY I'M DRIVING AWAY WITH THESE TASTY LITTLE NUGGETS AS MY INSURANCE POLICIES.
BUT MAN, IT'S BEEN SO LONG SINCE I KILLED JAILBAIT. IS IT WRONG THAT I'M KIND OF DYING FOR YOU TO MAKE A MOVE SO I CAN MURDER 'EM IN FRONT OF THEIR PARENTS?
HEH. 'COURSE IT'S WRONG. THAT'S WHY IT FEELS SO GOOD.
RAZOR-FIST. ONE OF THE HOOD'S MEN--PSYCHO ASSASSIN. FIFTY WAYS HE CAN KILL YOU WITHOUT THE KNIVES. WE LET HIM LEAVE WITH THE GIRLS, THEY'RE DEAD.
YOU HAVE A SHOT?
IF MY GUN WASN'T HOLSTERED.
I'LL DISTRACT HIM. YOU--
WHUD
GET OFF!
I JUST DID.
SSSSSH

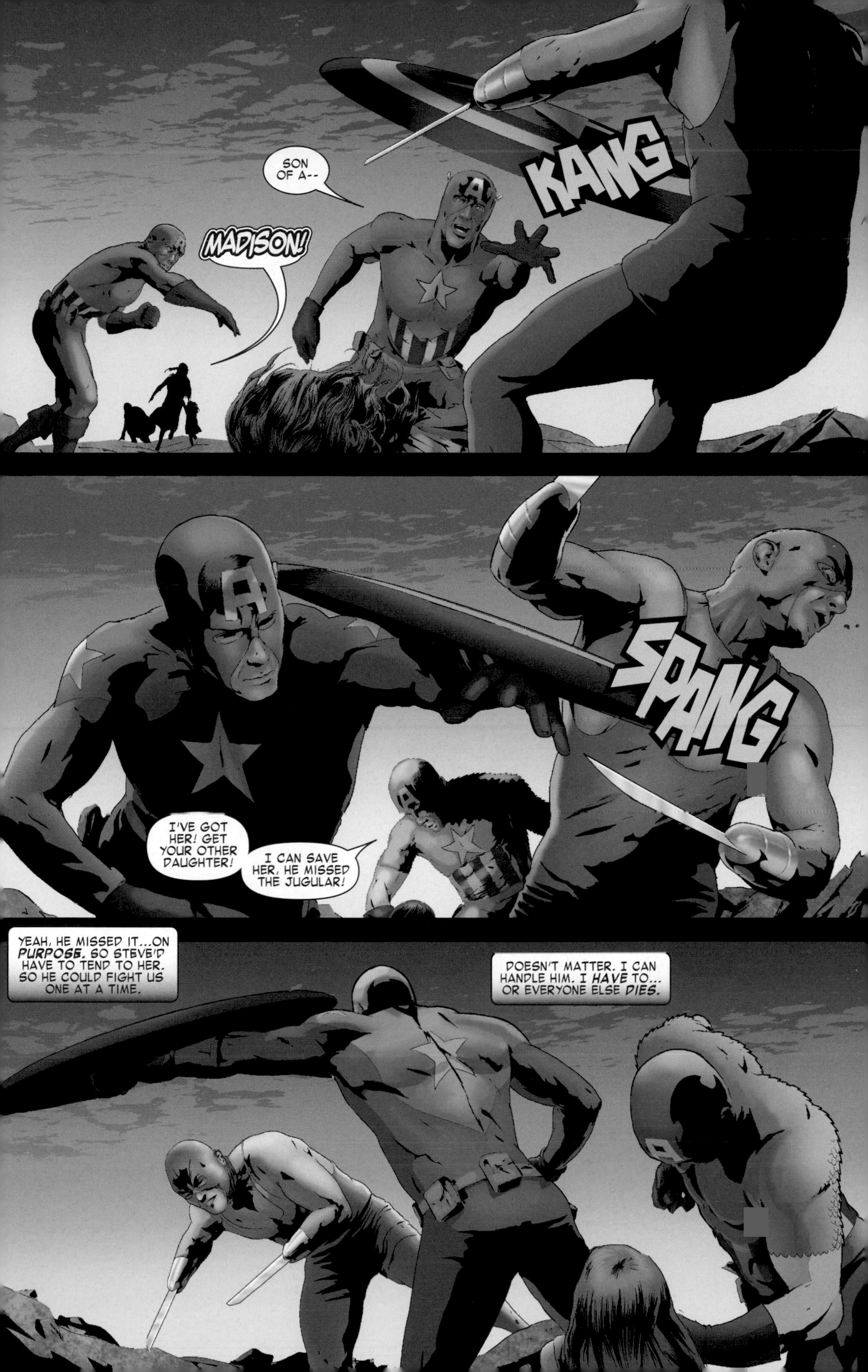

KANG
SON OF A--
MADISON!
SPANG
I'VE GOT HER! GET YOUR OTHER DAUGHTER!
I CAN SAVE HER, HE MISSED THE JUGULAR!
YEAH, HE MISSED IT...ON PURPOSE. SO STEVE'D HAVE TO TEND TO HER. SO HE COULD FIGHT US ONE AT A TIME.
DOESN'T MATTER. I CAN HANDLE HIM. I HAVE TO... OR EVERYONE ELSE DIES.

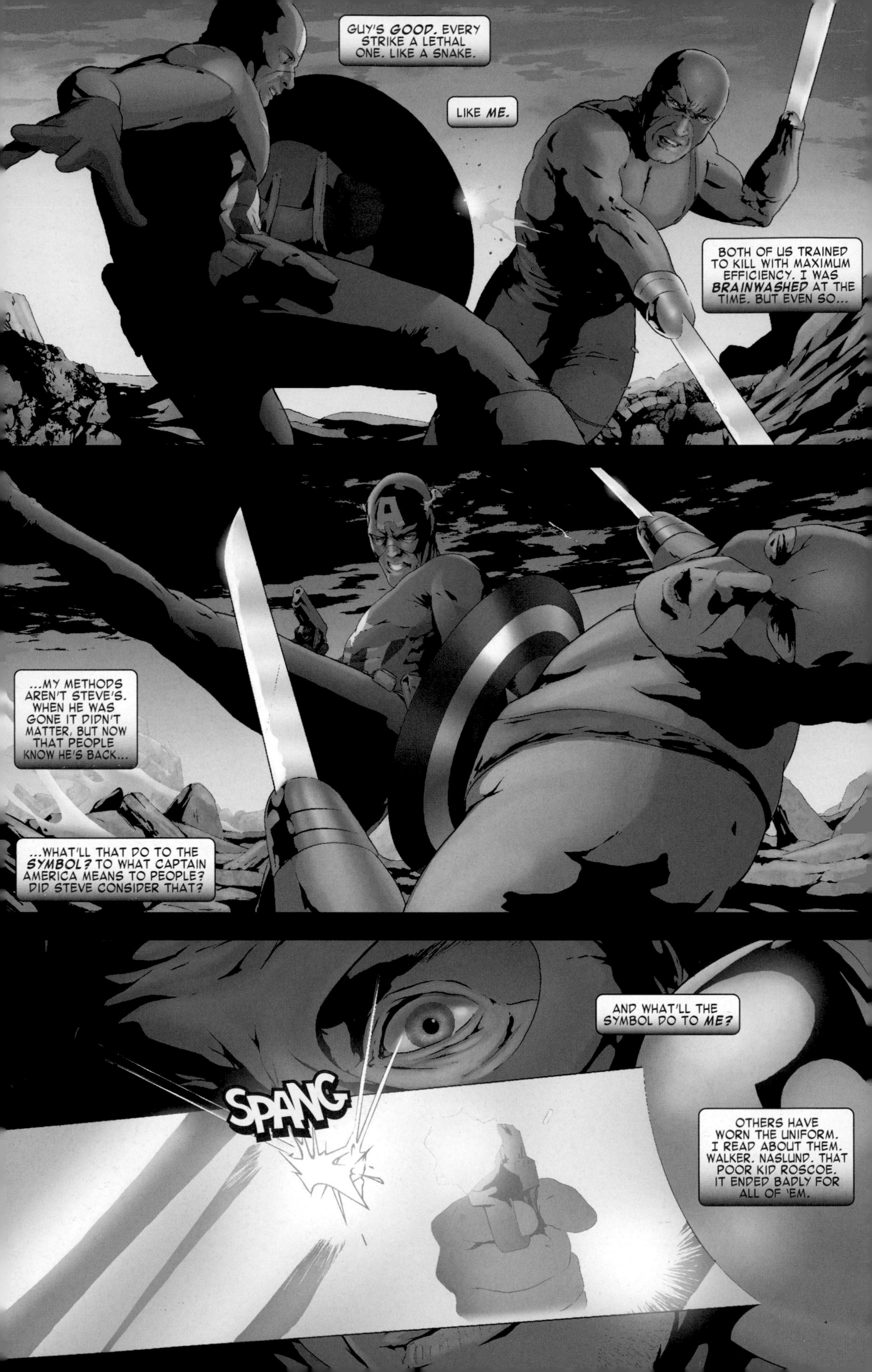
GUY'S GOOD. EVERY STRIKE A LETHAL ONE. LIKE A SNAKE.
LIKE ME.
BOTH OF US TRAINED TO KILL WITH MAXIMUM EFFICIENCY. I WAS BRAINWASHED AT THE TIME. BUT EVEN SO...
...MY METHODS AREN'T STEVE'S. WHEN HE WAS GONE IT DIDN'T MATTER, BUT NOW THAT PEOPLE KNOW HE'S BACK...
...WHAT'LL THAT DO TO THE SYMBOL? TO WHAT CAPTAIN AMERICA MEANS TO PEOPLE? DID STEVE CONSIDER THAT?
AND WHAT'LL THE SYMBOL DO TO ME?
SPANG
OTHERS HAVE WORN THE UNIFORM. I READ ABOUT THEM. WALKER. NASLUND. THAT POOR KID ROSCOE. IT ENDED BADLY FOR ALL OF 'EM.

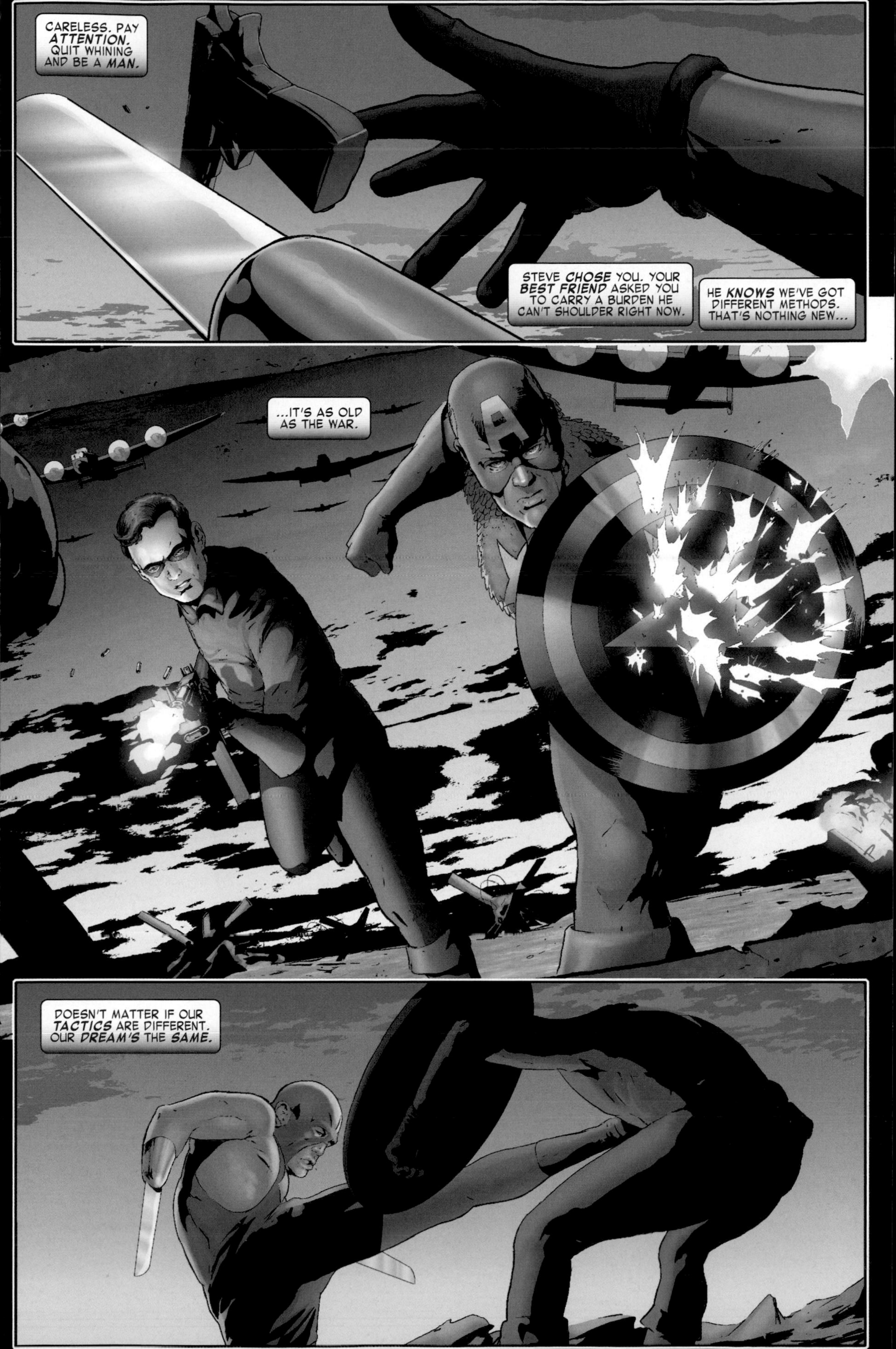
CARELESS. PAY ATTENTION. QUIT WHINING AND BE A MAN.
STEVE CHOSE YOU. YOUR BEST FRIEND ASKED YOU TO CARRY A BURDEN HE CAN'T SHOULDER RIGHT NOW.
HE KNOWS WE'VE GOT DIFFERENT METHODS. THAT'S NOTHING NEW...
...IT'S AS OLD AS THE WAR.
DOESN'T MATTER IF OUR TACTICS ARE DIFFERENT. OUR DREAM'S THE SAME.

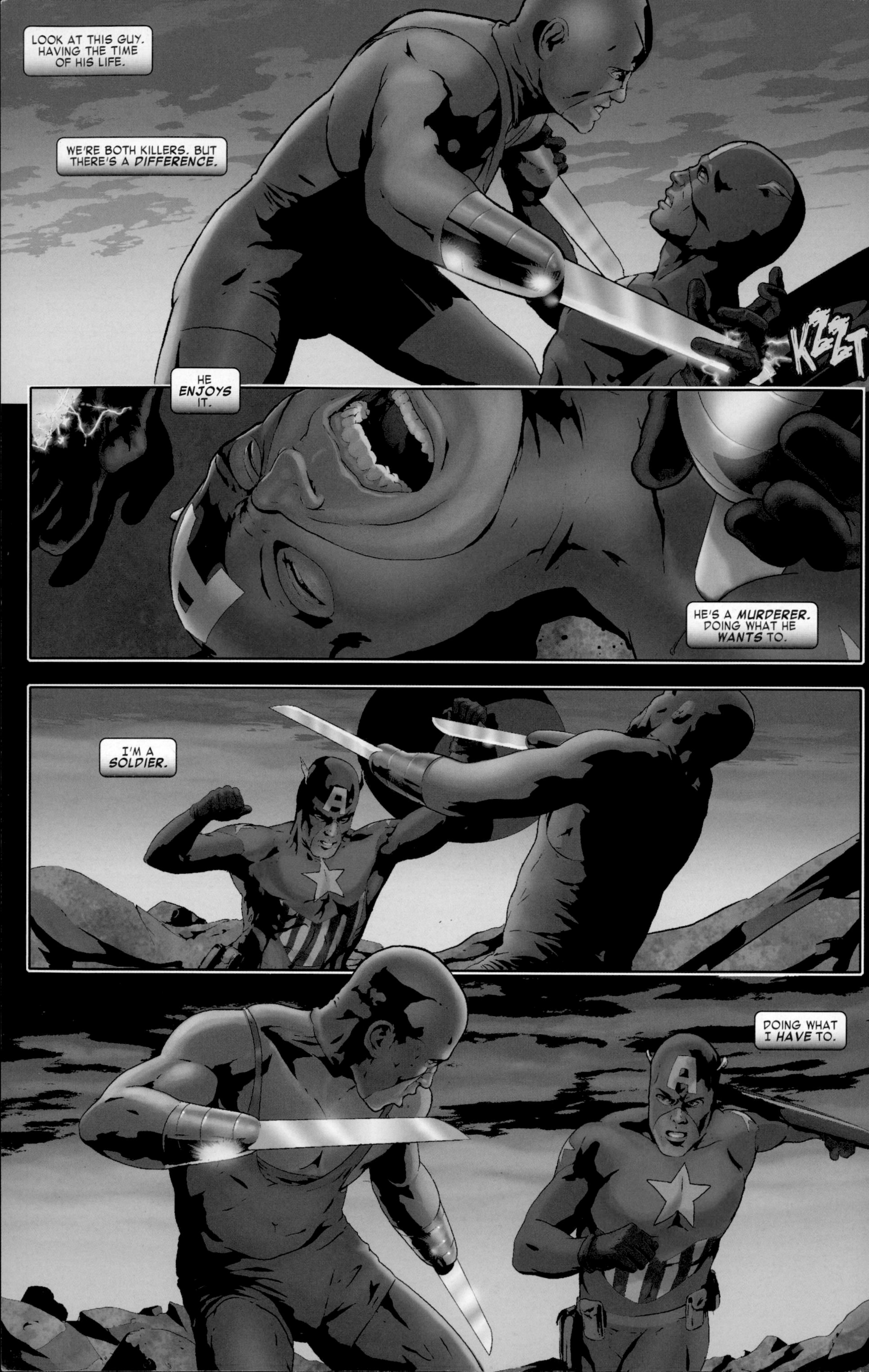
LOOK AT THIS GUY. HAVING THE TIME OF HIS LIFE.
WE'RE BOTH KILLERS. BUT THERE'S A *DIFFERENCE.*
KZZT
HE *ENJOYS* IT.
HE'S A *MURDERER.* DOING WHAT HE *WANTS* TO.
I'M A *SOLDIER.*
DOING WHAT I *HAVE* TO.

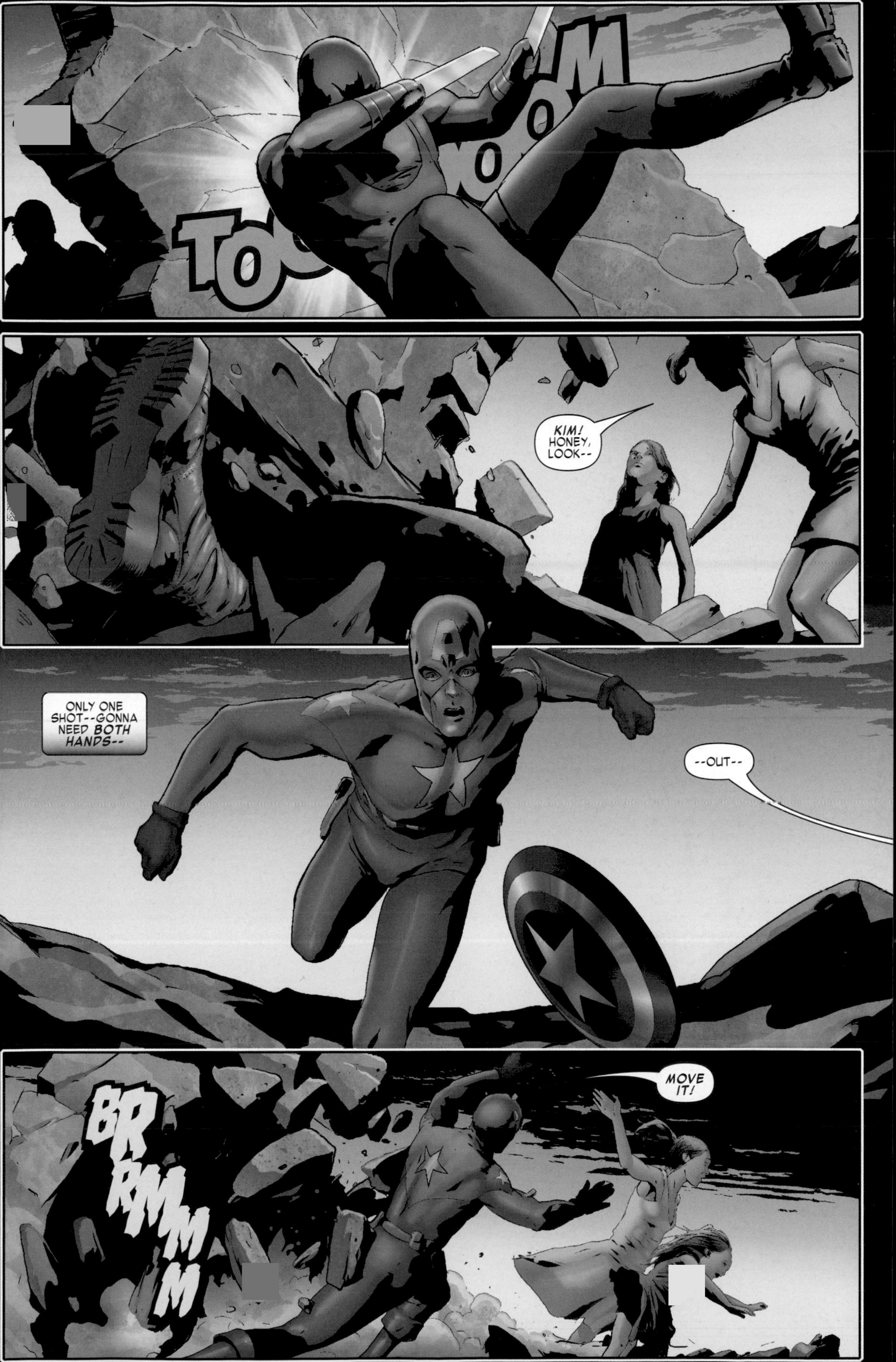
TOOOOM
KIM! HONEY, LOOK--
ONLY ONE SHOT--GONNA NEED BOTH HANDS--
--OUT--
MOVE IT!
BRRMMMM

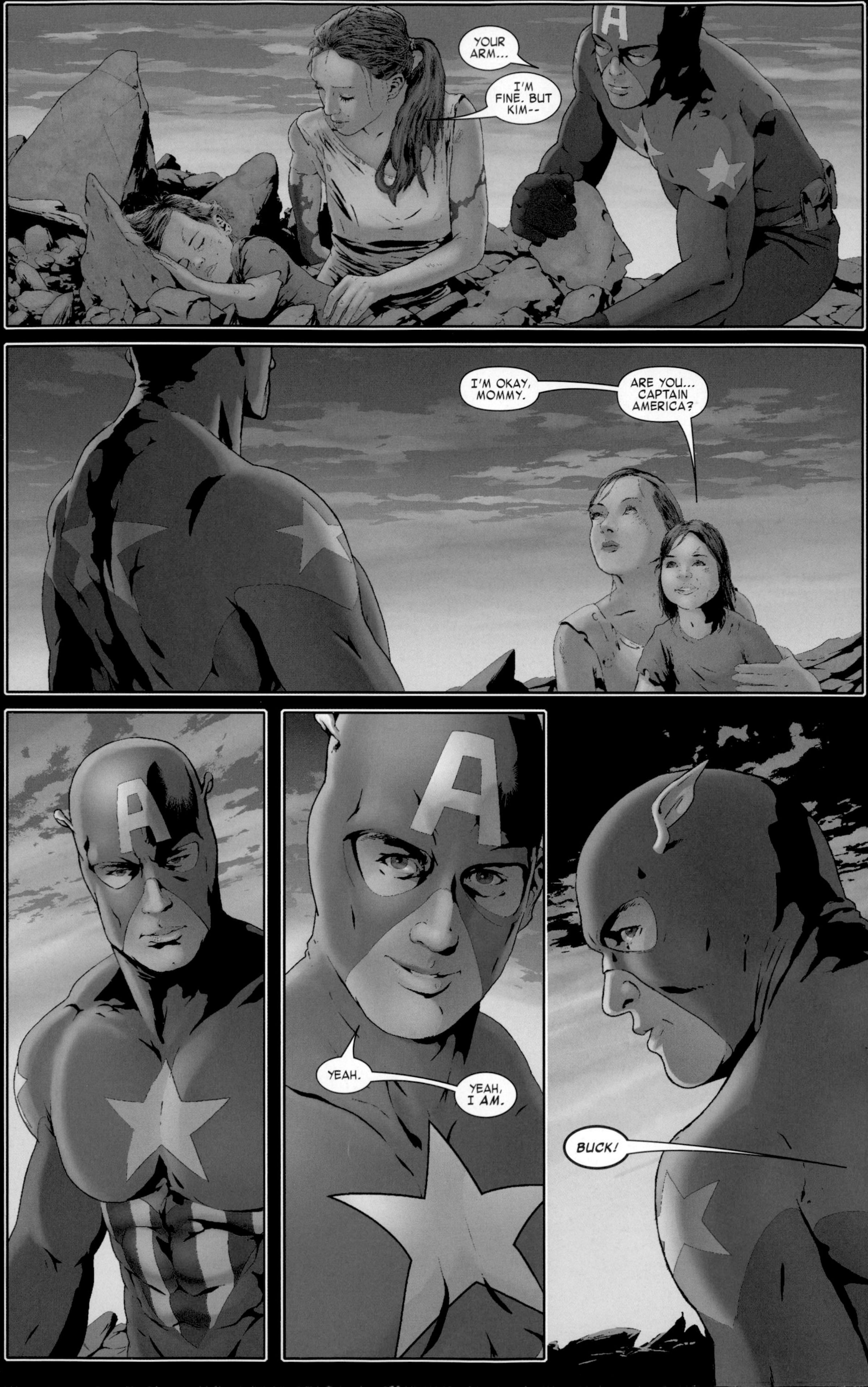
YOUR ARM...
I'M FINE. BUT KIM--
I'M OKAY, MOMMY.
ARE YOU... CAPTAIN AMERICA?
YEAH.
YEAH, I AM.
BUCK!

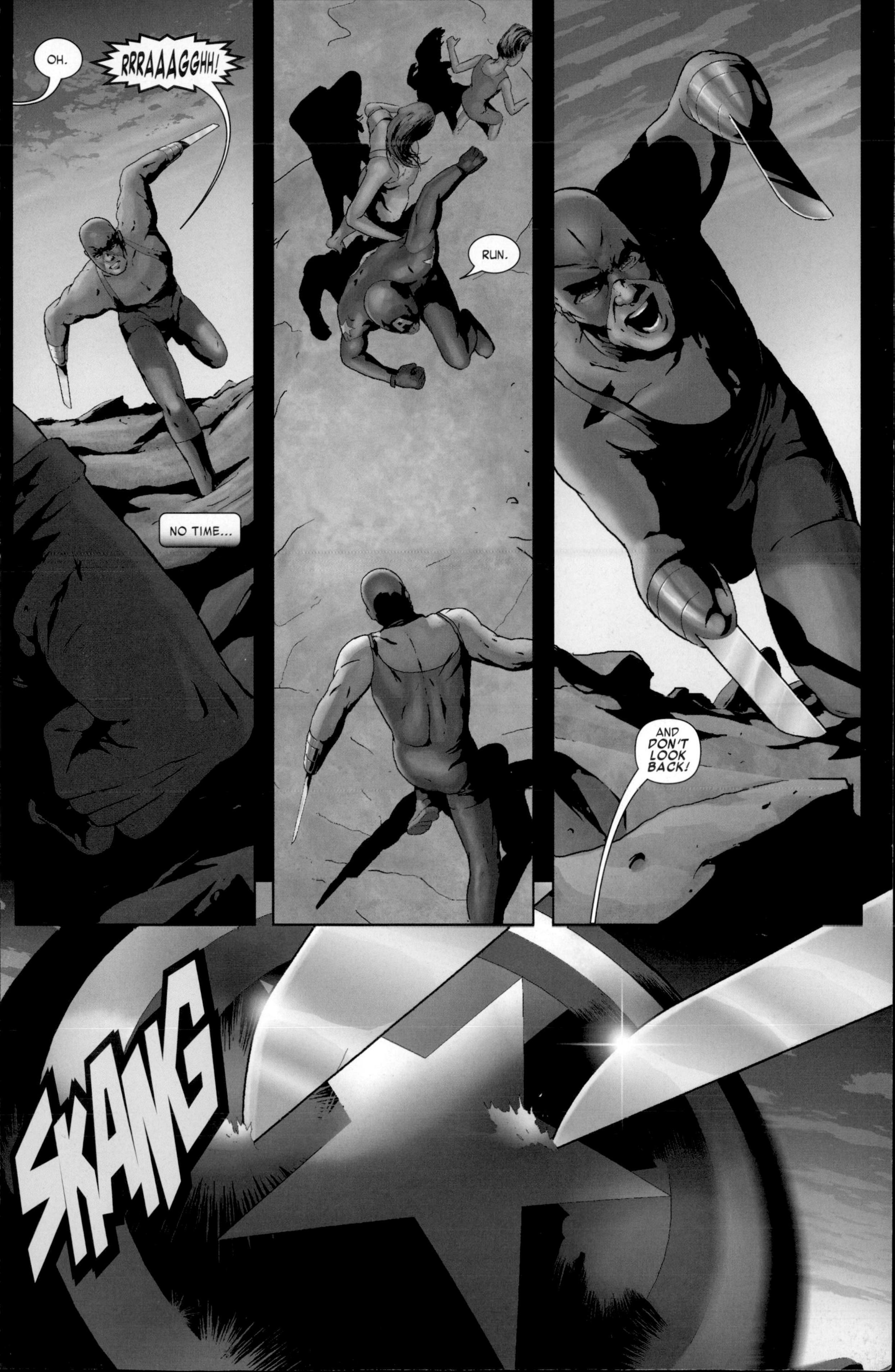

OH.
RRRAAAGGHH!
NO TIME...
RUN.
AND DON'T LOOK BACK!
SKANG

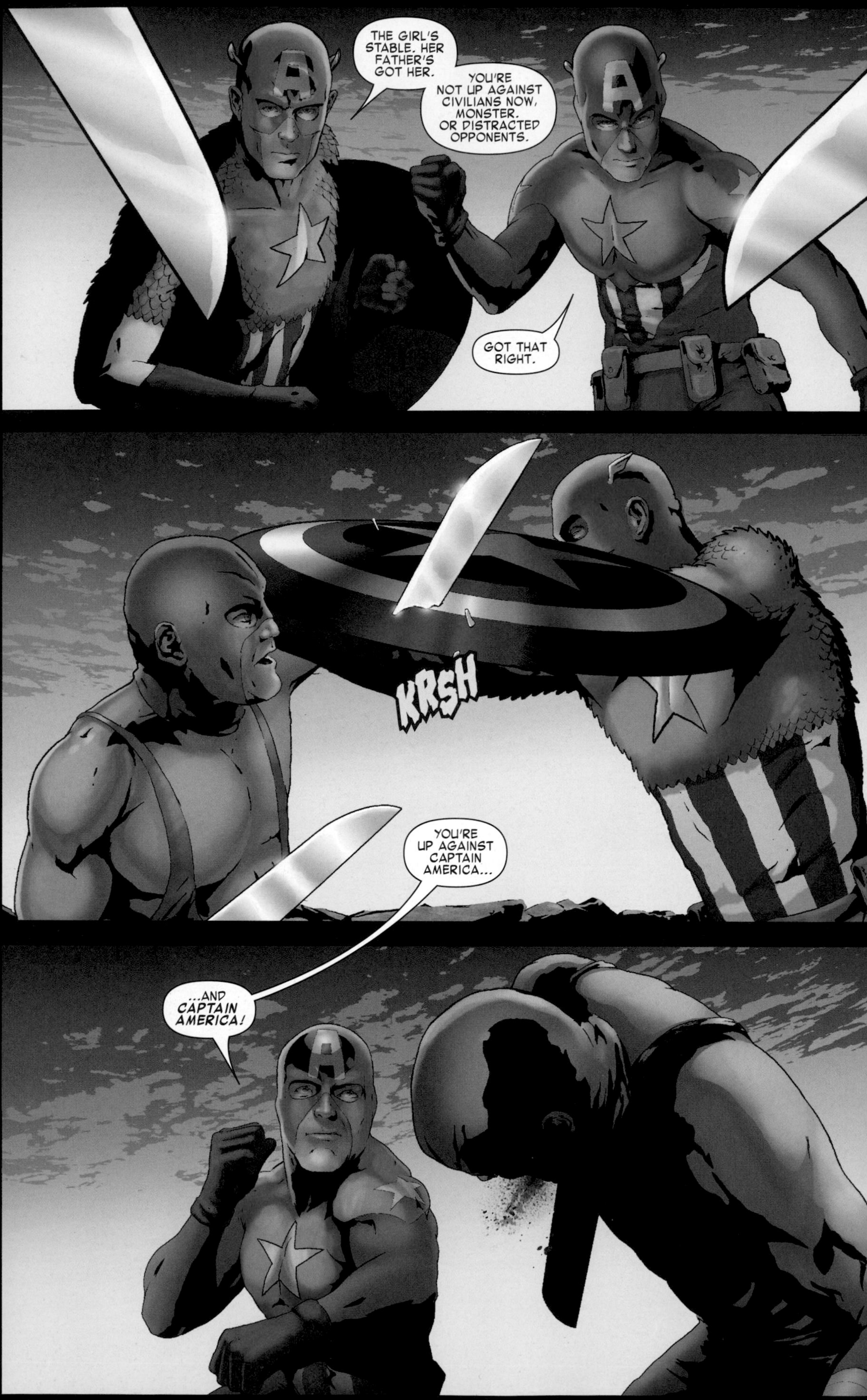
THE GIRL'S STABLE. HER FATHER'S GOT HER.
YOU'RE NOT UP AGAINST CIVILIANS NOW, MONSTER. OR DISTRACTED OPPONENTS.
GOT THAT RIGHT.
KRSH
YOU'RE UP AGAINST CAPTAIN AMERICA...
...AND CAPTAIN AMERICA!

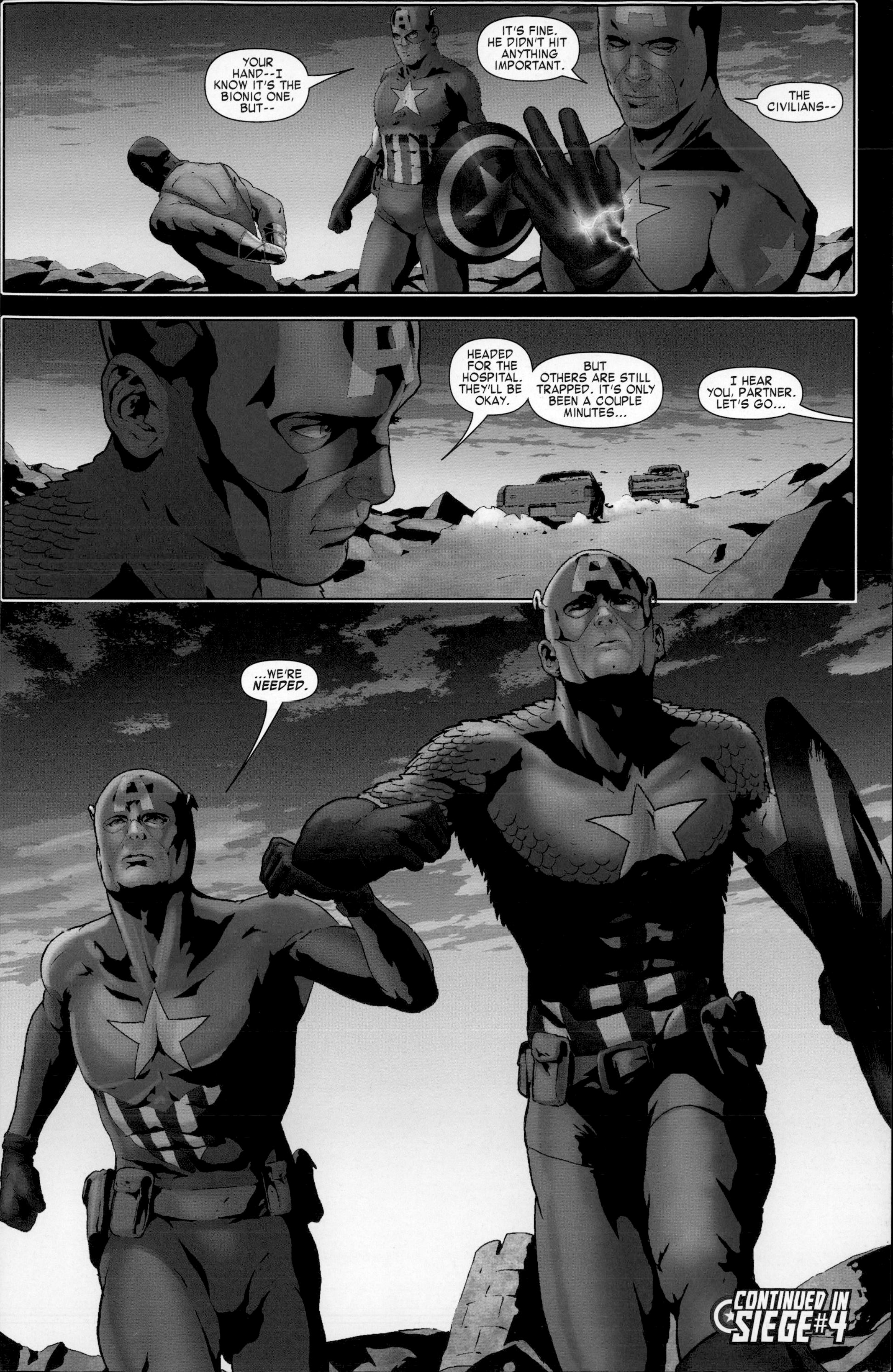
YOUR HAND--I KNOW IT'S THE BIONIC ONE, BUT--
IT'S FINE. HE DIDN'T HIT ANYTHING IMPORTANT.
THE CIVILIANS--
HEADED FOR THE HOSPITAL. THEY'LL BE OKAY.
BUT OTHERS ARE STILL TRAPPED. IT'S ONLY BEEN A COUPLE MINUTES...
I HEAR YOU, PARTNER. LET'S GO...
...WE'RE NEEDED.
CONTINUED IN SIEGE #4

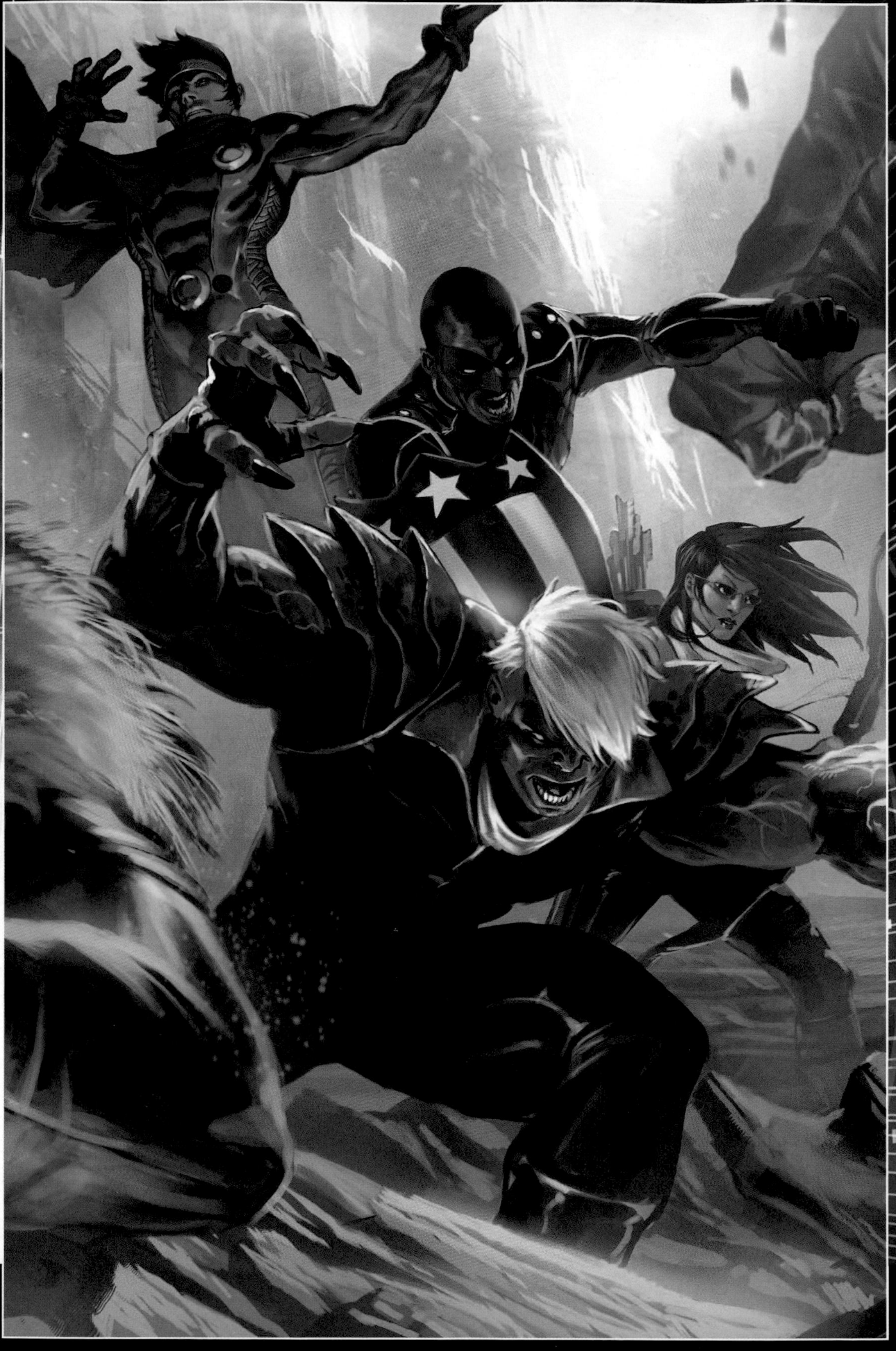

SIEGE: YOUNG AVENGERS

SIEGE

YOUNG AVENGERS

IN THE WAKE OF THE AVENGERS DISASSEMBLING, THE TIME TRAVELING TEENAGER WHO WOULD BECOME KANG THE CONQUEROR FOUND A FAILSAFE PROGRAM LEFT BEHIND BY THE DECEASED VISION DETAILING HOW TO FIND THE NEXT WAVE OF AVENGERS.

USING THIS PROGRAM, THE YOUNG KANG ADOPTED THE PERSONA OF IRON LAD, INITIALLY TEAMING WITH PATRIOT, ASGARDIAN AND HULKLING. AS TIME WENT ON, THE ROSTER GREW AND CHANGED WITH NEW MEMBERS, NEW IDENTITIES AND NEW RELATIONSHIPS.

NOW THE TEAM CONSISTS OF PATRIOT, HAWKEYE, WICCAN, HULKLING, SPEED, STATURE AND VISION. TO ONE ANOTHER, THEY ARE PARTNERS. SIBLINGS. FRIENDS. BUT TO THE WORLD AT LARGE, THEY ARE KNOWN AS THE YOUNG AVENGERS!

MEANWHILE, NORMAN OSBORN, FORMERLY KNOWN AS THE GREEN GOBLIN, HAS BECOME THE COMMANDER OF H.A.M.M.E.R. WITH THE NEW ALIAS IRON PATRIOT. HAVING FABRICATED AN EVENT REMINISCENT OF THE STAMFORD, CONNECTICUT TRAGEDY, OSBORN BEGAN HIS MAD SIEGE OF ASGARD. NOW THE YOUNG AVENGERS FIGHT ALONGSIDE CAPTAIN AMERICA AND THE ASGARDIAN GODS AGAINST OSBORN AND HIS INSANE ALLIES.

SEAN McKEEVER — WRITER

MAHMUD A. ASRAR — PENCILLER

SCOTT HANNA · VICTOR OLAZABA — INKERS

MATT MILLA · JORGE MAESE — COLORISTS

DAVE SHARPE — LETTERER

MARKO DJURDJEVIC COVER ART

RACHEL PINNELAS — ASSISTANT EDITOR

BILL ROSEMANN — EDITOR

JOE QUESADA — EDITOR IN CHIEF

DAN BUCKLEY — PUBLISHER

ALAN FINE — EXECUTIVE PRODUCER

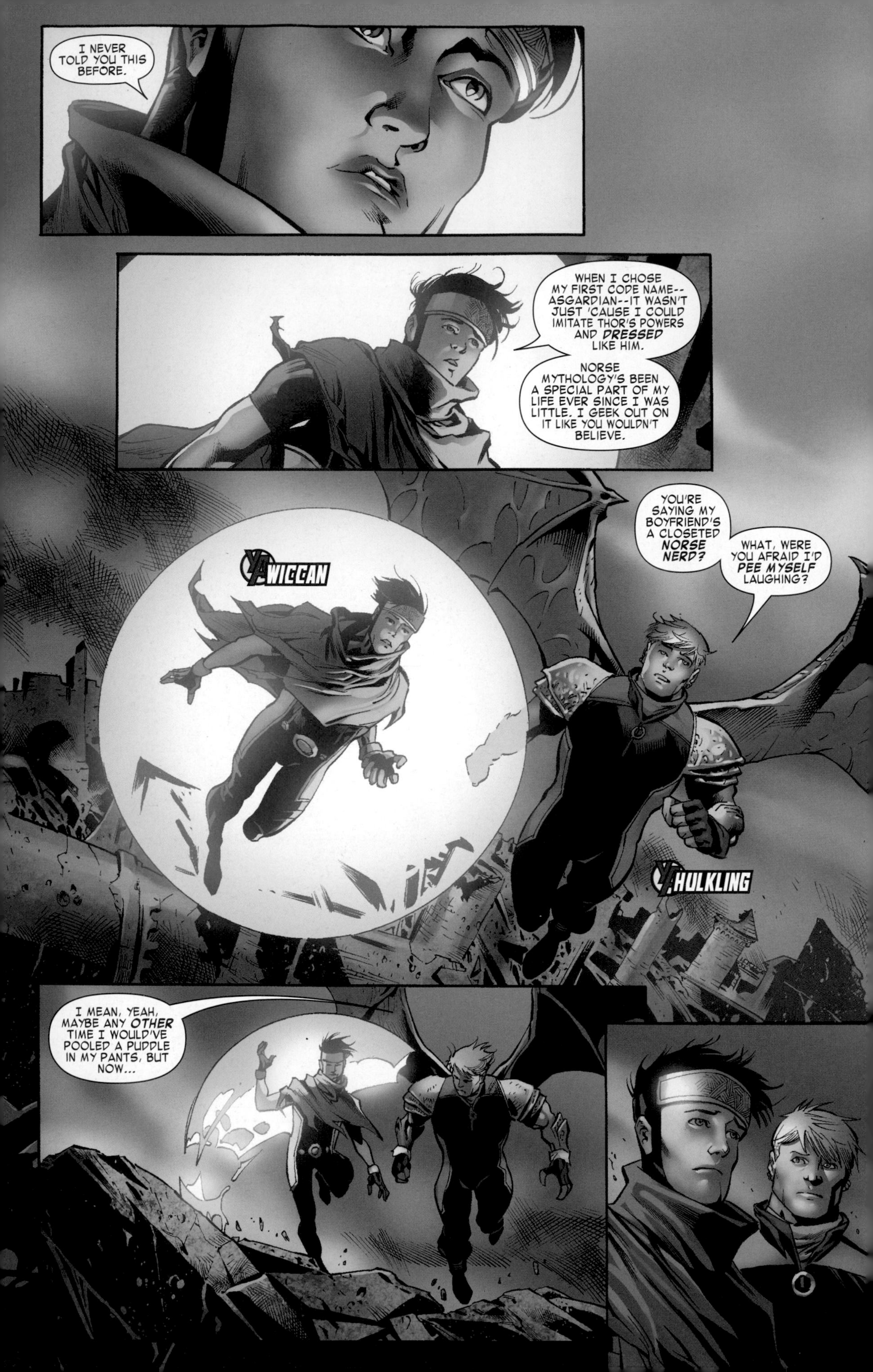
I NEVER TOLD YOU THIS BEFORE.
WHEN I CHOSE MY FIRST CODE NAME--ASGARDIAN--IT WASN'T JUST 'CAUSE I COULD IMITATE THOR'S POWERS AND DRESSED LIKE HIM.
NORSE MYTHOLOGY'S BEEN A SPECIAL PART OF MY LIFE EVER SINCE I WAS LITTLE. I GEEK OUT ON IT LIKE YOU WOULDN'T BELIEVE.
WICCAN
YOU'RE SAYING MY BOYFRIEND'S A CLOSETED NORSE NERD?
WHAT, WERE YOU AFRAID I'D PEE MYSELF LAUGHING?
HULKLING
I MEAN, YEAH, MAYBE ANY OTHER TIME I WOULD'VE POOLED A PUDDLE IN MY PANTS, BUT NOW...

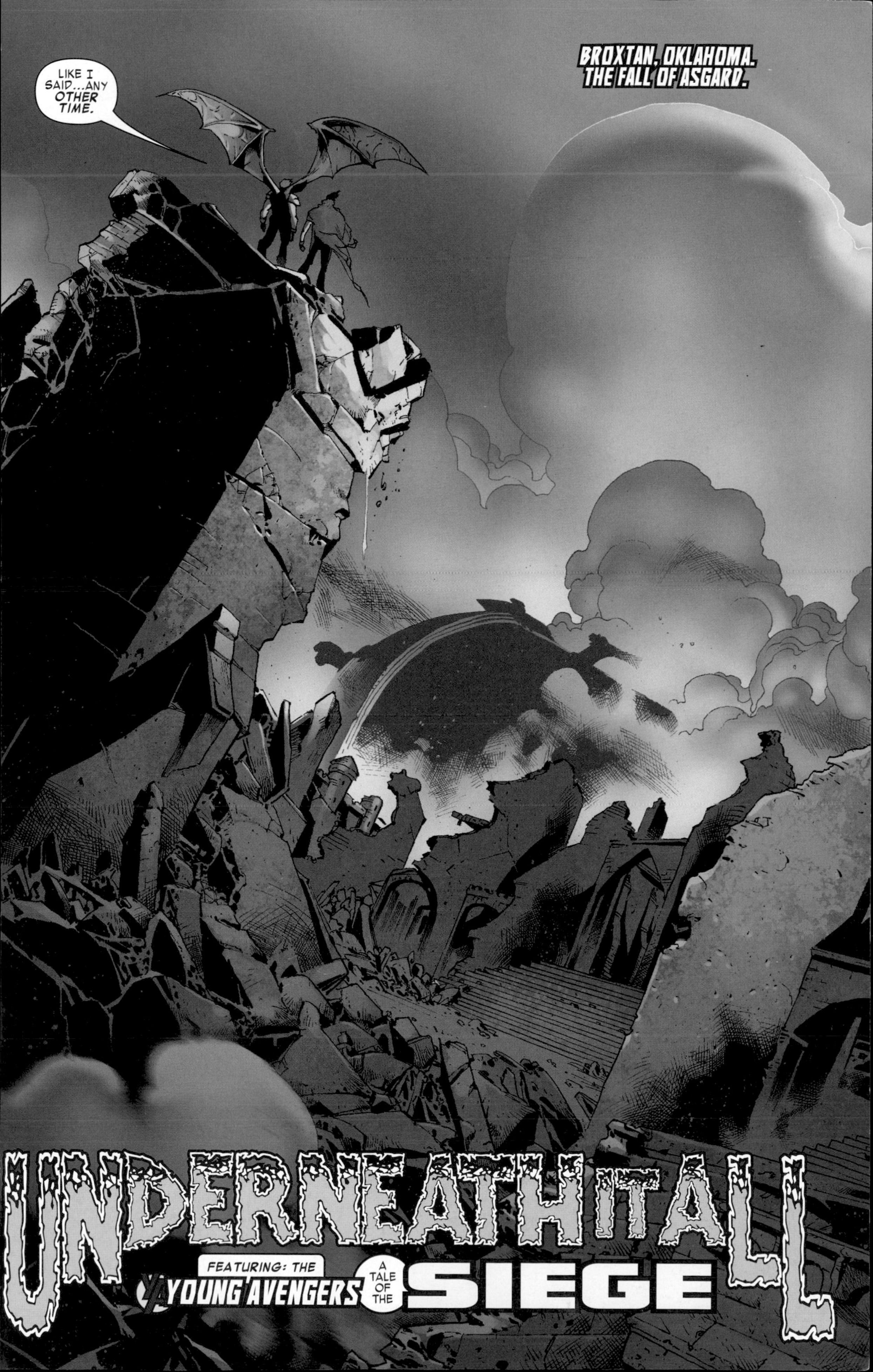
BROXTAN, OKLAHOMA. THE FALL OF ASGARD.
LIKE I SAID...ANY OTHER TIME.
UNDERNEATH IT ALL
FEATURING: THE YOUNG AVENGERS
A TALE OF THE SIEGE

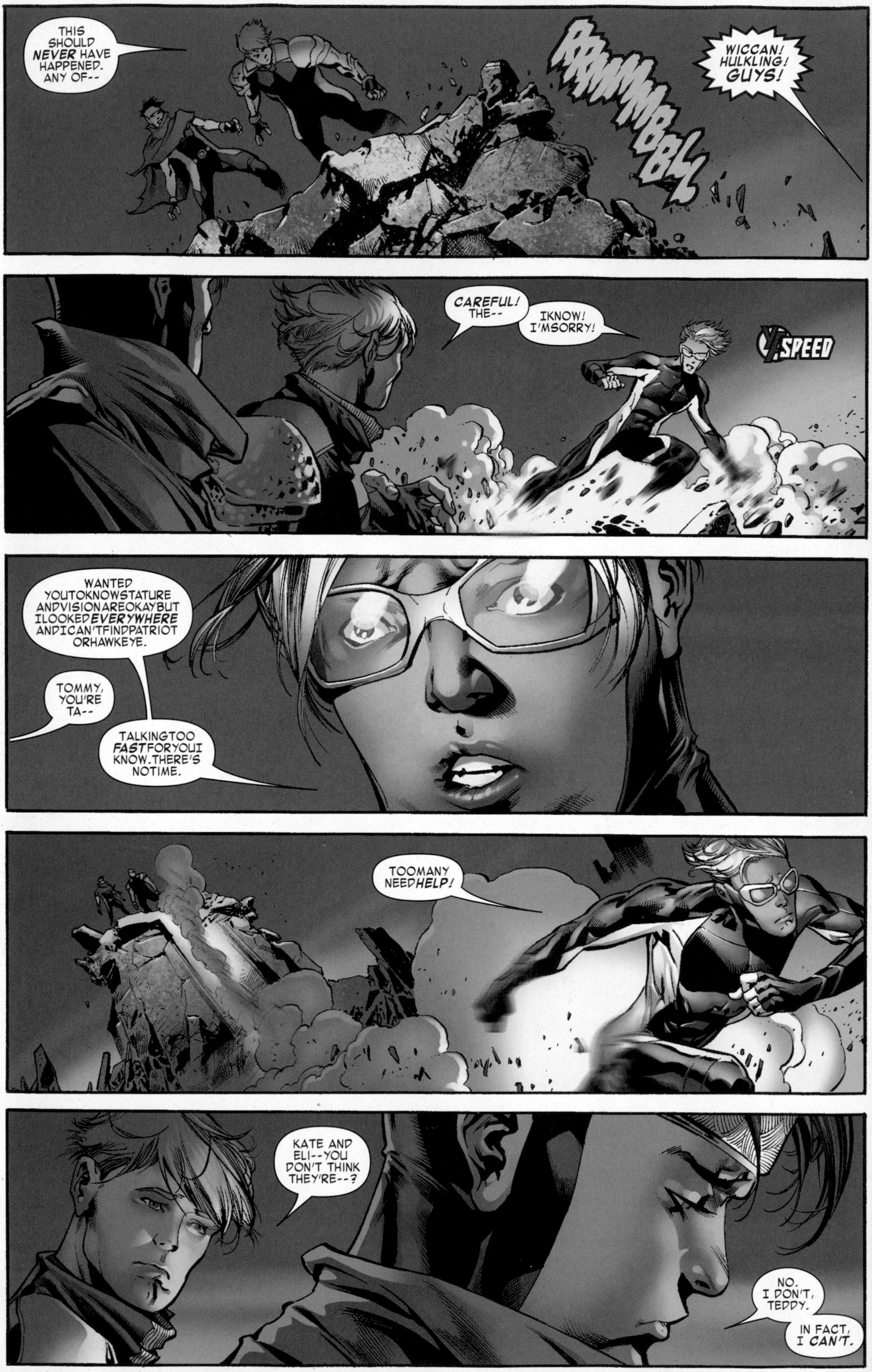
THIS SHOULD NEVER HAVE HAPPENED. ANY OF--
RRMMMBBLL
WICCAN! HULKLING! GUYS!
CAREFUL! THE--
IKNOW! I'MSORRY!
SPEED
WANTED YOUTOKNOWSTATURE ANDVISIONAREOKAYBUT ILOOKEDEVERYWHERE ANDICAN'TFINDPATRIOT ORHAWKEYE.
TOMMY, YOU'RE TA--
TALKINGTOO FASTFORYOUI KNOW.THERE'S NOTIME.
TOOMANY NEEDHELP!
KATE AND ELI--YOU DON'T THINK THEY'RE--?
NO. I DON'T, TEDDY.
IN FACT, I CAN'T.

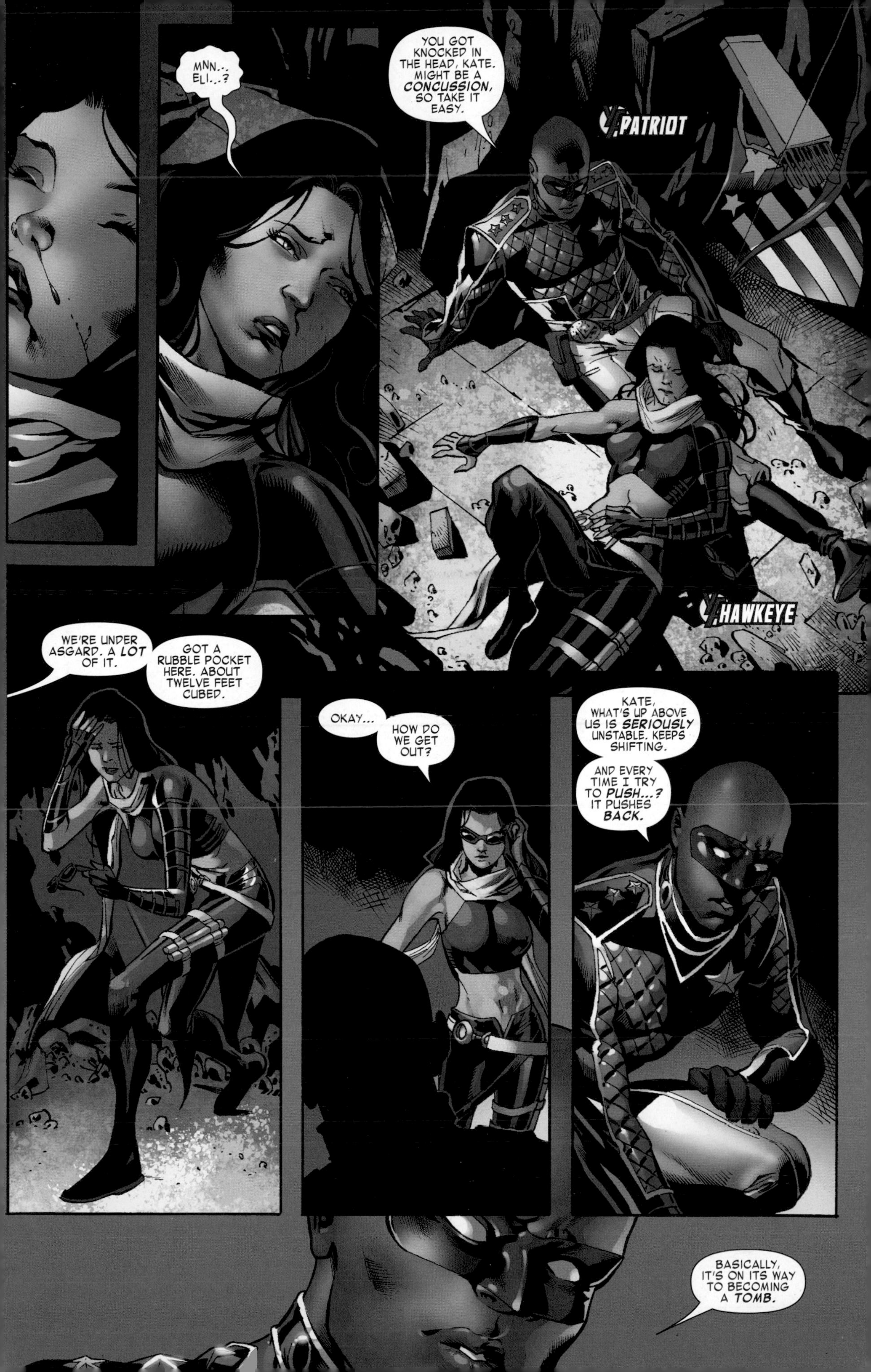
MNN... ELI...?
YOU GOT KNOCKED IN THE HEAD, KATE. MIGHT BE A CONCUSSION, SO TAKE IT EASY.
PATRIOT
HAWKEYE
WE'RE UNDER ASGARD. A LOT OF IT.
GOT A RUBBLE POCKET HERE. ABOUT TWELVE FEET CUBED.
OKAY...
HOW DO WE GET OUT?
KATE, WHAT'S UP ABOVE US IS SERIOUSLY UNSTABLE. KEEPS SHIFTING.
AND EVERY TIME I TRY TO PUSH...? IT PUSHES BACK.
BASICALLY, IT'S ON ITS WAY TO BECOMING A TOMB.

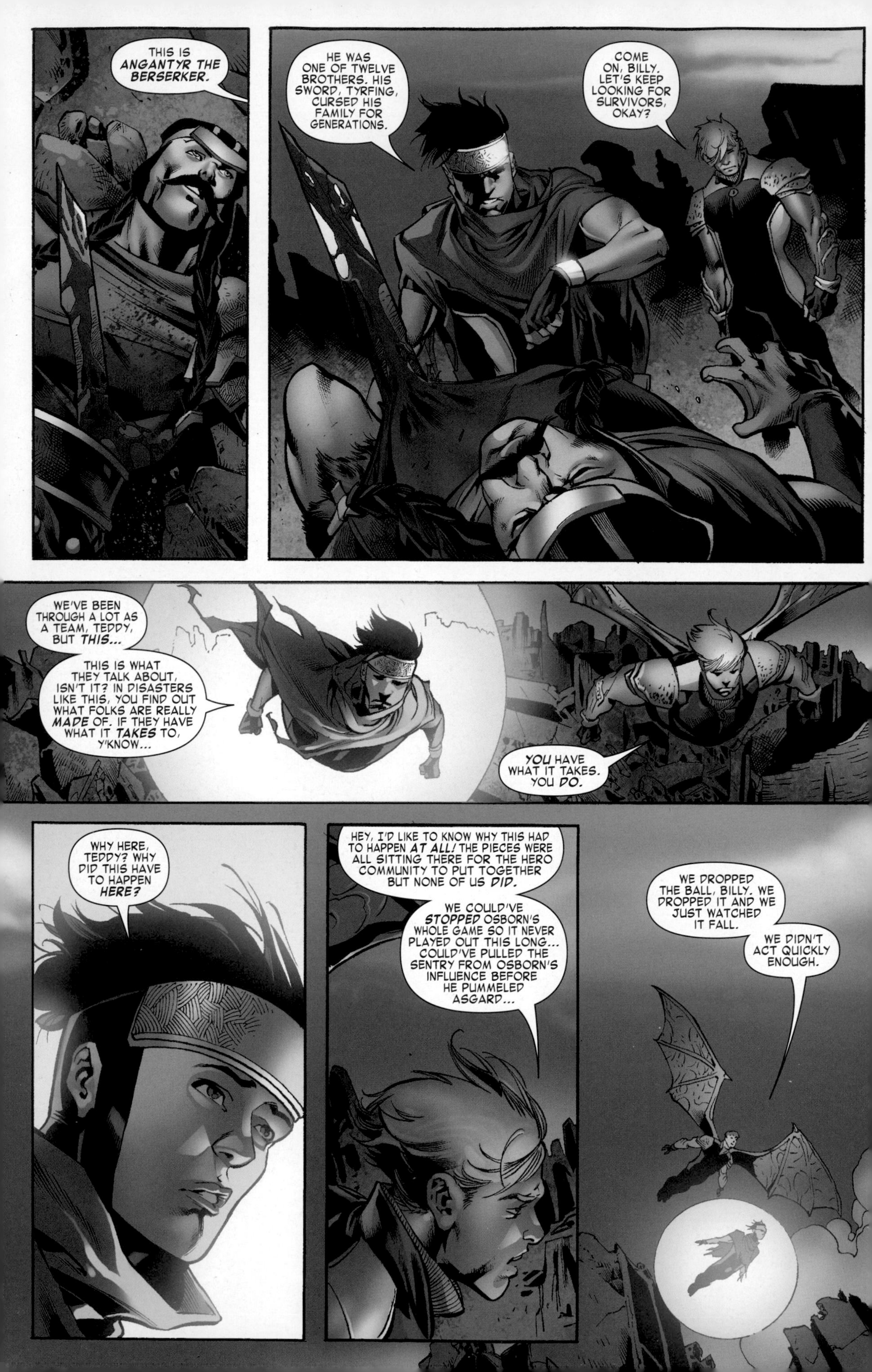
THIS IS *ANGANTYR THE BERSERKER.*
HE WAS ONE OF TWELVE BROTHERS. HIS SWORD, TYRFING, CURSED HIS FAMILY FOR GENERATIONS.
COME ON, BILLY. LET'S KEEP LOOKING FOR SURVIVORS, OKAY?
WE'VE BEEN THROUGH A LOT AS A TEAM, TEDDY, BUT *THIS...*
THIS IS WHAT THEY TALK ABOUT, ISN'T IT? IN DISASTERS LIKE THIS, YOU FIND OUT WHAT FOLKS ARE REALLY *MADE* OF. IF THEY HAVE WHAT IT *TAKES* TO, Y'KNOW...
YOU HAVE WHAT IT TAKES. YOU *DO.*
WHY HERE, TEDDY? WHY DID THIS HAVE TO HAPPEN *HERE?*
HEY, I'D LIKE TO KNOW WHY THIS HAD TO HAPPEN *AT ALL!* THE PIECES WERE ALL SITTING THERE FOR THE HERO COMMUNITY TO PUT TOGETHER BUT NONE OF US *DID.*
WE COULD'VE *STOPPED* OSBORN'S WHOLE GAME SO IT NEVER PLAYED OUT THIS LONG... COULD'VE PULLED THE SENTRY FROM OSBORN'S INFLUENCE BEFORE HE PUMMELED ASGARD...
WE DROPPED THE BALL, BILLY. WE DROPPED IT AND WE JUST WATCHED IT FALL.
WE DIDN'T ACT QUICKLY ENOUGH.

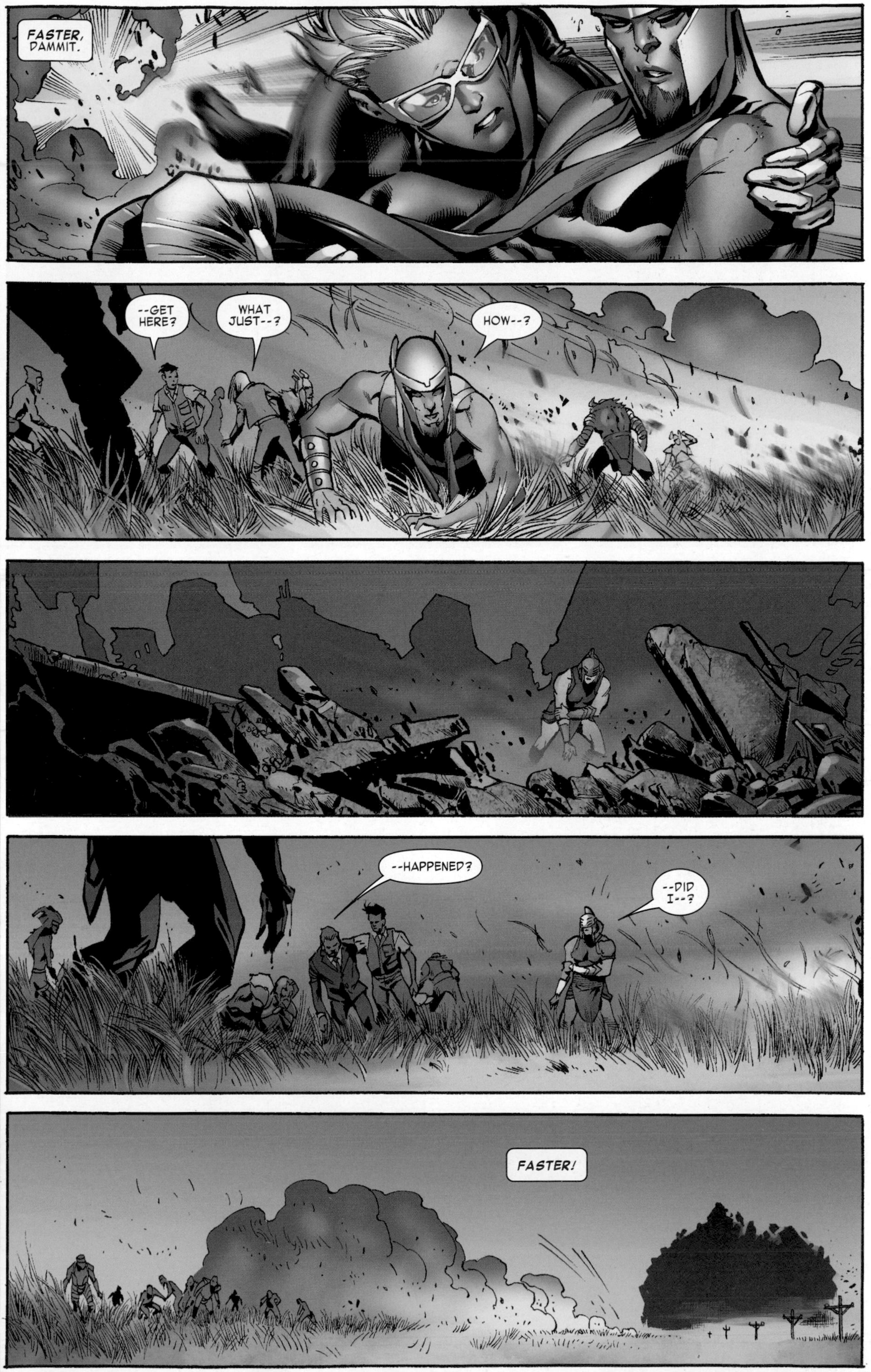
FASTER, DAMMIT.
--GET HERE?
WHAT JUST--?
HOW--?
--HAPPENED?
--DID I--?
FASTER!

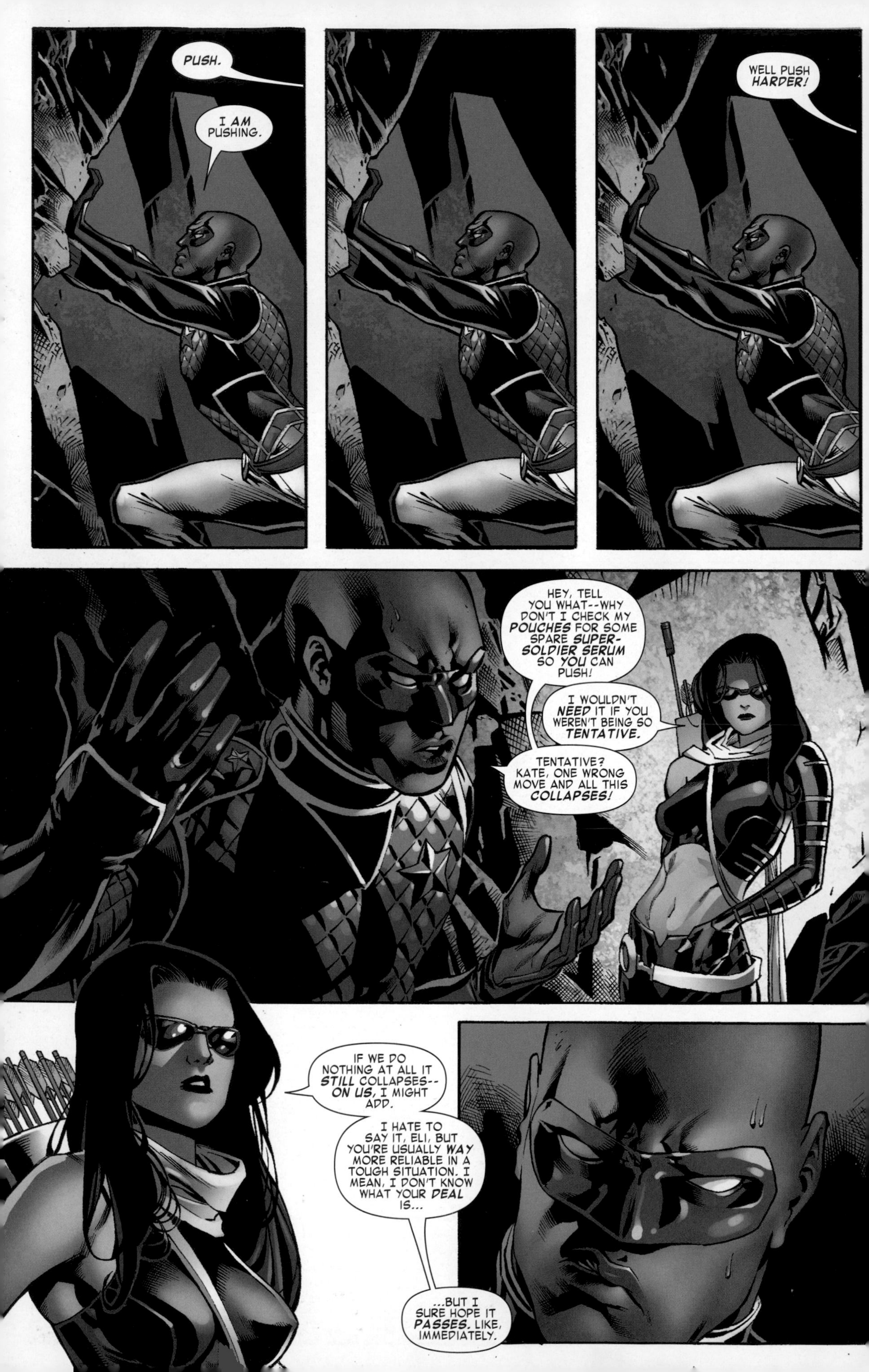
PUSH.
I AM PUSHING.
WELL PUSH HARDER!
HEY, TELL YOU WHAT--WHY DON'T I CHECK MY POUCHES FOR SOME SPARE SUPER-SOLDIER SERUM SO YOU CAN PUSH!
I WOULDN'T NEED IT IF YOU WEREN'T BEING SO TENTATIVE.
TENTATIVE? KATE, ONE WRONG MOVE AND ALL THIS COLLAPSES!
IF WE DO NOTHING AT ALL IT STILL COLLAPSES-- ON US, I MIGHT ADD.
I HATE TO SAY IT, ELI, BUT YOU'RE USUALLY WAY MORE RELIABLE IN A TOUGH SITUATION. I MEAN, I DON'T KNOW WHAT YOUR DEAL IS...
...BUT I SURE HOPE IT PASSES. LIKE, IMMEDIATELY.

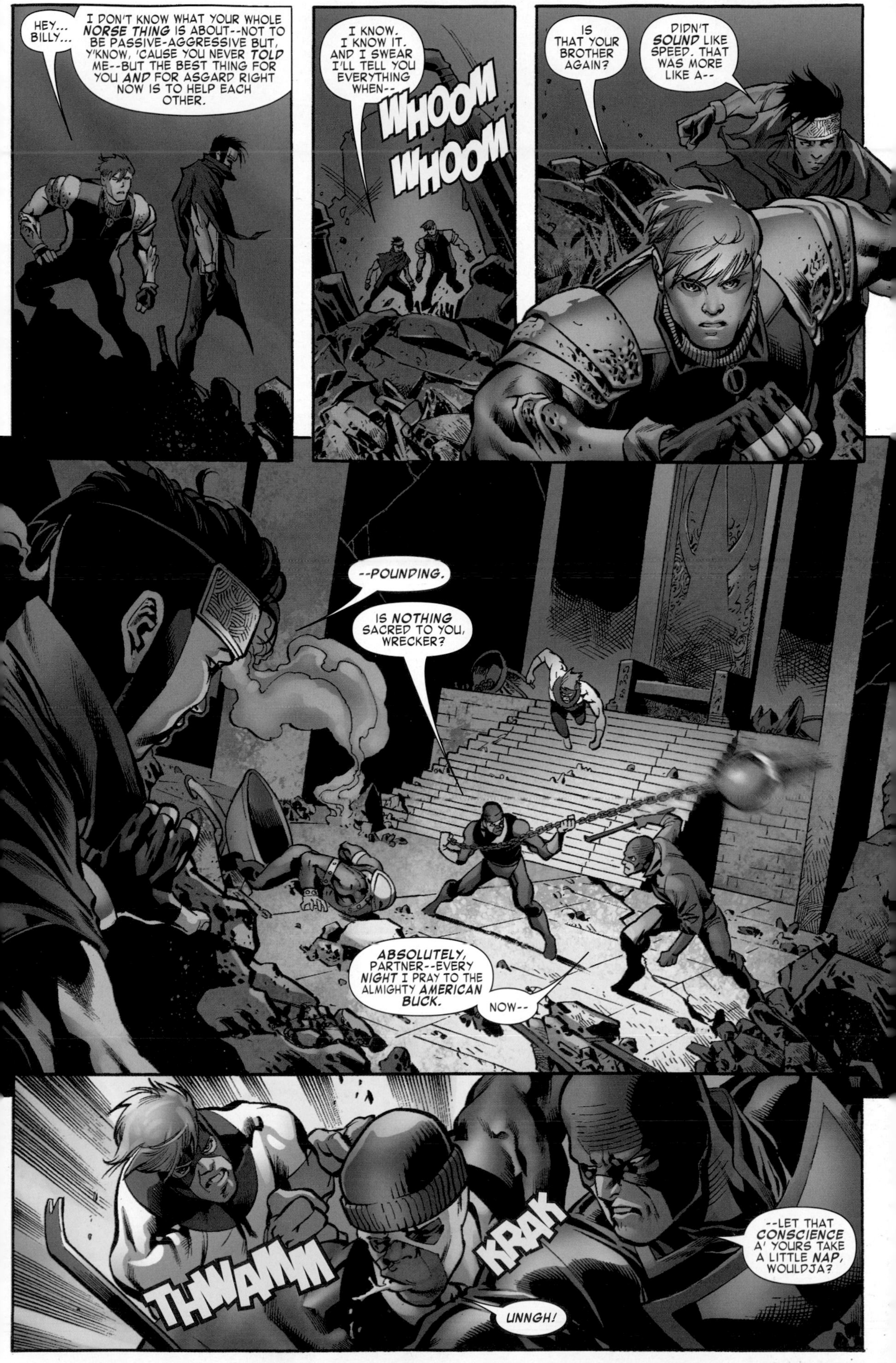
HEY... BILLY...
I DON'T KNOW WHAT YOUR WHOLE NORSE THING IS ABOUT--NOT TO BE PASSIVE-AGGRESSIVE BUT, Y'KNOW, 'CAUSE YOU NEVER TOLD ME--BUT THE BEST THING FOR YOU AND FOR ASGARD RIGHT NOW IS TO HELP EACH OTHER.
I KNOW. I KNOW IT. AND I SWEAR I'LL TELL YOU EVERYTHING WHEN--
WHOOM
WHOOM
IS THAT YOUR BROTHER AGAIN?
DIDN'T SOUND LIKE SPEED. THAT WAS MORE LIKE A--
--POUNDING.
IS NOTHING SACRED TO YOU, WRECKER?
ABSOLUTELY, PARTNER--EVERY NIGHT I PRAY TO THE ALMIGHTY AMERICAN BUCK.
NOW--
THWAMM
KRAK
--LET THAT CONSCIENCE A' YOURS TAKE A LITTLE NAP, WOULDJA?
UNNGH!

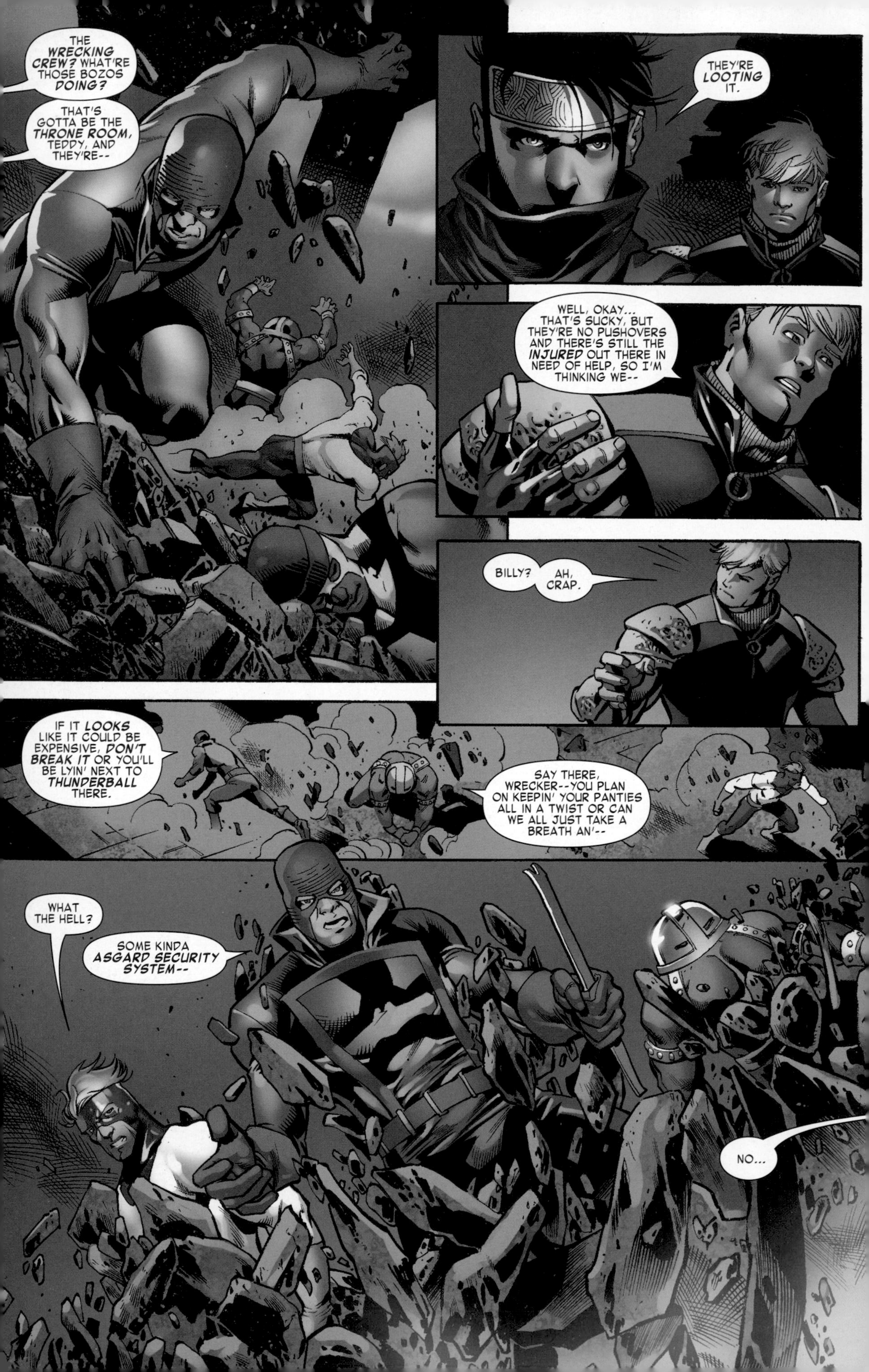
THE WRECKING CREW? WHAT'RE THOSE BOZOS DOING?
THAT'S GOTTA BE THE THRONE ROOM, TEDDY, AND THEY'RE--
THEY'RE LOOTING IT.
WELL, OKAY... THAT'S SUCKY, BUT THEY'RE NO PUSHOVERS AND THERE'S STILL THE INJURED OUT THERE IN NEED OF HELP, SO I'M THINKING WE--
BILLY?
AH, CRAP.
IF IT LOOKS LIKE IT COULD BE EXPENSIVE, DON'T BREAK IT OR YOU'LL BE LYIN' NEXT TO THUNDERBALL THERE.
SAY THERE, WRECKER--YOU PLAN ON KEEPIN' YOUR PANTIES ALL IN A TWIST OR CAN WE ALL JUST TAKE A BREATH AN'--
WHAT THE HELL?
SOME KINDA ASGARD SECURITY SYSTEM--
NO...

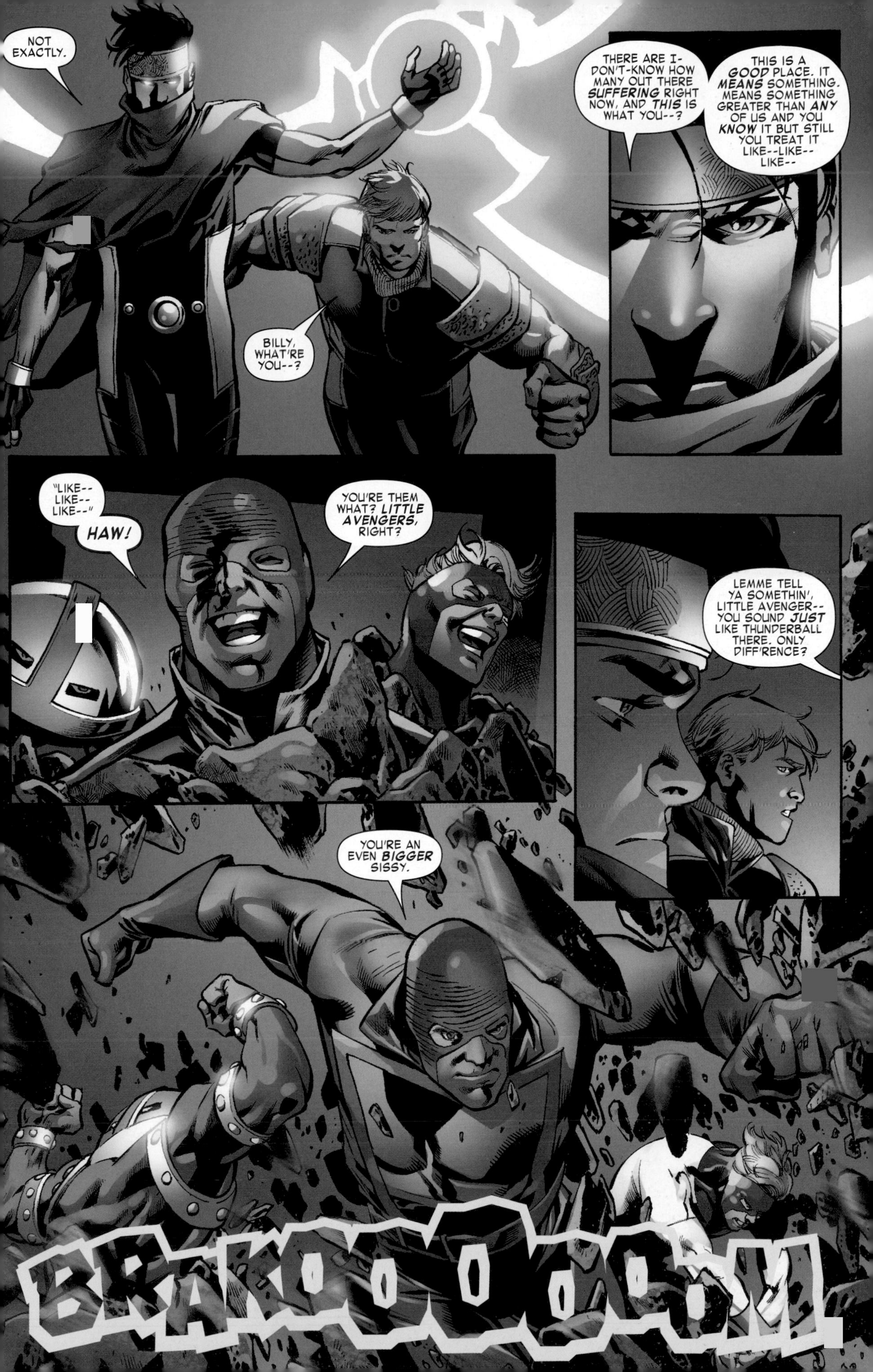

NOT EXACTLY.
BILLY, WHAT'RE YOU--?
THERE ARE I-DON'T-KNOW HOW MANY OUT THERE SUFFERING RIGHT NOW, AND THIS IS WHAT YOU--?
THIS IS A GOOD PLACE. IT MEANS SOMETHING. MEANS SOMETHING GREATER THAN ANY OF US AND YOU KNOW IT BUT STILL YOU TREAT IT LIKE--LIKE--LIKE--
"LIKE--LIKE--LIKE--"
HAW!
YOU'RE THEM WHAT? LITTLE AVENGERS, RIGHT?
LEMME TELL YA SOMETHIN', LITTLE AVENGER--YOU SOUND JUST LIKE THUNDERBALL THERE. ONLY DIFF'RENCE?
YOU'RE AN EVEN BIGGER SISSY.

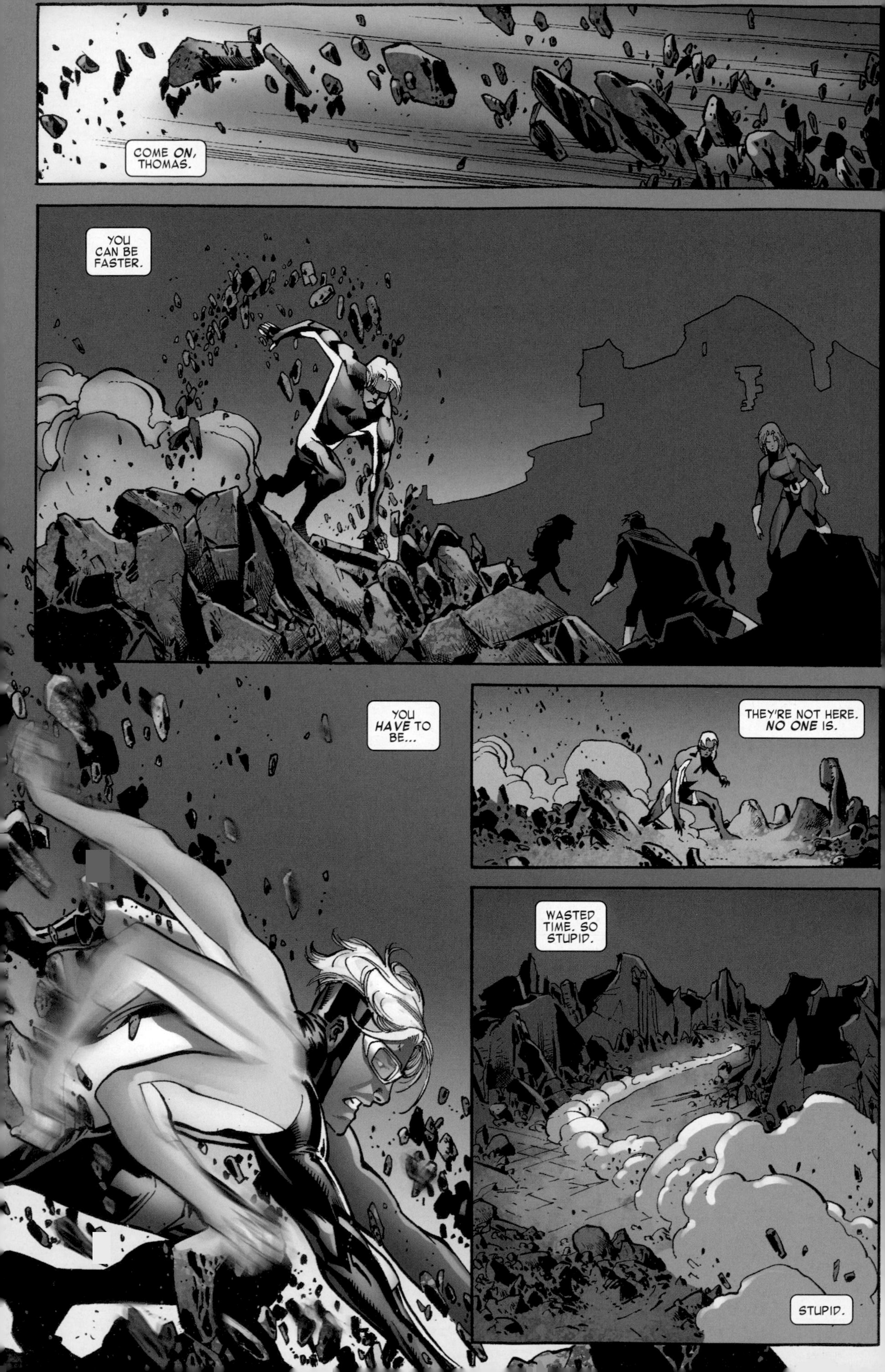
COME *ON*, THOMAS.
YOU CAN BE FASTER.
YOU *HAVE* TO BE...
THEY'RE NOT HERE. *NO ONE* IS.
WASTED TIME. SO STUPID.
STUPID.

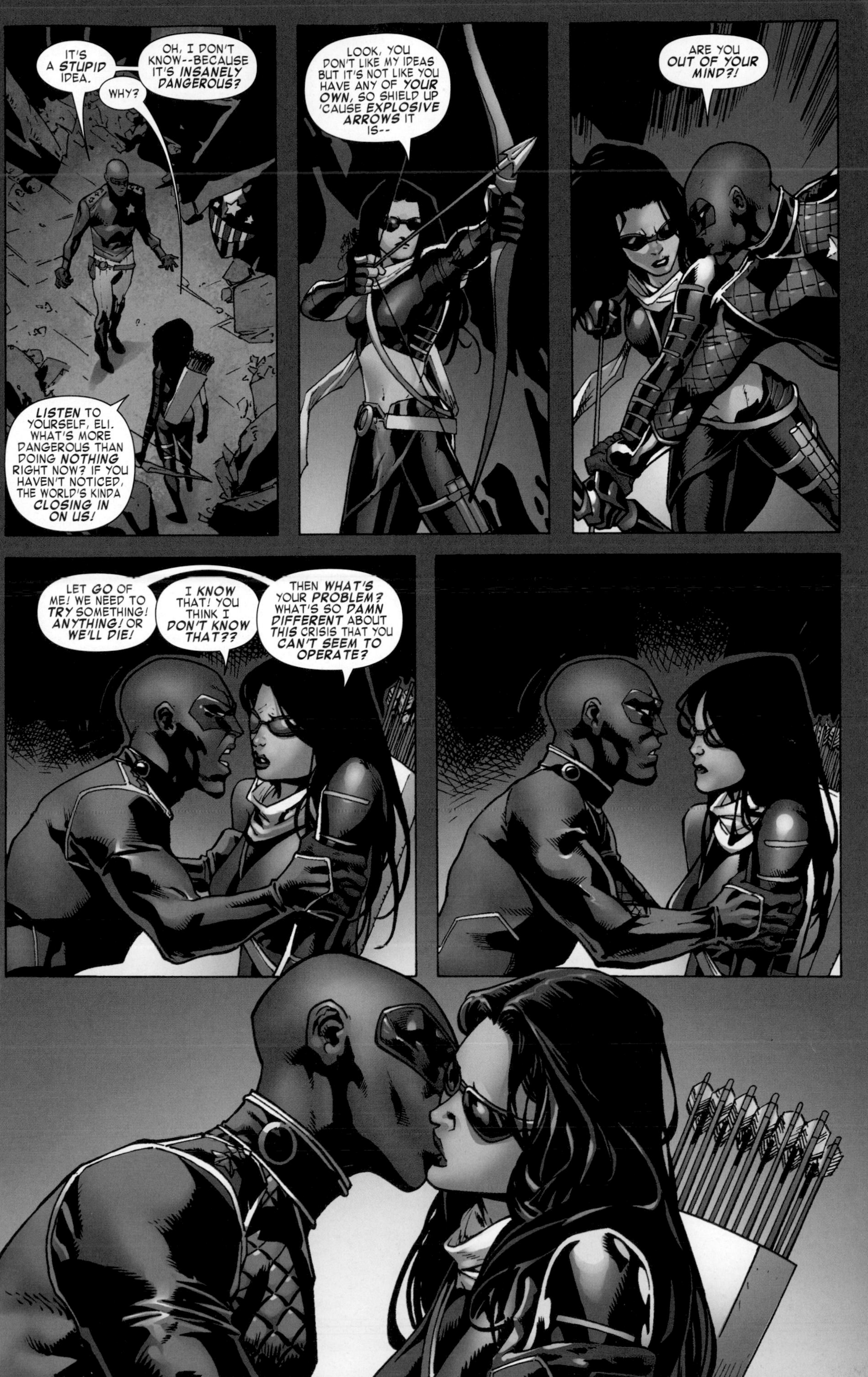
IT'S A STUPID IDEA.
WHY?
OH, I DON'T KNOW--BECAUSE IT'S INSANELY DANGEROUS?
LISTEN TO YOURSELF, ELI. WHAT'S MORE DANGEROUS THAN DOING NOTHING RIGHT NOW? IF YOU HAVEN'T NOTICED, THE WORLD'S KINDA CLOSING IN ON US!
LOOK, YOU DON'T LIKE MY IDEAS BUT IT'S NOT LIKE YOU HAVE ANY OF YOUR OWN, SO SHIELD UP 'CAUSE EXPLOSIVE ARROWS IT IS--
ARE YOU OUT OF YOUR MIND?!
LET GO OF ME! WE NEED TO TRY SOMETHING! ANYTHING! OR WE'LL DIE!
I KNOW THAT! YOU THINK I DON'T KNOW THAT??
THEN WHAT'S YOUR PROBLEM? WHAT'S SO DAMN DIFFERENT ABOUT THIS CRISIS THAT YOU CAN'T SEEM TO OPERATE?

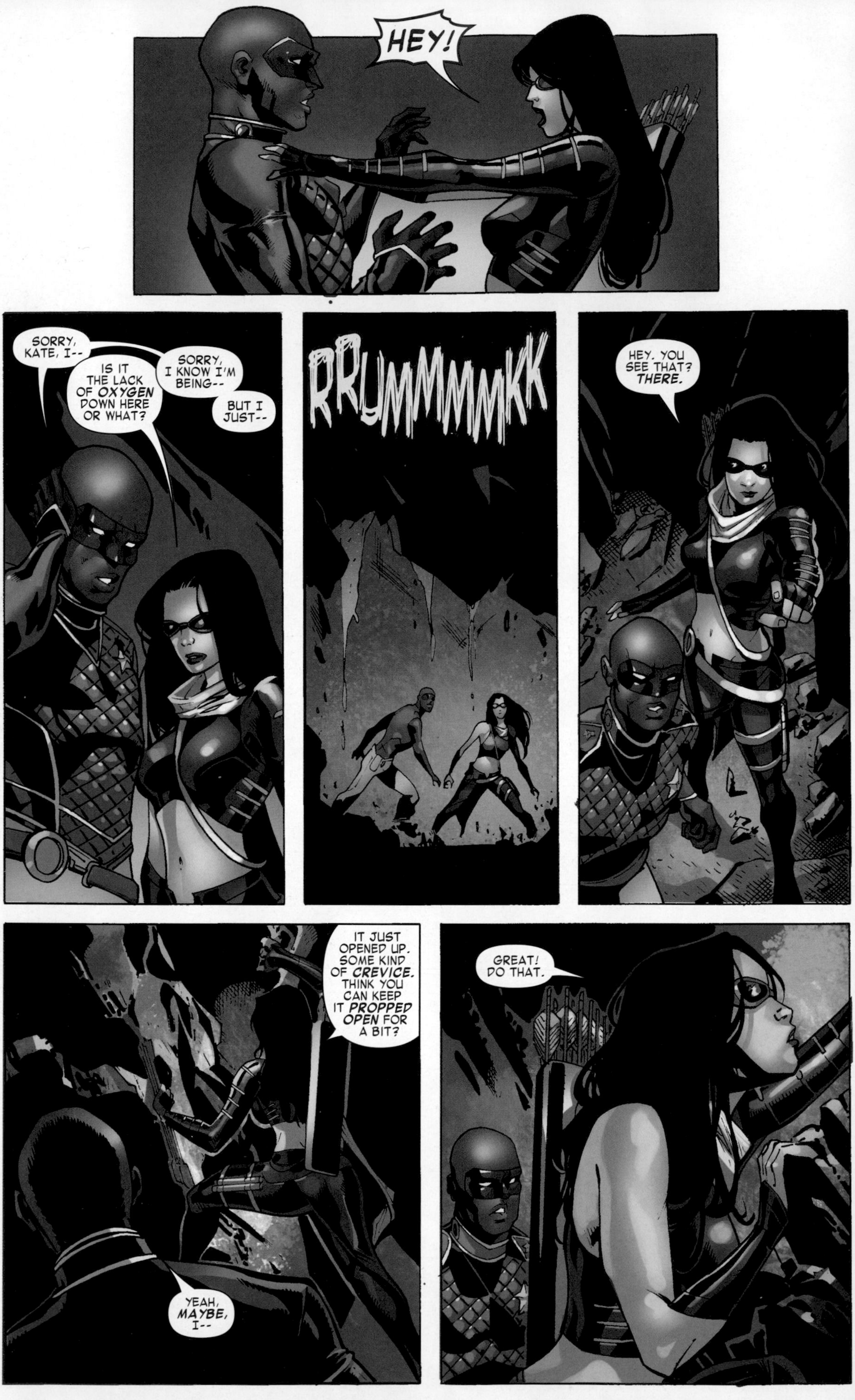
HEY!
SORRY, KATE, I--
IS IT THE LACK OF OXYGEN DOWN HERE OR WHAT?
SORRY, I KNOW I'M BEING--
BUT I JUST--
RRUMMMMKK
HEY. YOU SEE THAT? THERE.
IT JUST OPENED UP. SOME KIND OF CREVICE. THINK YOU CAN KEEP IT PROPPED OPEN FOR A BIT?
YEAH, MAYBE, I--
GREAT! DO THAT.

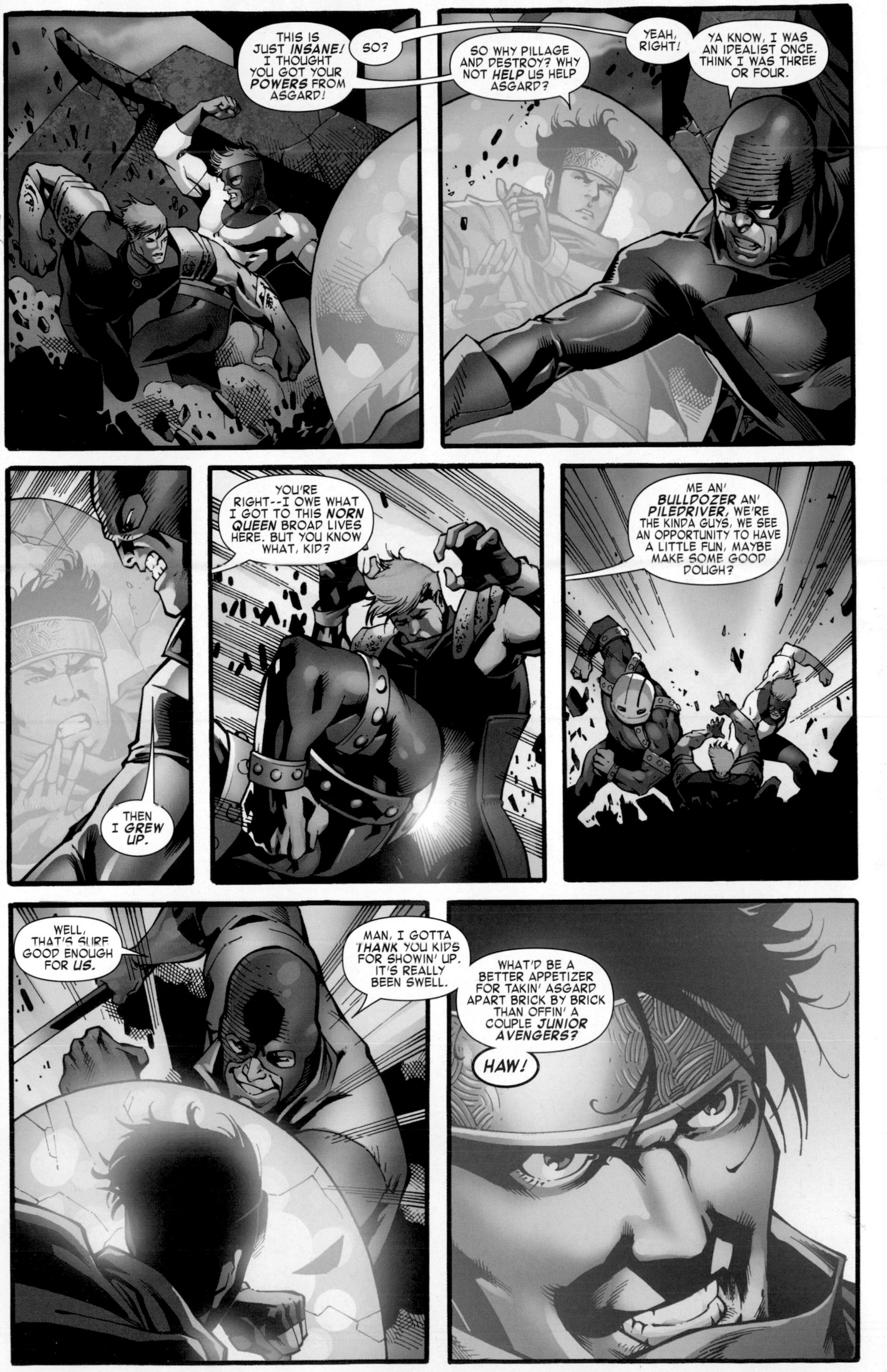
THIS IS JUST INSANE! I THOUGHT YOU GOT YOUR POWERS FROM ASGARD!
SO?
SO WHY PILLAGE AND DESTROY? WHY NOT HELP US HELP ASGARD?
YEAH, RIGHT!
YA KNOW, I WAS AN IDEALIST ONCE. THINK I WAS THREE OR FOUR.
THEN I GREW UP.
YOU'RE RIGHT--I OWE WHAT I GOT TO THIS NORN QUEEN BROAD LIVES HERE. BUT YOU KNOW WHAT, KID?
ME AN' BULLDOZER AN' PILEDRIVER, WE'RE THE KINDA GUYS, WE SEE AN OPPORTUNITY TO HAVE A LITTLE FUN, MAYBE MAKE SOME GOOD DOUGH?
WELL, THAT'S SURE GOOD ENOUGH FOR US.
MAN, I GOTTA THANK YOU KIDS FOR SHOWIN' UP. IT'S REALLY BEEN SWELL.
WHAT'D BE A BETTER APPETIZER FOR TAKIN' ASGARD APART BRICK BY BRICK THAN OFFIN' A COUPLE JUNIOR AVENGERS?
HAW!

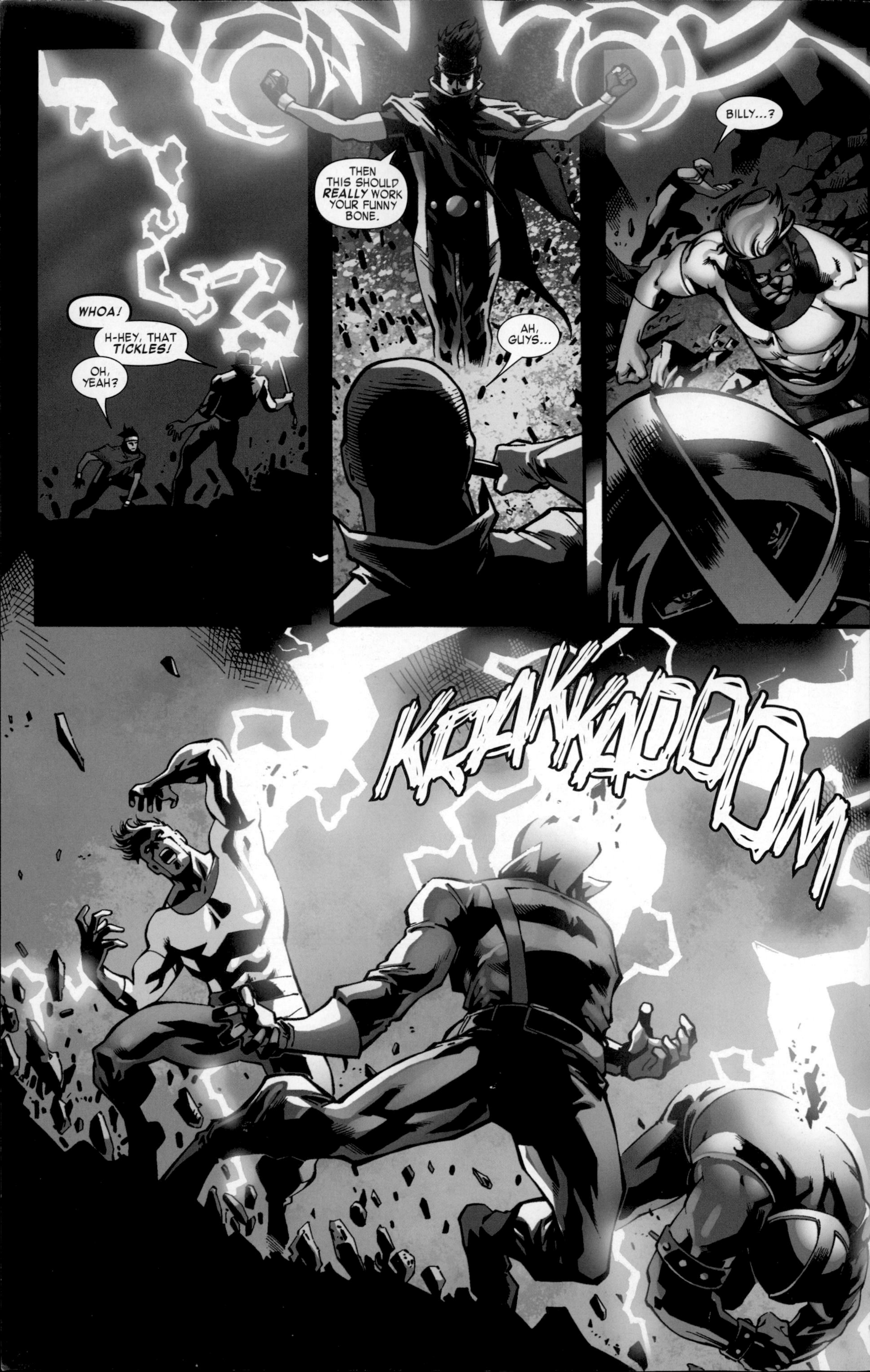
WHOA!
H-HEY, THAT TICKLES!
OH, YEAH?
THEN THIS SHOULD REALLY WORK YOUR FUNNY BONE.
AH, GUYS...
BILLY...?
KRAKKADOOOM

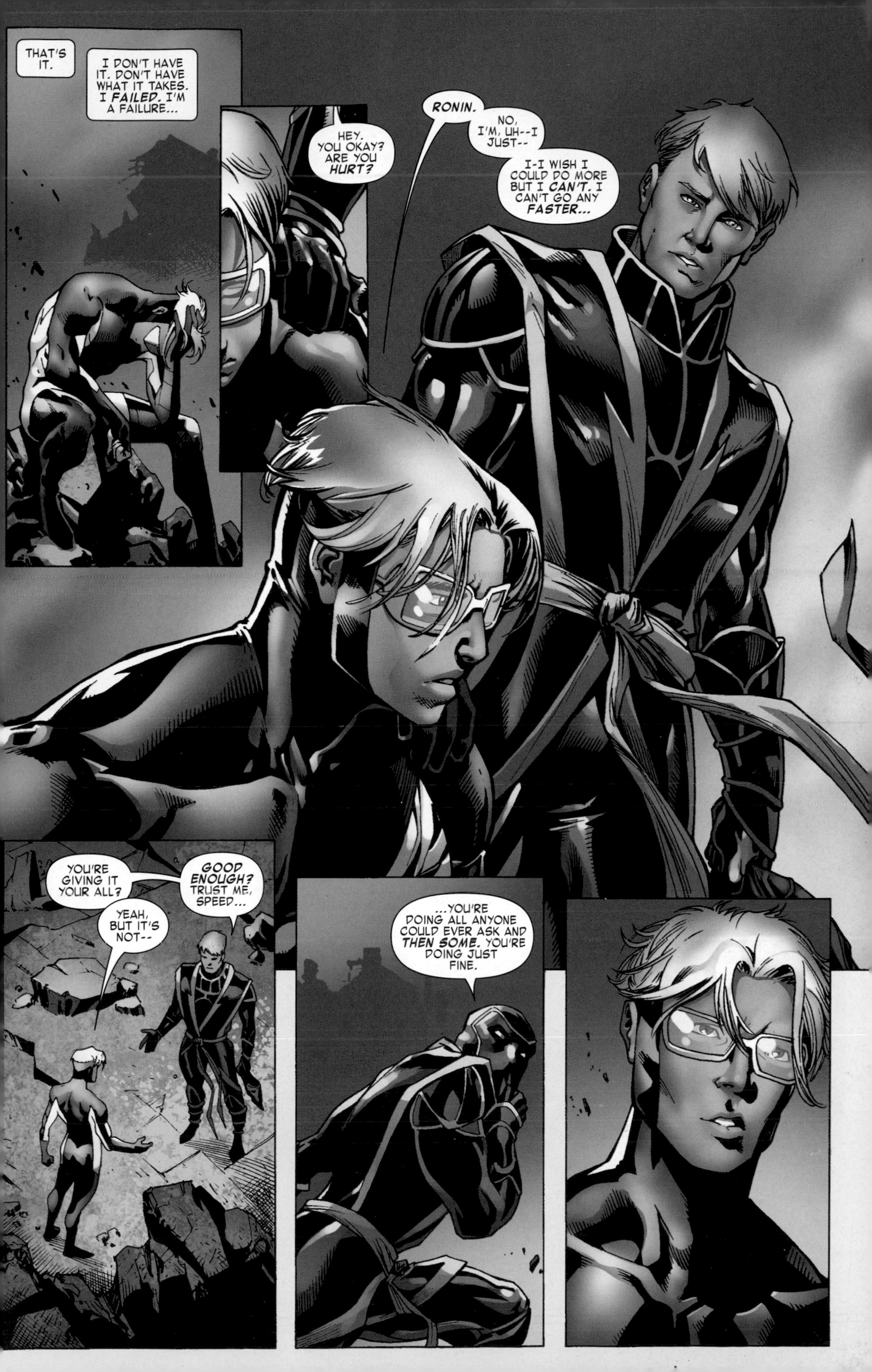
THAT'S IT.
I DON'T HAVE IT. DON'T HAVE WHAT IT TAKES. I FAILED. I'M A FAILURE...
HEY. YOU OKAY? ARE YOU HURT?
RONIN.
NO, I'M, UH--I JUST--
I-I WISH I COULD DO MORE BUT I CAN'T. I CAN'T GO ANY FASTER...
YOU'RE GIVING IT YOUR ALL?
YEAH, BUT IT'S NOT--
GOOD ENOUGH? TRUST ME, SPEED...
...YOU'RE DOING ALL ANYONE COULD EVER ASK AND THEN SOME. YOU'RE DOING JUST FINE.

UH...
DID YOU
JUST...?

THEY'LL
BE OKAY.

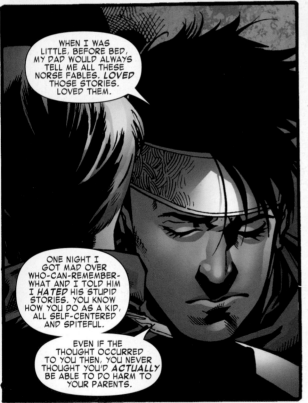

ARE
YOU
OKAY?

NO NO NO.
IT'S NOT YOU
WHO GETS TO
WORRY ABOUT
ME RIGHT
NOW.

WHEN I WAS
LITTLE, BEFORE BED,
MY DAD WOULD ALWAYS
TELL ME ALL THESE
NORSE FABLES. LOVED
THOSE STORIES.
LOVED THEM.

ONE NIGHT I
GOT MAD OVER
WHO-CAN-REMEMBER-
WHAT AND I TOLD HIM
I HATED HIS STUPID
STORIES. YOU KNOW
HOW YOU DO AS A KID,
ALL SELF-CENTERED
AND SPITEFUL.

EVEN IF THE
THOUGHT OCCURRED
TO YOU THEN, YOU NEVER
THOUGHT YOU'D ACTUALLY
BE ABLE TO DO HARM TO
YOUR PARENTS.

HE NEVER
TOLD ME THOSE
STORIES AGAIN AFTER
THAT, AND NOW THAT
I'M OLDER ALL I CAN
THINK IS HOW I HURT
HIM AND I WISH
IT NEVER--

HEY.
DON'T DO THAT.
WHAT'S PASSED
IS PAST.

YEAH, WE
MAKE MISTAKES,
BUT EVEN IF WE DON'T
GET THE CHANCE TO
CORRECT THEM WE
CAN STILL LEARN
FROM THEM,
RIGHT?

COME ON,
SOFTIE. 'PORT
THESE BOZOS
TO SAFETY SO
WE CAN GO
FIND OUR
FRIENDS.

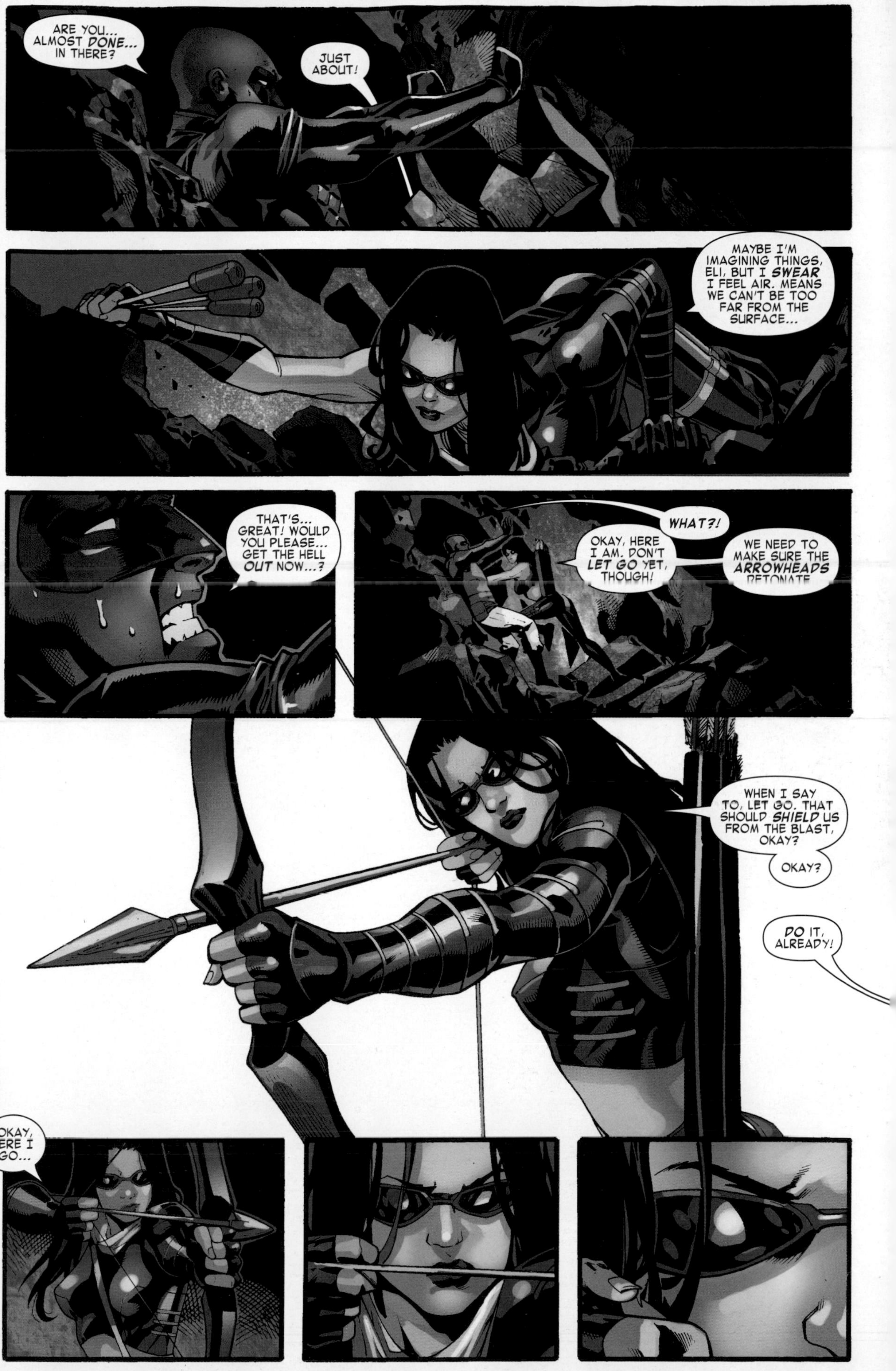
ARE YOU... ALMOST DONE... IN THERE?
JUST ABOUT!
MAYBE I'M IMAGINING THINGS, ELI, BUT I SWEAR I FEEL AIR. MEANS WE CAN'T BE TOO FAR FROM THE SURFACE...
THAT'S... GREAT! WOULD YOU PLEASE... GET THE HELL OUT NOW...?
WHAT?!
OKAY, HERE I AM. DON'T LET GO YET, THOUGH!
WE NEED TO MAKE SURE THE ARROWHEADS DETONATE
WHEN I SAY TO, LET GO. THAT SHOULD SHIELD US FROM THE BLAST, OKAY?
OKAY?
DO IT, ALREADY!
OKAY, HERE I GO...

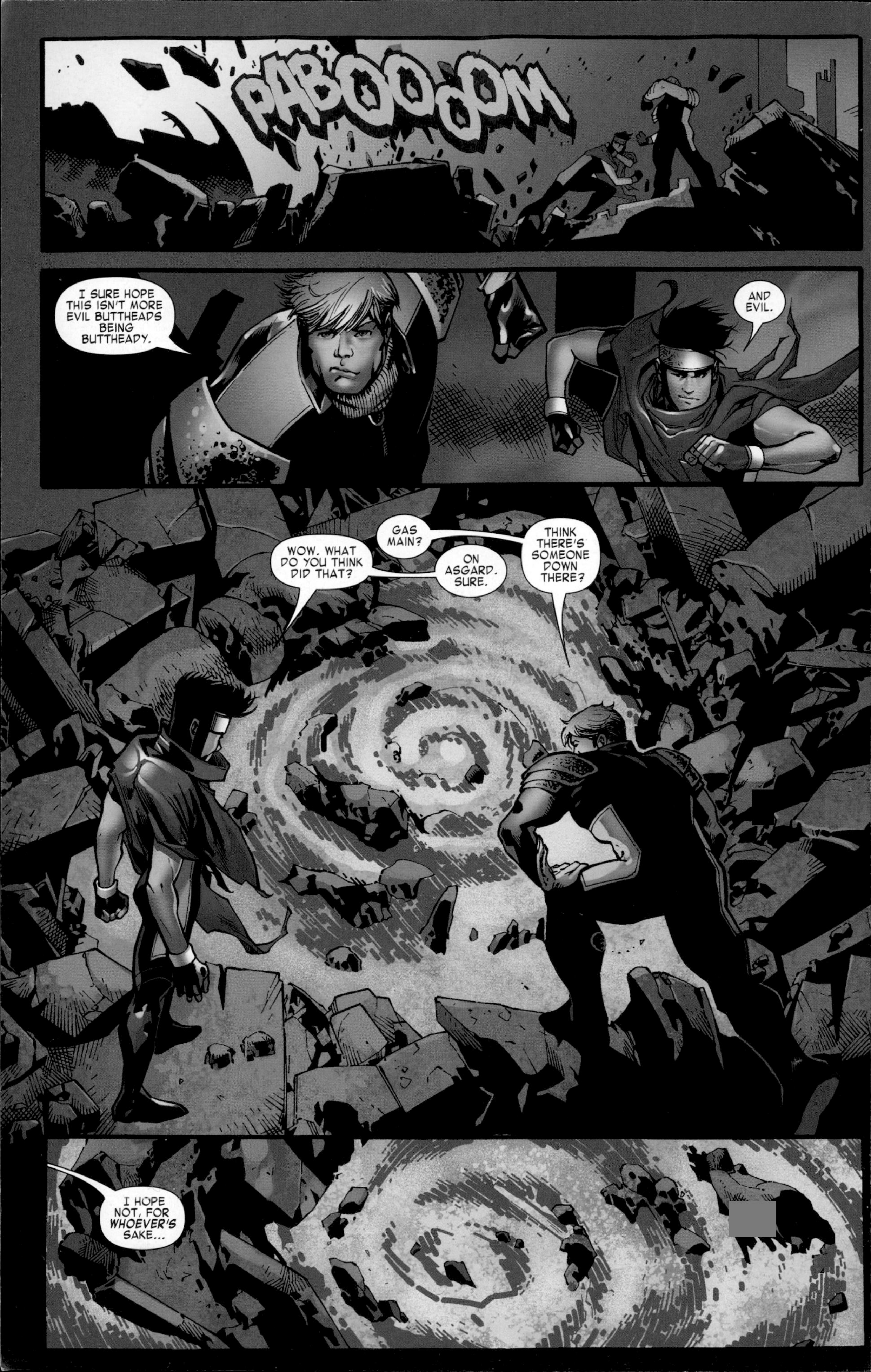
PABOOOOM
I SURE HOPE THIS ISN'T MORE EVIL BUTTHEADS BEING BUTTHEADY.
AND EVIL.
WOW. WHAT DO YOU THINK DID THAT?
GAS MAIN?
ON ASGARD. SURE.
THINK THERE'S SOMEONE DOWN THERE?
I HOPE NOT, FOR WHOEVER'S SAKE...

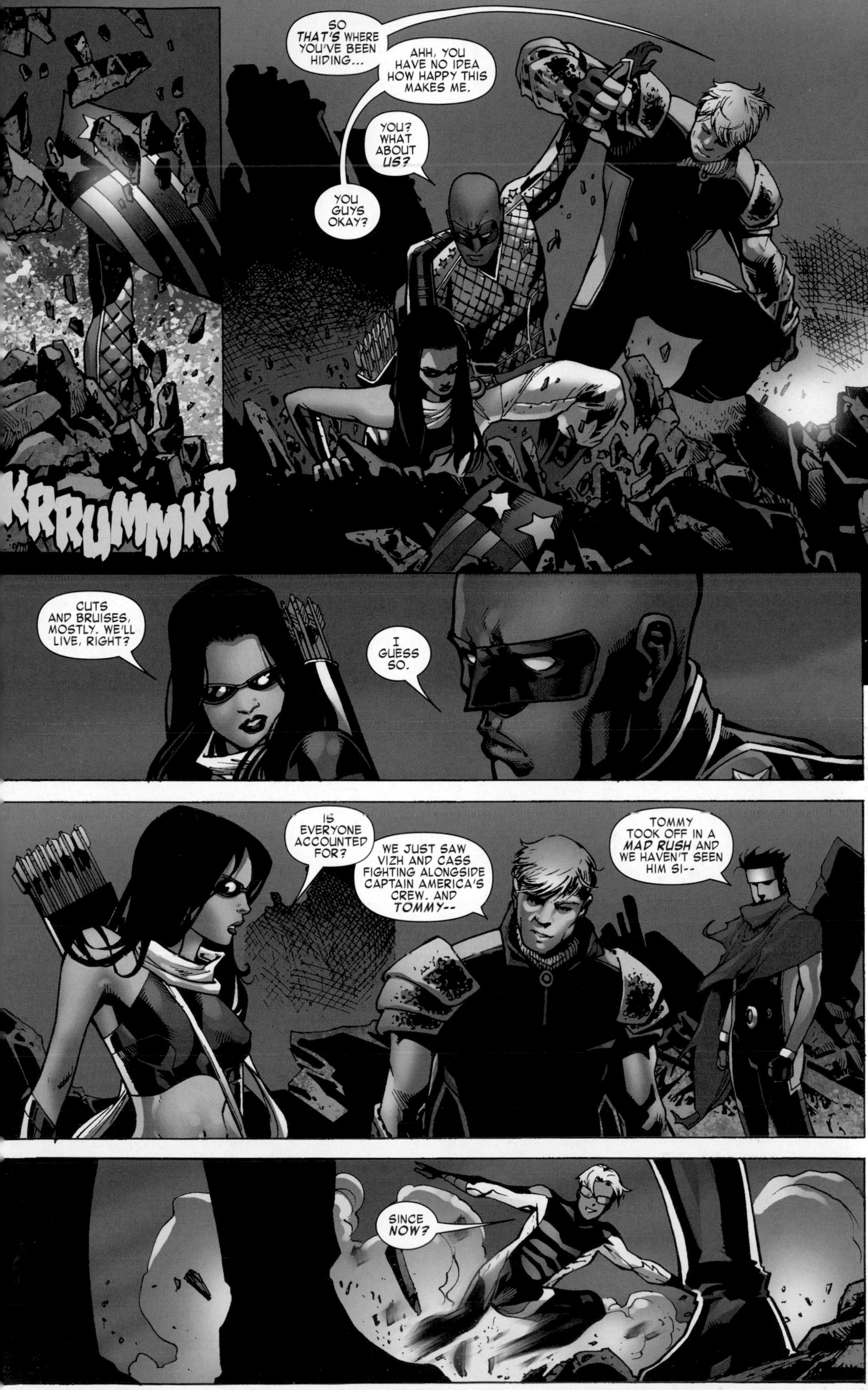
SO THAT'S WHERE YOU'VE BEEN HIDING...
AHH, YOU HAVE NO IDEA HOW HAPPY THIS MAKES ME.
YOU? WHAT ABOUT US?
YOU GUYS OKAY?
KRRUMMKT
CUTS AND BRUISES, MOSTLY. WE'LL LIVE, RIGHT?
I GUESS SO.
IS EVERYONE ACCOUNTED FOR?
WE JUST SAW VIZH AND CASS FIGHTING ALONGSIDE CAPTAIN AMERICA'S CREW. AND TOMMY--
TOMMY TOOK OFF IN A MAD RUSH AND WE HAVEN'T SEEN HIM SI--
SINCE NOW?

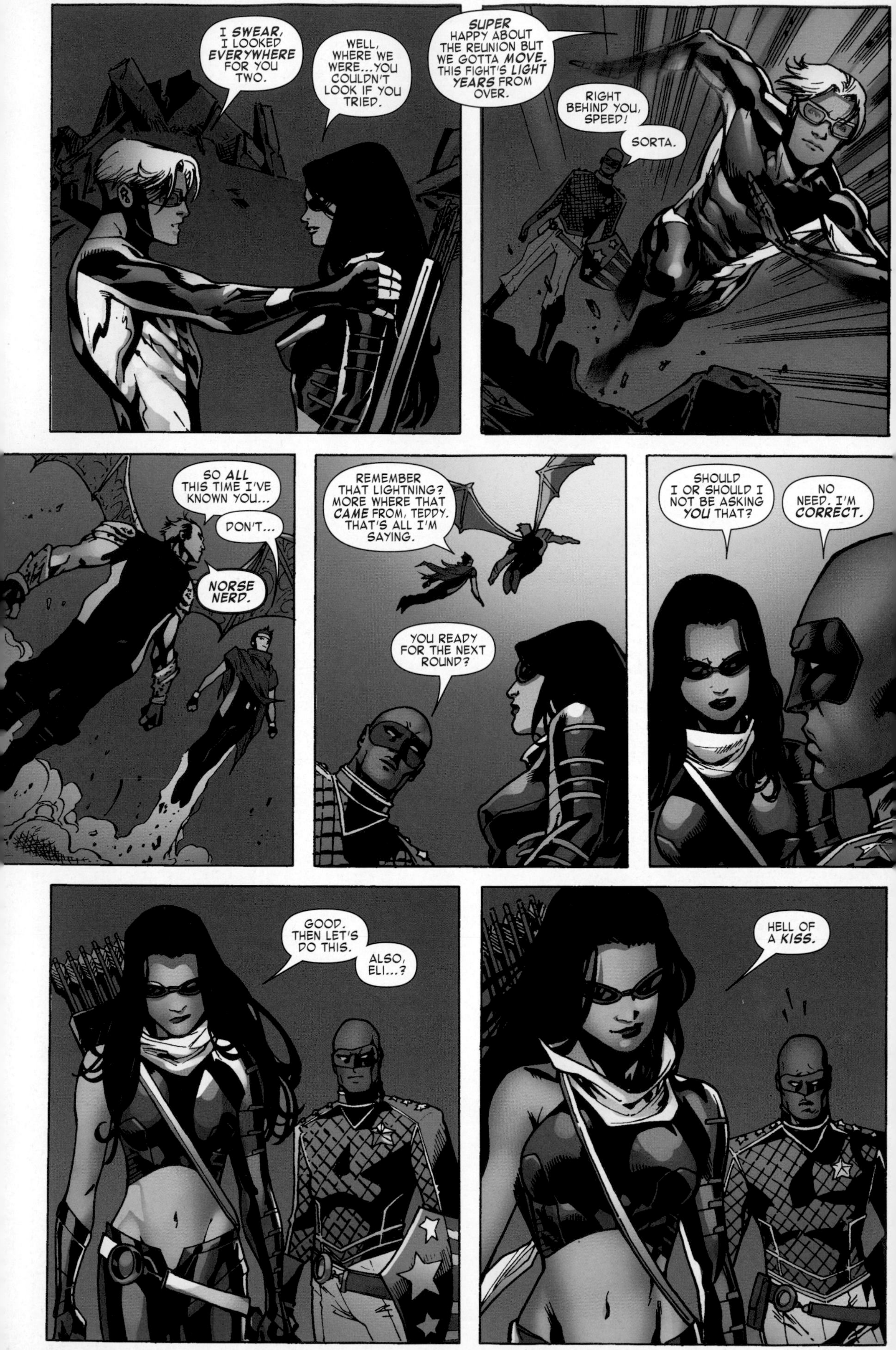
I SWEAR, I LOOKED EVERYWHERE FOR YOU TWO.
WELL, WHERE WE WERE...YOU COULDN'T LOOK IF YOU TRIED.
SUPER HAPPY ABOUT THE REUNION BUT WE GOTTA MOVE. THIS FIGHT'S LIGHT YEARS FROM OVER.
RIGHT BEHIND YOU, SPEED!
SORTA.
SO ALL THIS TIME I'VE KNOWN YOU...
DON'T...
NORSE NERD.
REMEMBER THAT LIGHTNING? MORE WHERE THAT CAME FROM, TEDDY. THAT'S ALL I'M SAYING.
YOU READY FOR THE NEXT ROUND?
SHOULD I OR SHOULD I NOT BE ASKING YOU THAT?
NO NEED. I'M CORRECT.
GOOD. THEN LET'S DO THIS.
ALSO, ELI...?
HELL OF A KISS.

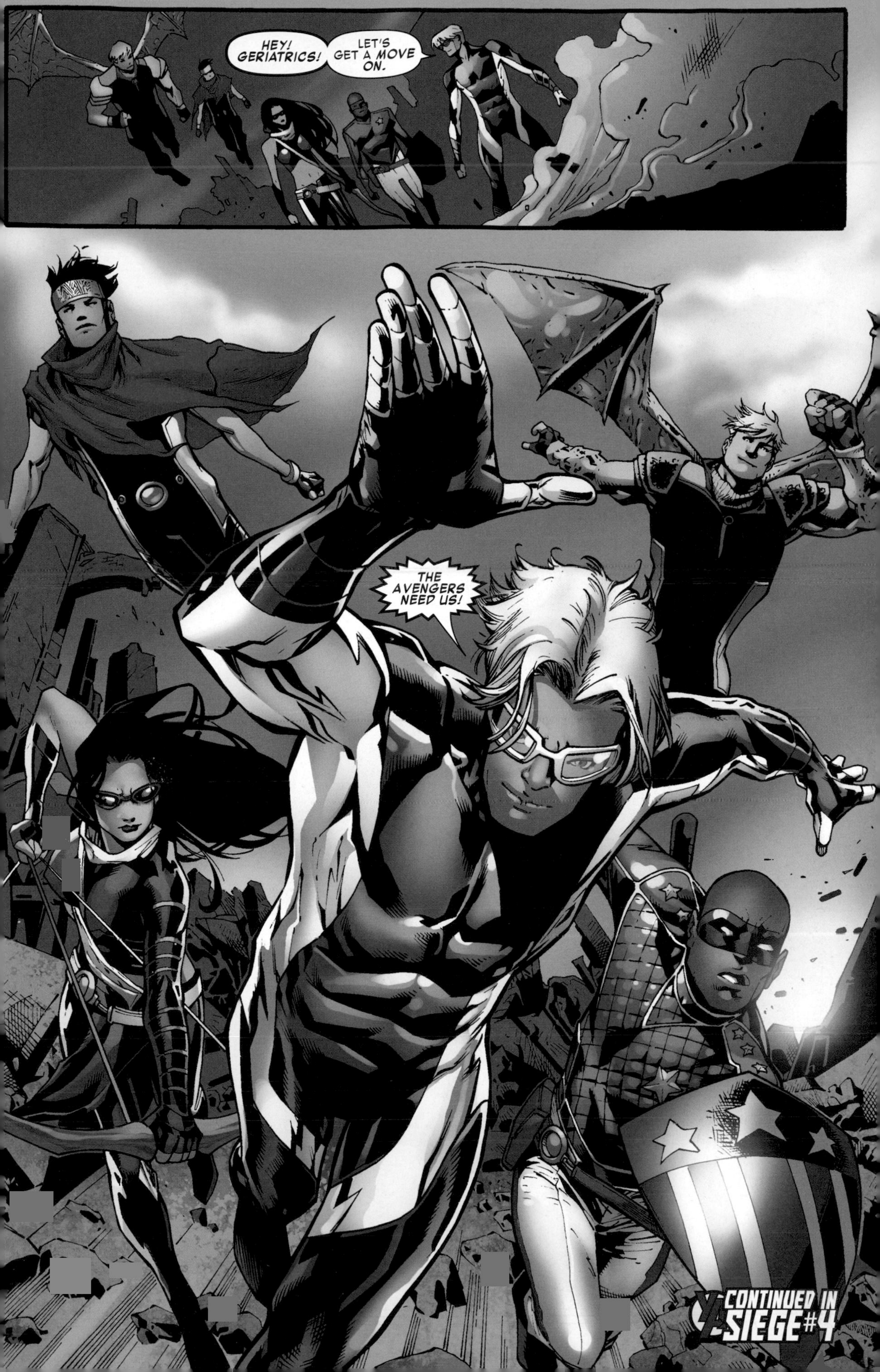
HEY! GERIATRICS!
LET'S GET A MOVE ON.
THE AVENGERS NEED US!
CONTINUED IN SIEGE #4

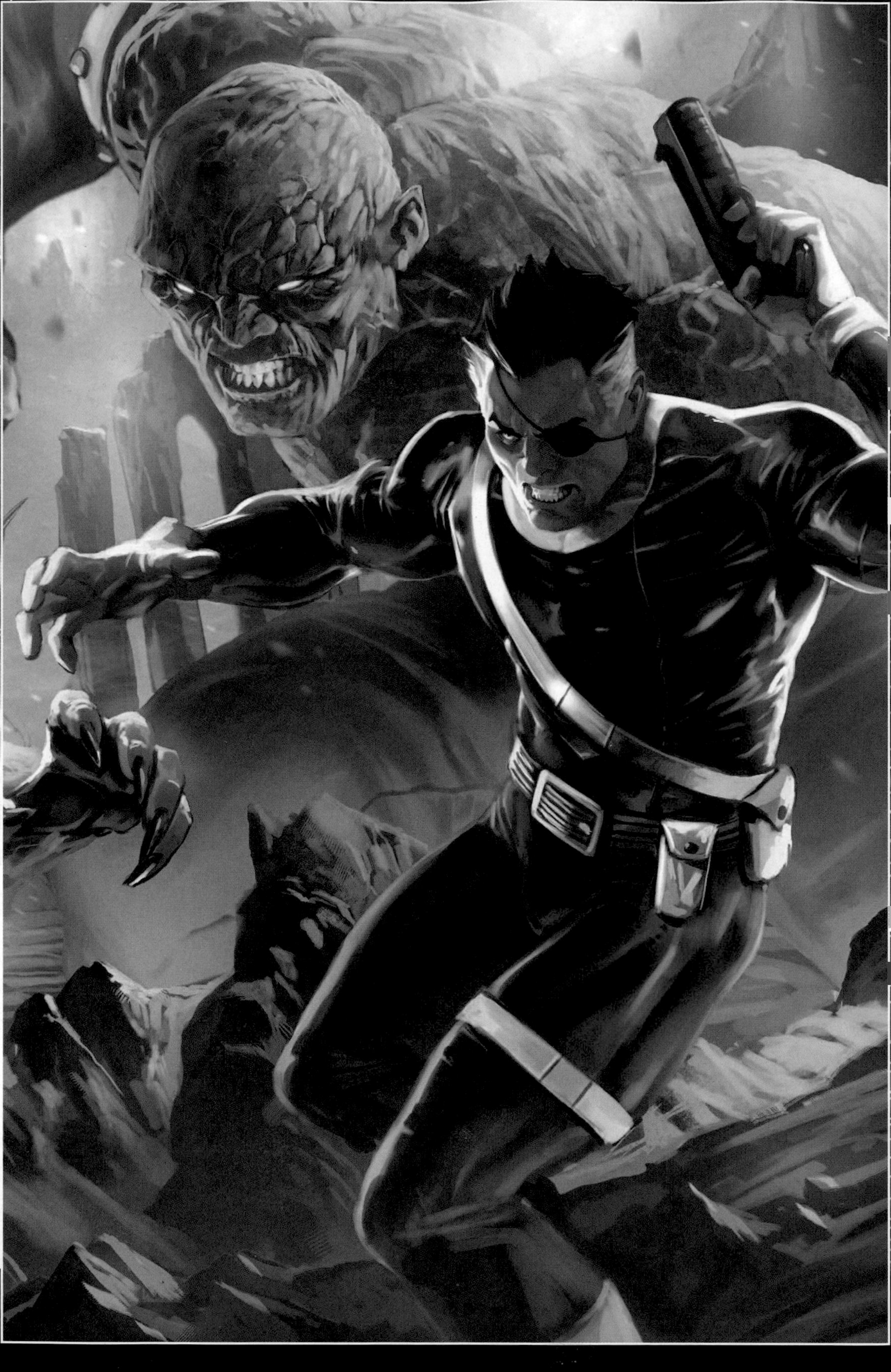

SIEGE: SECRET WARRIORS

SIEGE
SECRET WARRIORS

SECRET AGENT NICK FURY, AFTER LEAVING HIS POST AS LEADER OF THE ESPIONAGE AGENCY KNOWN AS S.H.I.E.L.D., WENT UNDERGROUND AND UNCOVERD EVIDENCE OF A SECRET INVASION CARRIED OUT BY THE SHAPE-SHIFTING SKRULLS. KNOWING THAT MANY ACTIVE HEROES MAY HAVE BEEN COMPROMISED, HE GATHERED A NEW TEAM OF "CATEPILLARS"— YOUNG, UNTESTED SUPERHUMANS, WHOSE EXISTENCE WAS KNOWN TO FURY ALONE.

THIS TEAM OF SECRET WARRIORS—WHO ARE ALL THE OFFSPRING OF OR WERE RAISED BY KNOWN SUPERHUMANS—INCLUDE QUAKE (DAUGHTER OF MR. HYDE), DRUID (SON OF DR. DRUID), SLINGSHOT (DAUGHTER OF THE GRIFFIN), HELLFIRE (GRANDSON OF THE PHANTOM RIDER), STONEWALL (SON OF THE ABSORBING MAN), EDEN FESI (TRAINED BY GATEWAY), AND PHOBOS (SON OF ARES, THE GOD OF WAR).

MONTHS AGO, NORMAN OSBORN DISSOLVED S.H.I.E.L.D. AND REPLACED IT WITH H.A.M.M.E.R. OPERATING UNDER THE ALIAS OF IRON PATRIOT, OSBORN FABRICATED AN EVENT REMINISCENT OF THE STAMFORD TRAGEDY THAT LED TO THE CIVIL WAR, THIS TIME LAYING SIEGE TO ASGARD. DURING THE BATTLE, THE SENTRY KILLED ARES. NOW PHOBOS MUST AVENGE HIS FALLEN FATHER, BEGGING THE QUESTION: WILL ANY SURVIVE HIS VENGEANCE?

JONATHAN HICKMAN
WRITER

ALESSANDRO VITTI
ARTIST

JOSE VILLARRUBIA
COLORIST

DAVE LANPHEAR
LETTERER

MARKO DJURDJEVIC COVER ART

RACHEL PINNELAS
ASSISTANT EDITOR

BILL ROSEMANN
EDITOR

JOE QUESADA
EDITOR IN CHIEF

DAN BUCKLEY
PUBLISHER

ALAN FINE
EXECUTIVE PRODUCER

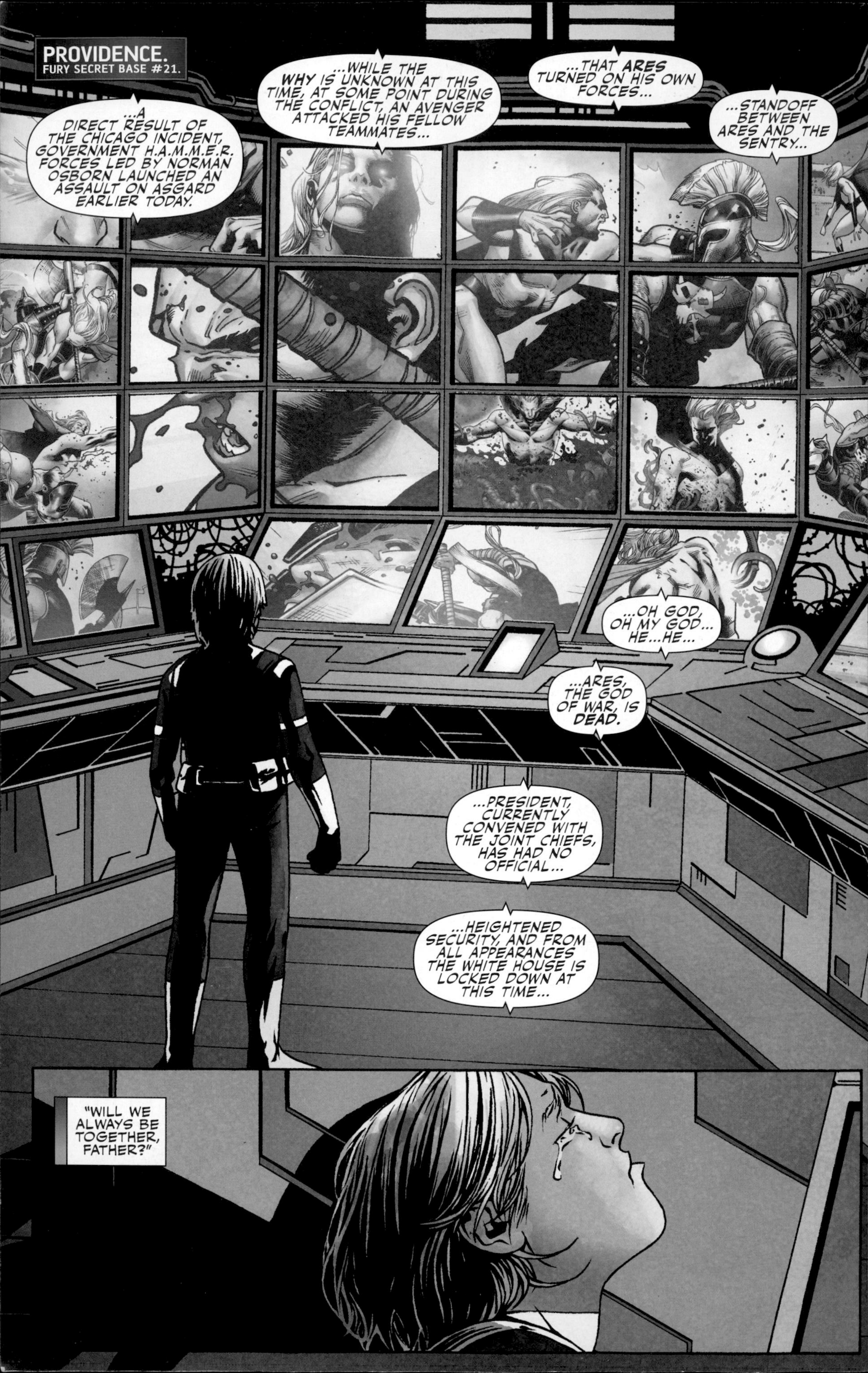
PROVIDENCE.
FURY SECRET BASE #21.
...A DIRECT RESULT OF THE CHICAGO INCIDENT, GOVERNMENT H.A.M.M.E.R. FORCES LED BY NORMAN OSBORN LAUNCHED AN ASSAULT ON ASGARD EARLIER TODAY.
...WHILE THE WHY IS UNKNOWN AT THIS TIME, AT SOME POINT DURING THE CONFLICT, AN AVENGER ATTACKED HIS FELLOW TEAMMATES...
...THAT ARES TURNED ON HIS OWN FORCES...
...STANDOFF BETWEEN ARES AND THE SENTRY...
...OH GOD, OH MY GOD... HE...HE...
...ARES, THE GOD OF WAR, IS DEAD.
...PRESIDENT, CURRENTLY CONVENED WITH THE JOINT CHIEFS, HAS HAD NO OFFICIAL...
...HEIGHTENED SECURITY, AND FROM ALL APPEARANCES THE WHITE HOUSE IS LOCKED DOWN AT THIS TIME...
"WILL WE ALWAYS BE TOGETHER, FATHER?"

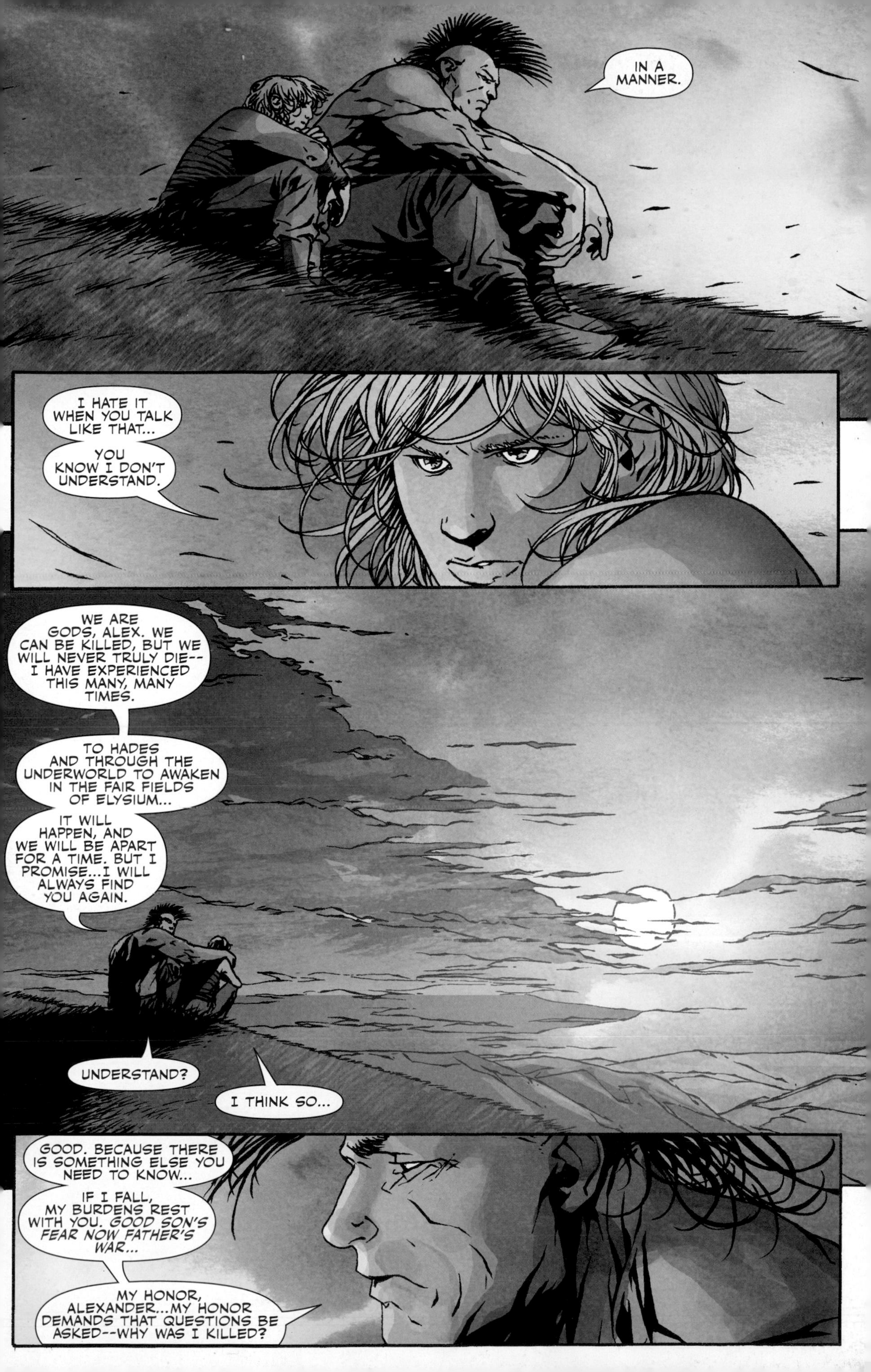
IN A MANNER.
I HATE IT WHEN YOU TALK LIKE THAT...
YOU KNOW I DON'T UNDERSTAND.
WE ARE GODS, ALEX. WE CAN BE KILLED, BUT WE WILL NEVER TRULY DIE-- I HAVE EXPERIENCED THIS MANY, MANY TIMES.
TO HADES AND THROUGH THE UNDERWORLD TO AWAKEN IN THE FAIR FIELDS OF ELYSIUM...
IT WILL HAPPEN, AND WE WILL BE APART FOR A TIME. BUT I PROMISE...I WILL ALWAYS FIND YOU AGAIN.
UNDERSTAND?
I THINK SO...
GOOD. BECAUSE THERE IS SOMETHING ELSE YOU NEED TO KNOW...
IF I FALL, MY BURDENS REST WITH YOU. *GOOD SON'S FEAR NOW FATHER'S WAR*...
MY HONOR, ALEXANDER...MY HONOR DEMANDS THAT QUESTIONS BE ASKED--WHY WAS I KILLED?

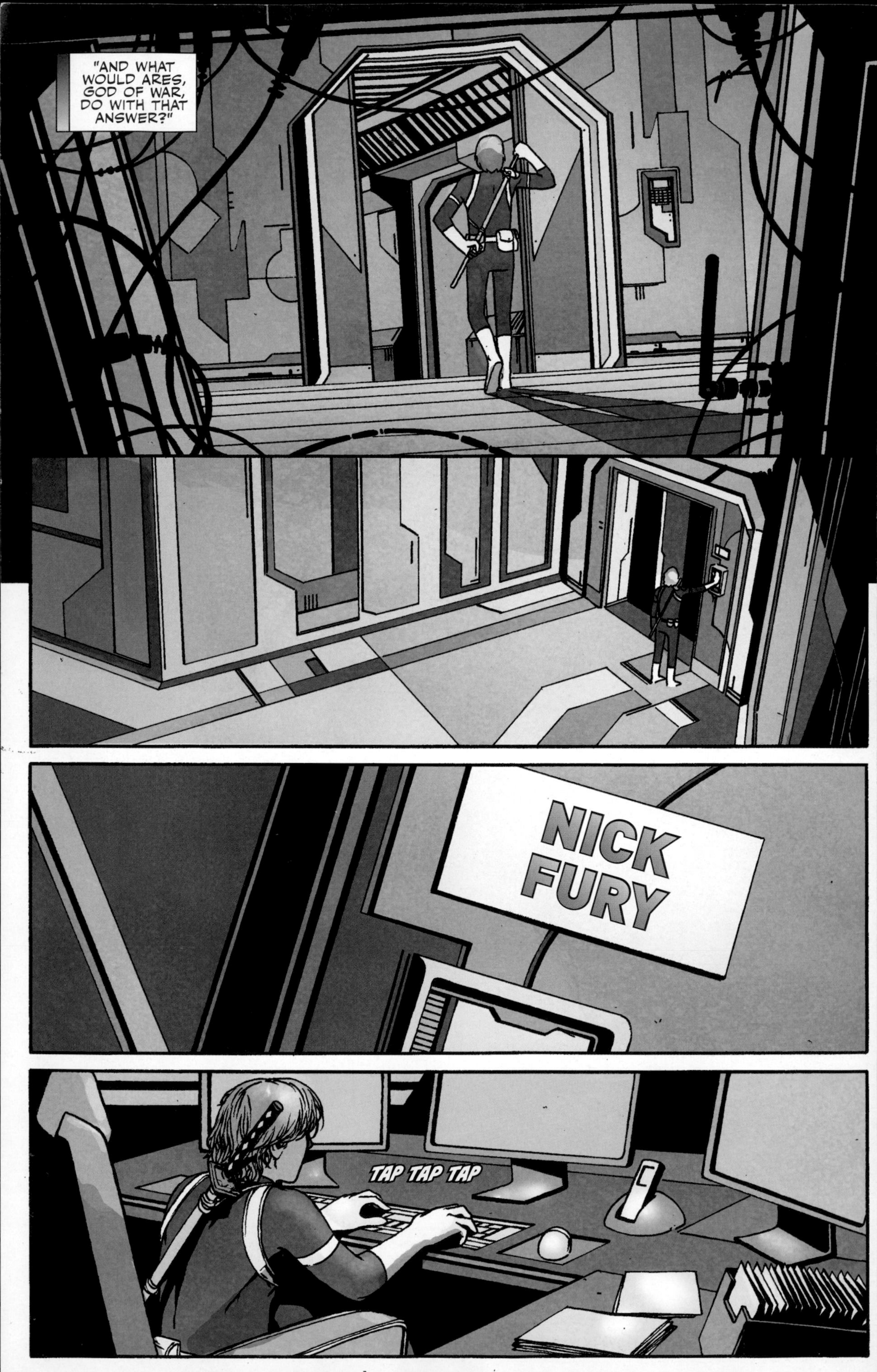
"AND WHAT WOULD ARES, GOD OF WAR, DO WITH THAT ANSWER?"
NICK FURY
TAP TAP TAP

LOGIN: NICHOLAS FURY
PASSWORD: ************

ACCEPTED

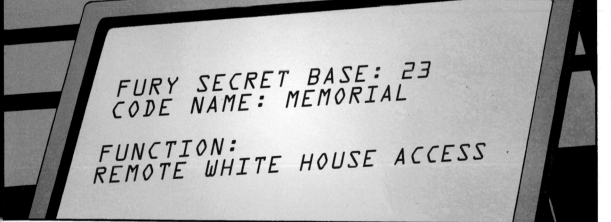

FURY SECRET BASE: 23
CODE NAME: MEMORIAL

FUNCTION:
REMOTE WHITE HOUSE ACCESS

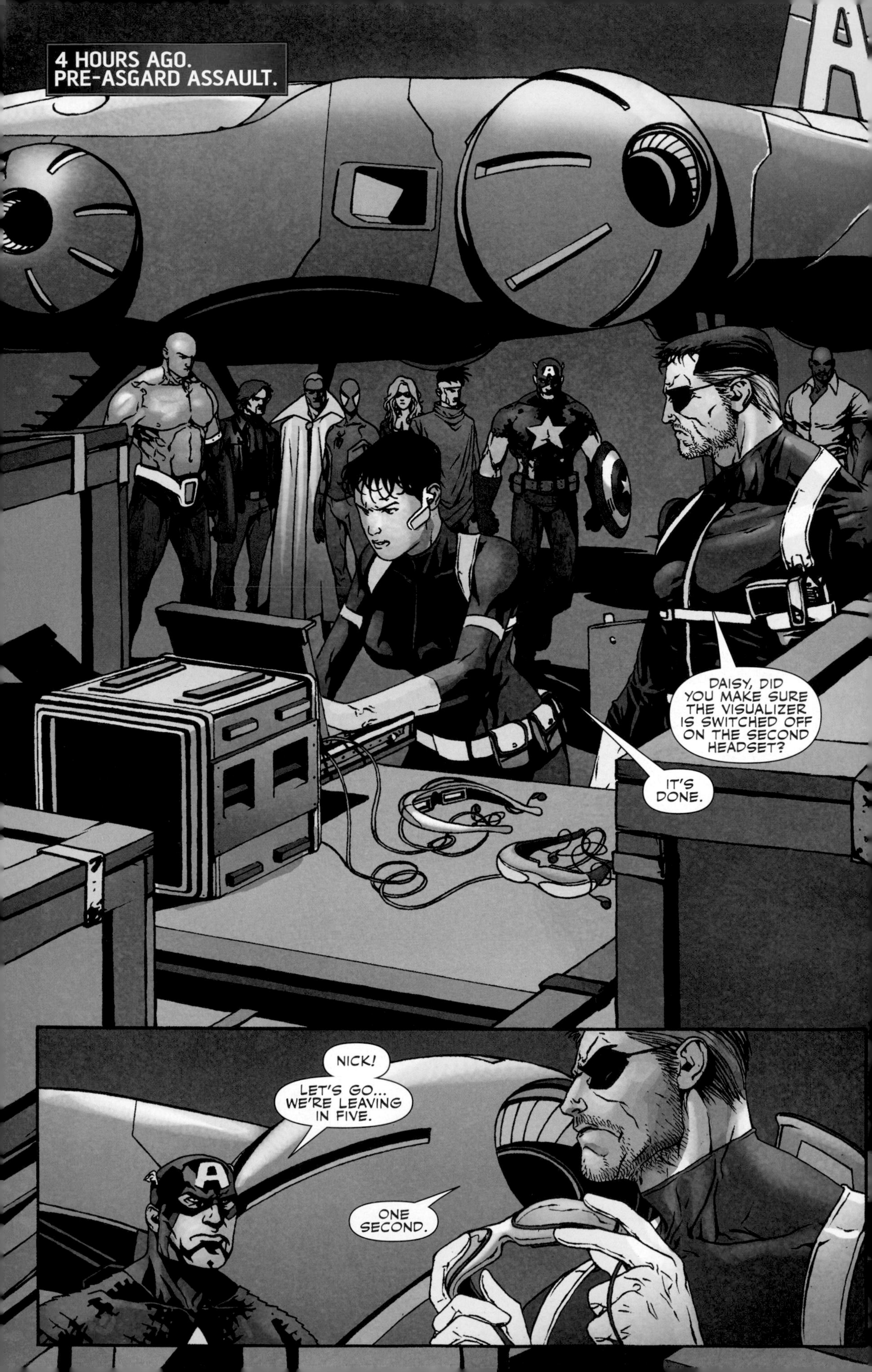
4 HOURS AGO.
PRE-ASGARD ASSAULT.
DAISY, DID YOU MAKE SURE THE VISUALIZER IS SWITCHED OFF ON THE SECOND HEADSET?
IT'S DONE.
NICK!
LET'S GO... WE'RE LEAVING IN FIVE.
ONE SECOND.

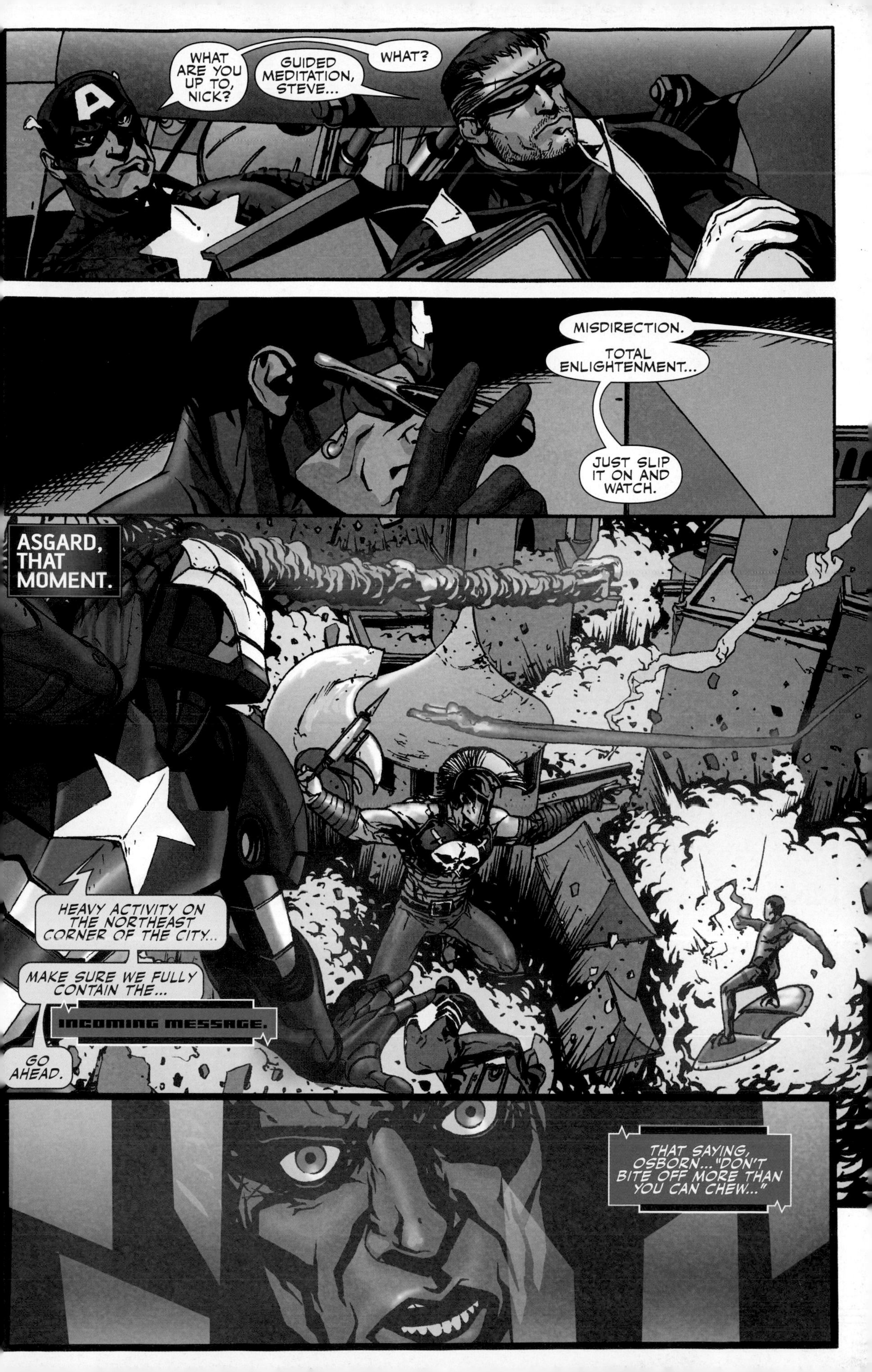
WHAT ARE YOU UP TO, NICK?
GUIDED MEDITATION, STEVE...
WHAT?
MISDIRECTION.
TOTAL ENLIGHTENMENT...
JUST SLIP IT ON AND WATCH.
ASGARD, THAT MOMENT.
HEAVY ACTIVITY ON THE NORTHEAST CORNER OF THE CITY...
MAKE SURE WE FULLY CONTAIN THE...
INCOMING MESSAGE.
GO AHEAD.
THAT SAYING, OSBORN... "DON'T BITE OFF MORE THAN YOU CAN CHEW..."

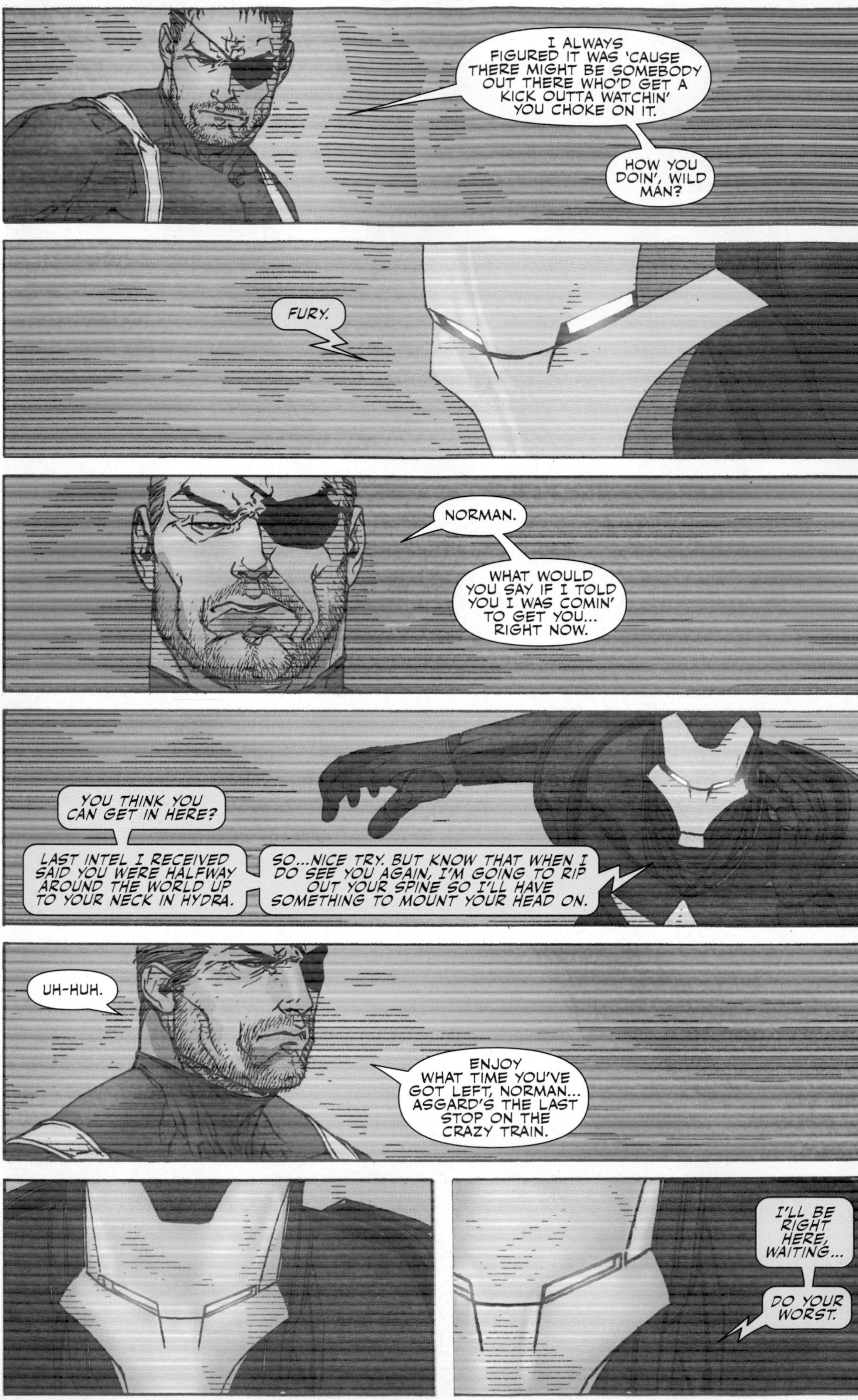
I ALWAYS FIGURED IT WAS 'CAUSE THERE MIGHT BE SOMEBODY OUT THERE WHO'D GET A KICK OUTTA WATCHIN' YOU CHOKE ON IT.
HOW YOU DOIN', WILD MAN?
FURY.
NORMAN.
WHAT WOULD YOU SAY IF I TOLD YOU I WAS COMIN' TO GET YOU... RIGHT NOW.
YOU THINK YOU CAN GET IN HERE?
LAST INTEL I RECEIVED SAID YOU WERE HALFWAY AROUND THE WORLD UP TO YOUR NECK IN HYDRA.
SO...NICE TRY. BUT KNOW THAT WHEN I DO SEE YOU AGAIN, I'M GOING TO RIP OUT YOUR SPINE SO I'LL HAVE SOMETHING TO MOUNT YOUR HEAD ON.
UH-HUH.
ENJOY WHAT TIME YOU'VE GOT LEFT, NORMAN... ASGARD'S THE LAST STOP ON THE CRAZY TRAIN.
I'LL BE RIGHT HERE, WAITING...
DO YOUR WORST.

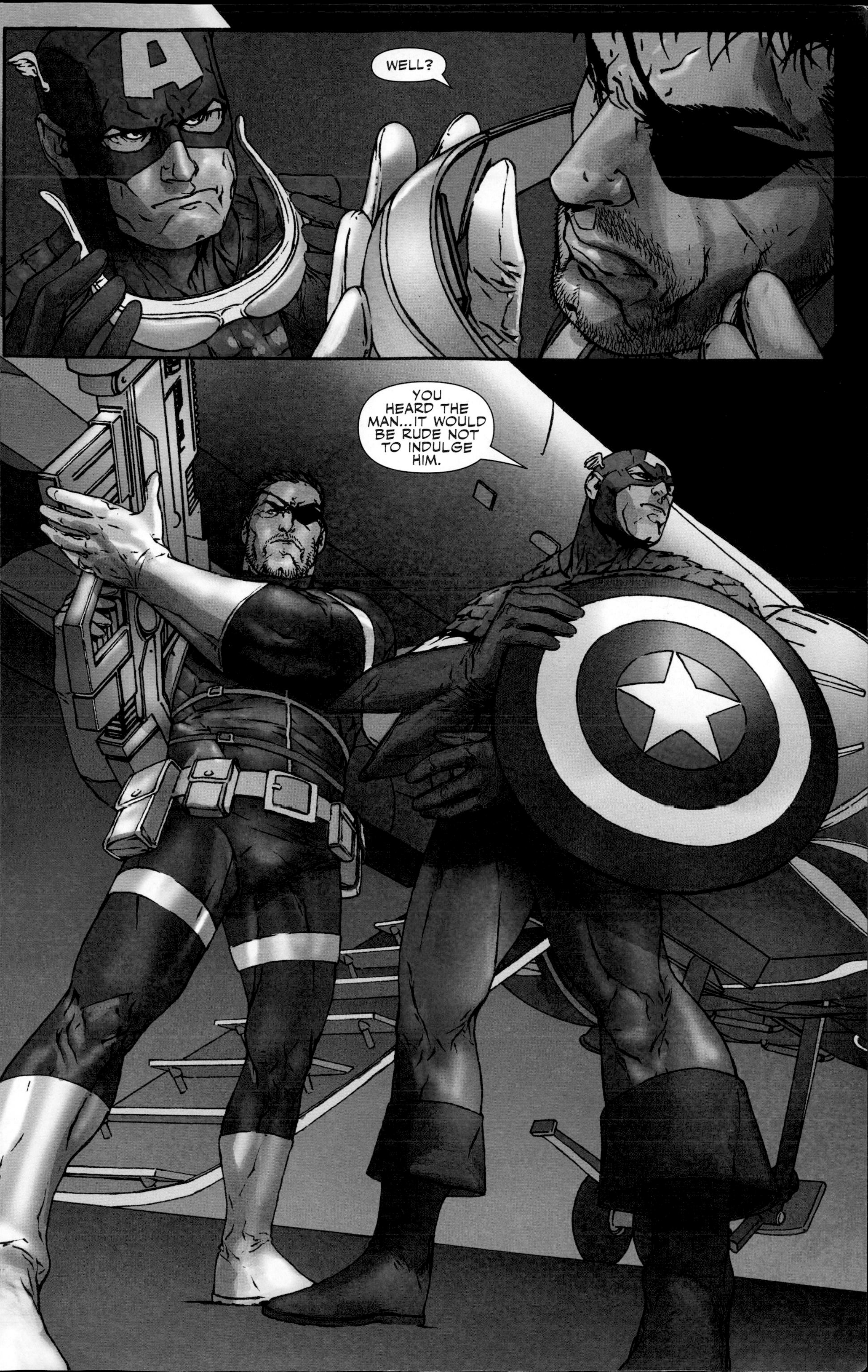
WELL?
YOU HEARD THE MAN...IT WOULD BE RUDE NOT TO INDULGE HIM.

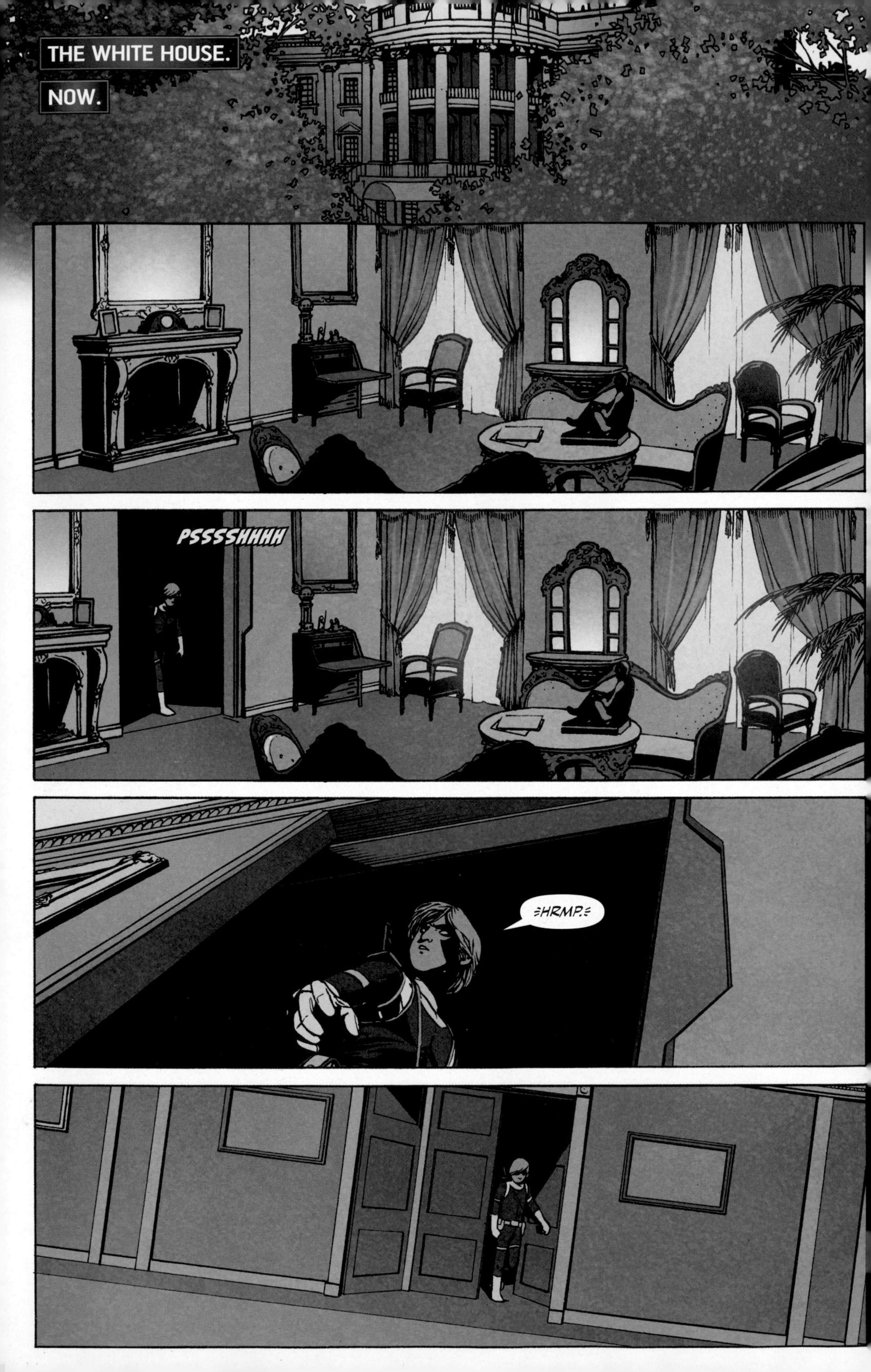
THE WHITE HOUSE.
NOW.
PSSSSHHHH
HRMP.

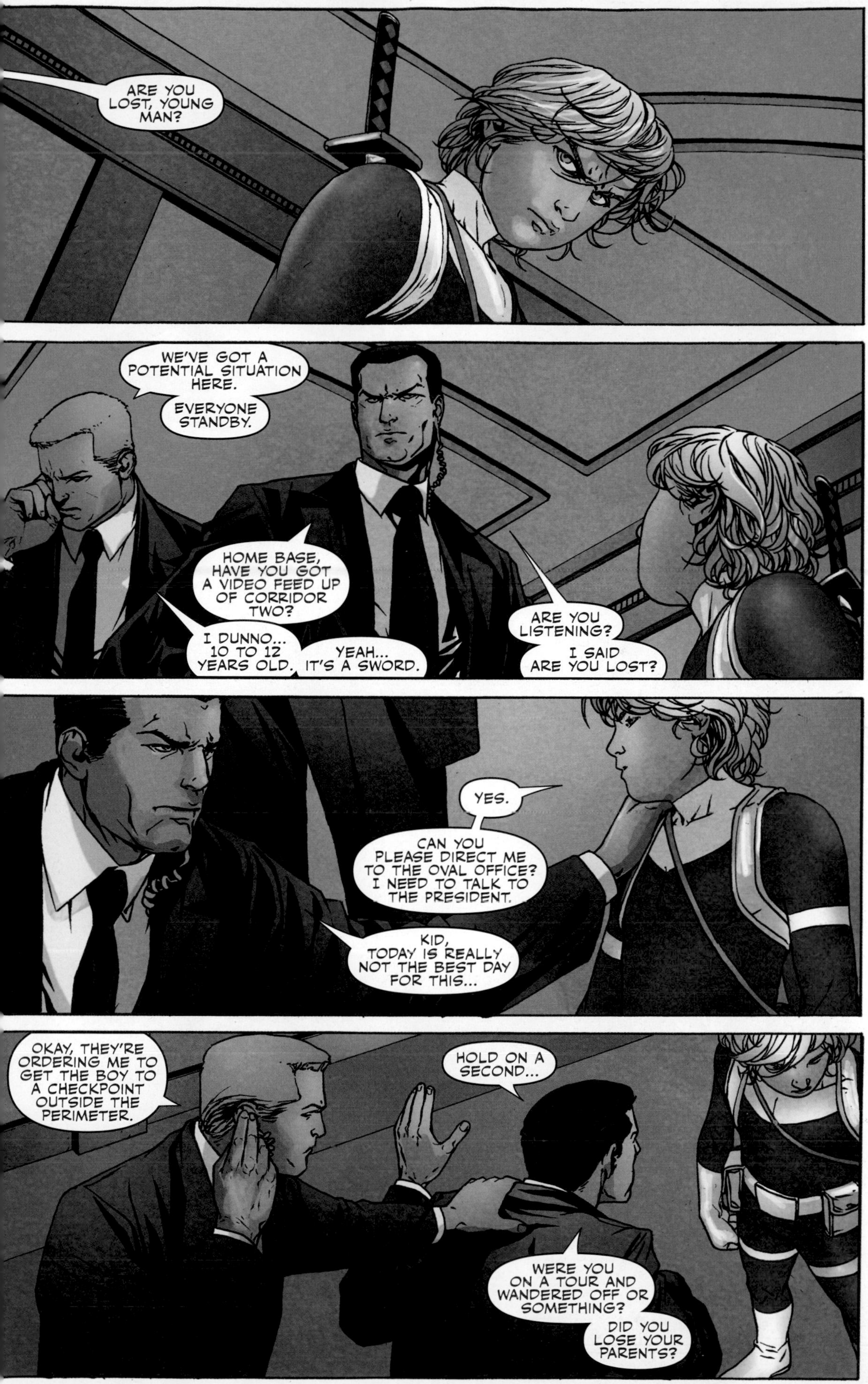

ARE YOU LOST, YOUNG MAN?
WE'VE GOT A POTENTIAL SITUATION HERE.
EVERYONE STANDBY.
HOME BASE, HAVE YOU GOT A VIDEO FEED UP OF CORRIDOR TWO?
I DUNNO... 10 TO 12 YEARS OLD.
YEAH... IT'S A SWORD.
ARE YOU LISTENING?
I SAID ARE YOU LOST?
YES.
CAN YOU PLEASE DIRECT ME TO THE OVAL OFFICE? I NEED TO TALK TO THE PRESIDENT.
KID, TODAY IS REALLY NOT THE BEST DAY FOR THIS...
OKAY, THEY'RE ORDERING ME TO GET THE BOY TO A CHECKPOINT OUTSIDE THE PERIMETER.
HOLD ON A SECOND...
WERE YOU ON A TOUR AND WANDERED OFF OR SOMETHING?
DID YOU LOSE YOUR PARENTS?

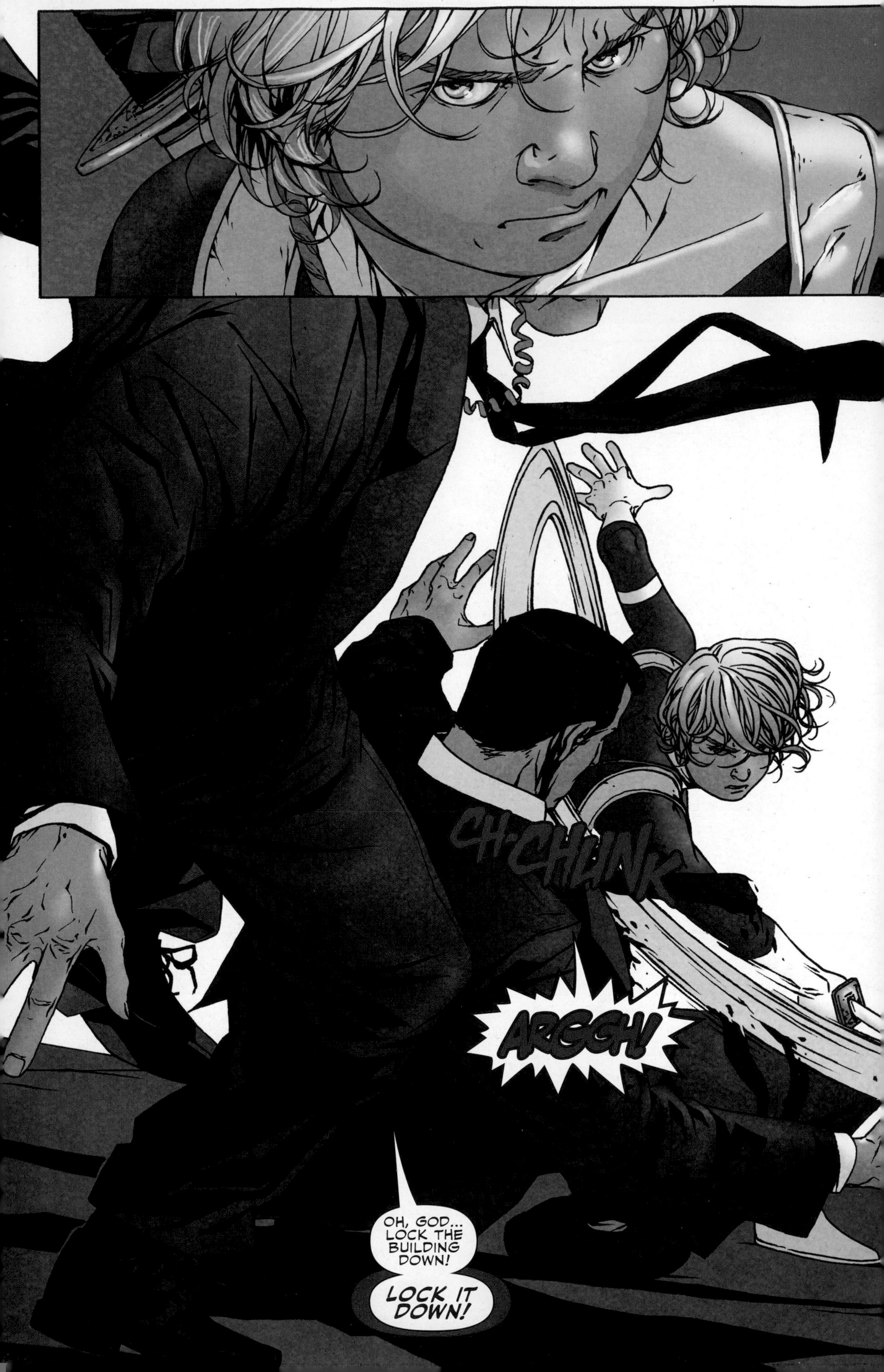
CH-CHUNK
ARGGH!
OH, GOD... LOCK THE BUILDING DOWN!
LOCK IT DOWN!

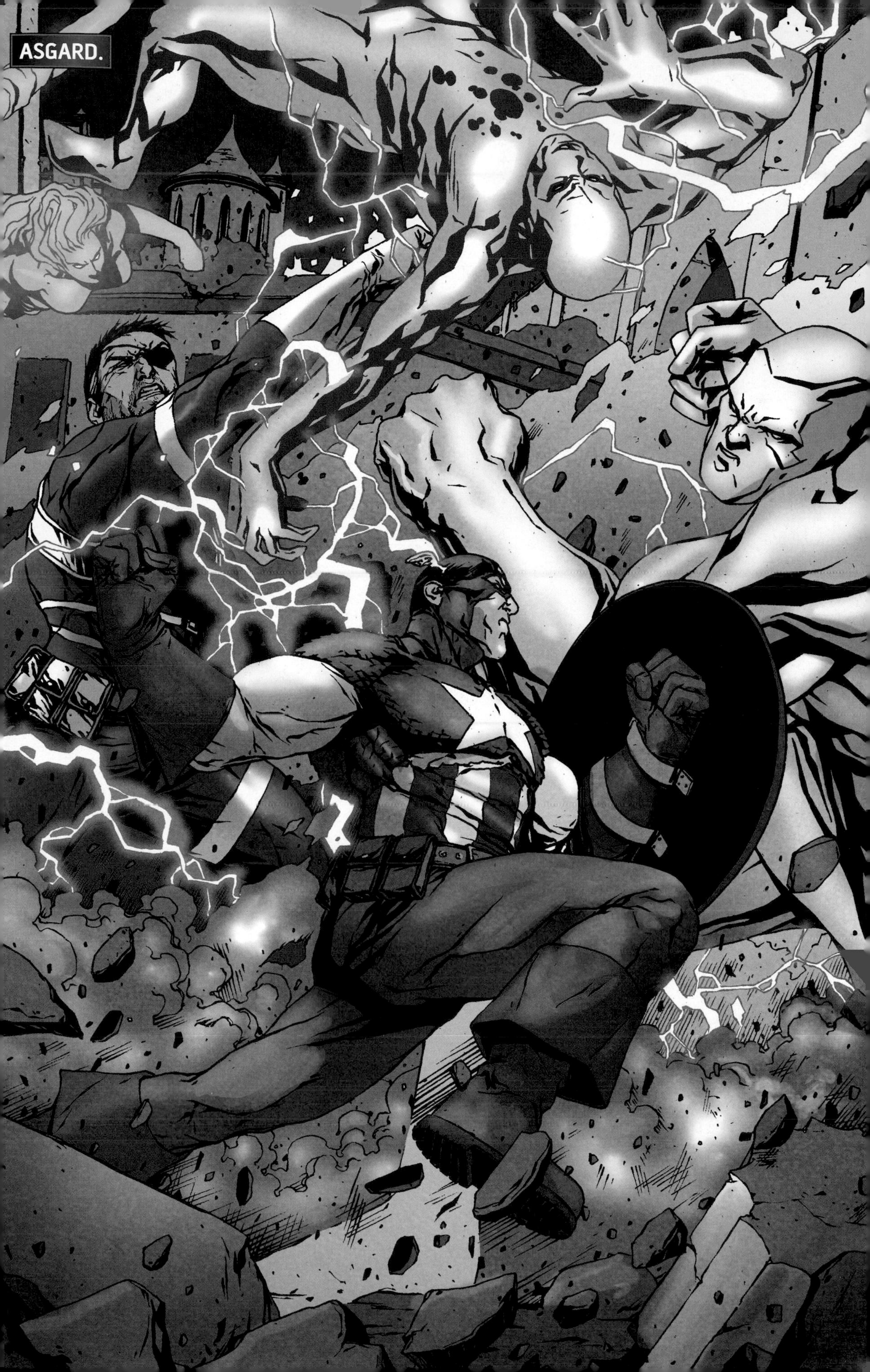
ASGARD.

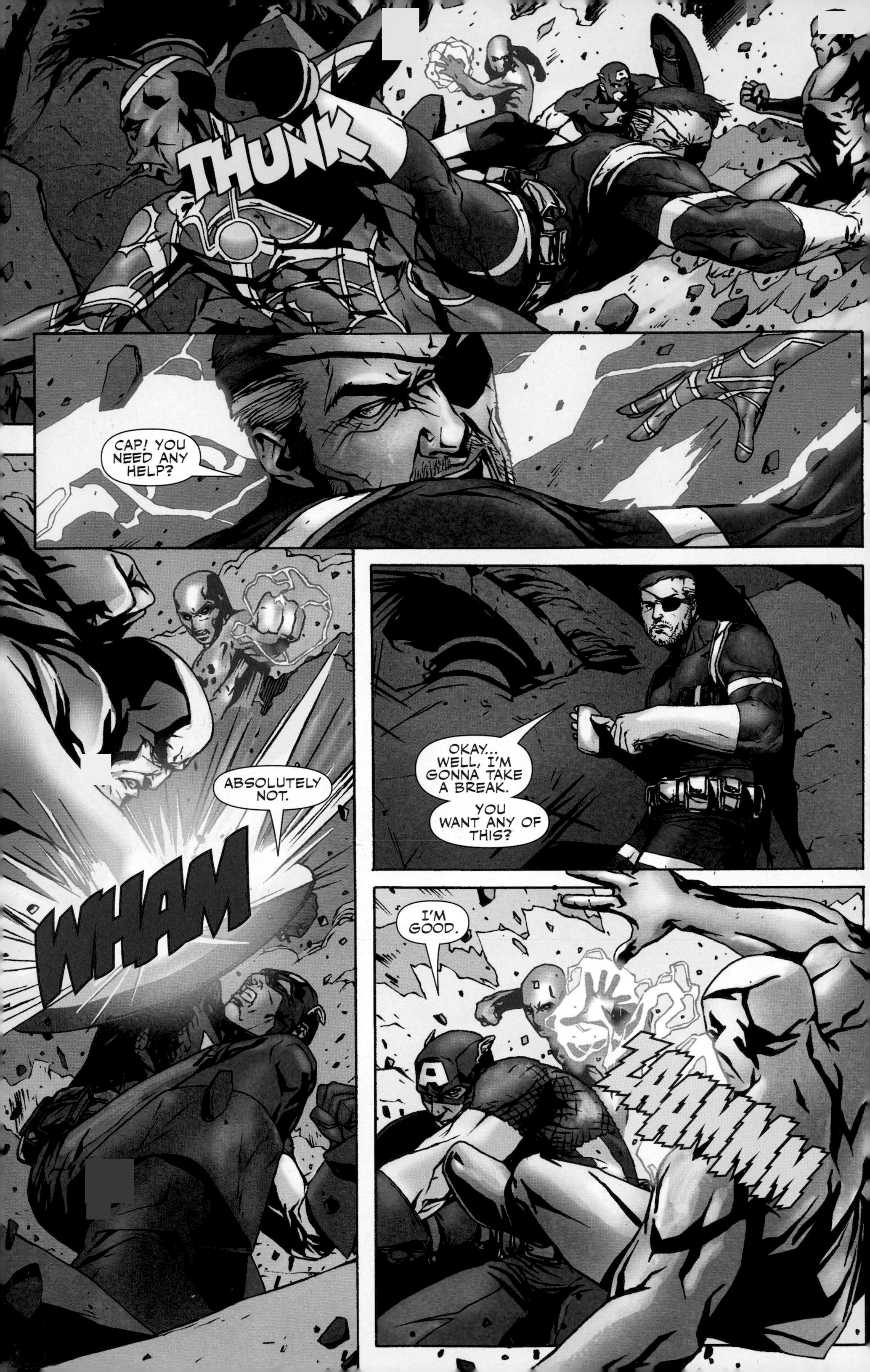
THUNK
CAP! YOU NEED ANY HELP?
ABSOLUTELY NOT.
WHAM
OKAY... WELL, I'M GONNA TAKE A BREAK.
YOU WANT ANY OF THIS?
I'M GOOD.
ZAMMMM

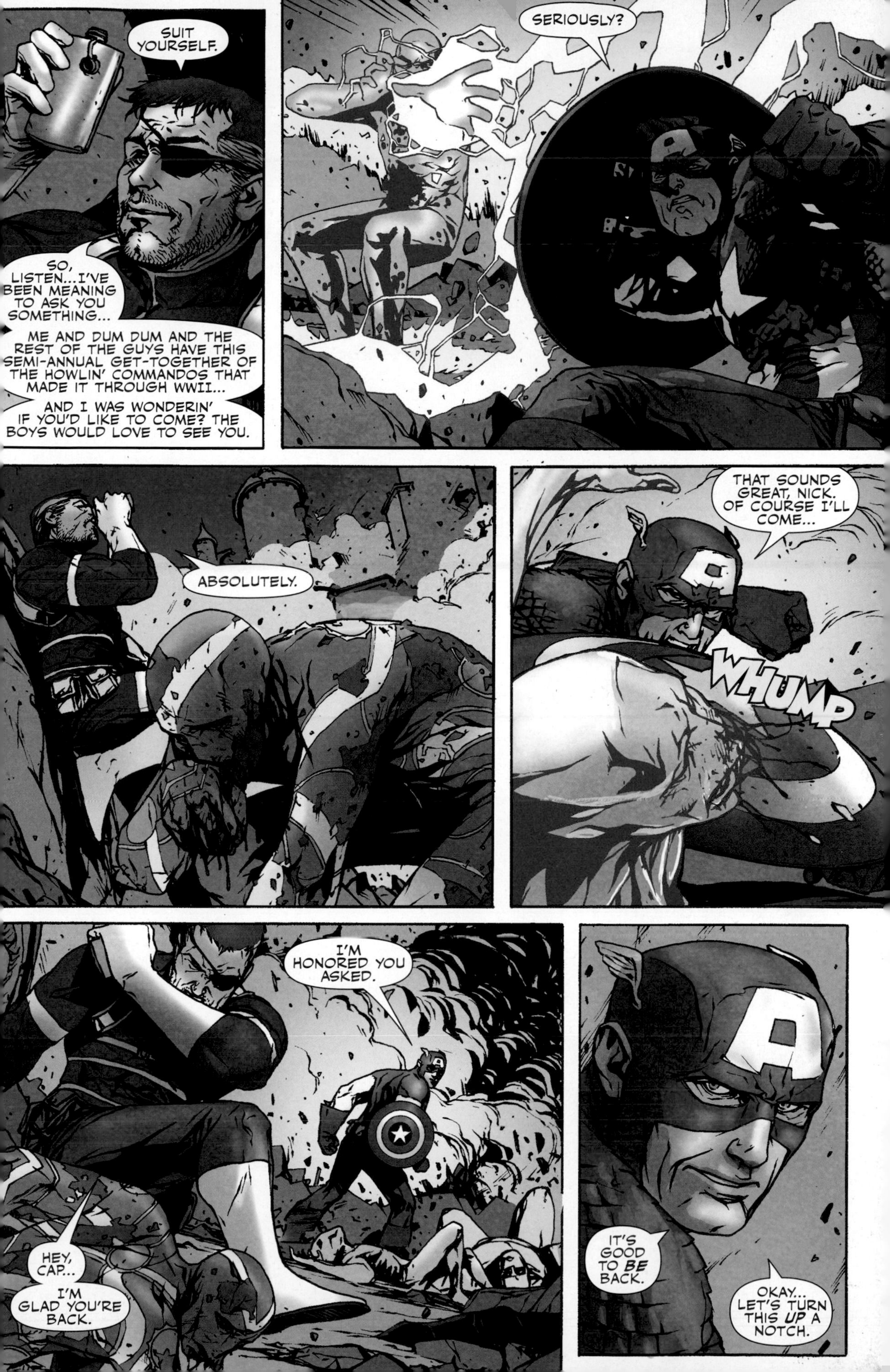
SUIT YOURSELF.
SO, LISTEN...I'VE BEEN MEANING TO ASK YOU SOMETHING...
ME AND DUM DUM AND THE REST OF THE GUYS HAVE THIS SEMI-ANNUAL GET-TOGETHER OF THE HOWLIN' COMMANDOS THAT MADE IT THROUGH WWII...
AND I WAS WONDERIN' IF YOU'D LIKE TO COME? THE BOYS WOULD LOVE TO SEE YOU.
SERIOUSLY?
ABSOLUTELY.
THAT SOUNDS GREAT, NICK. OF COURSE I'LL COME...
WHUMP
I'M HONORED YOU ASKED.
HEY, CAP...
I'M GLAD YOU'RE BACK.
IT'S GOOD TO *BE* BACK.
OKAY... LET'S TURN THIS *UP* A NOTCH.

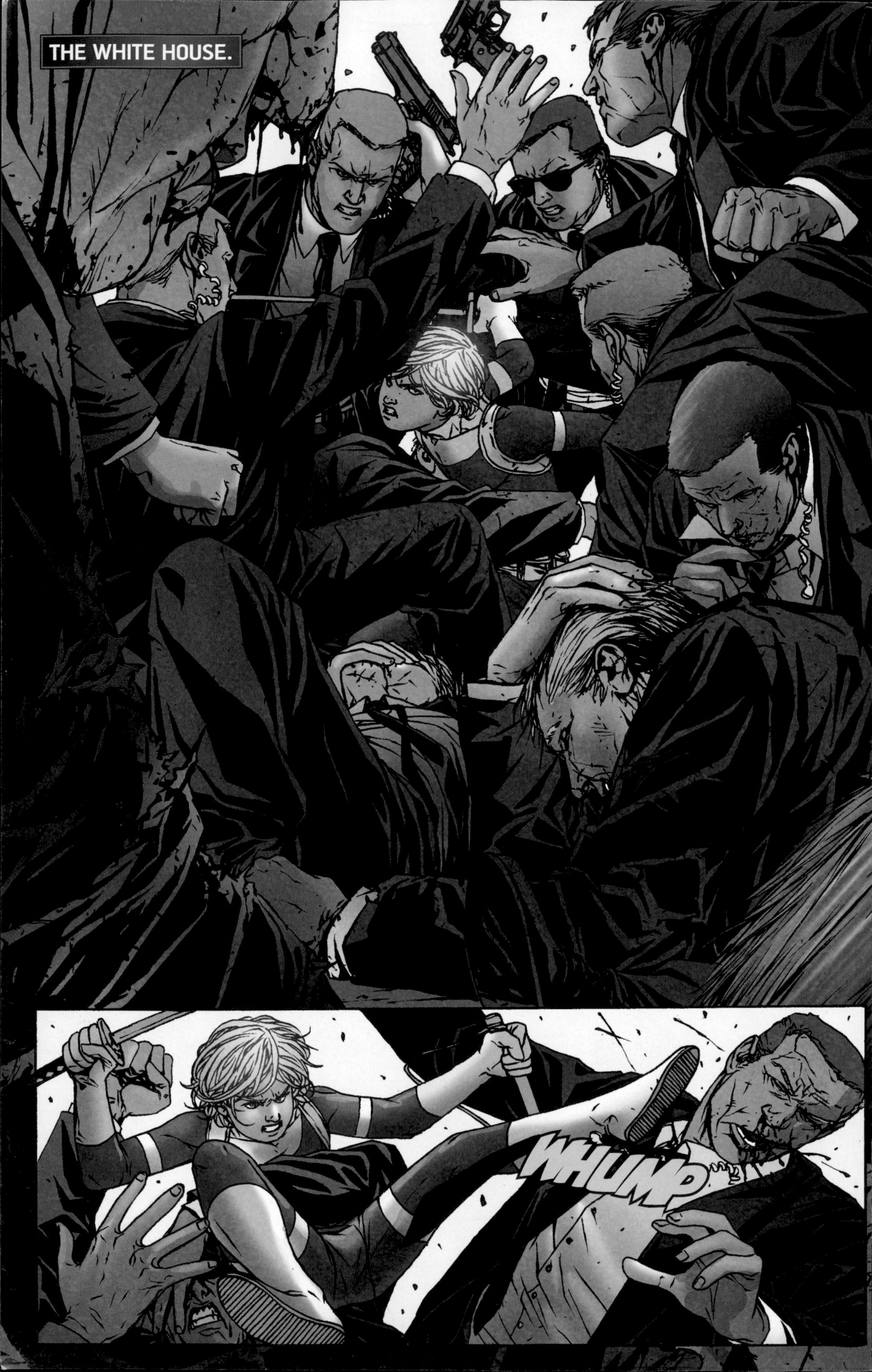
THE WHITE HOUSE.
WHUMP

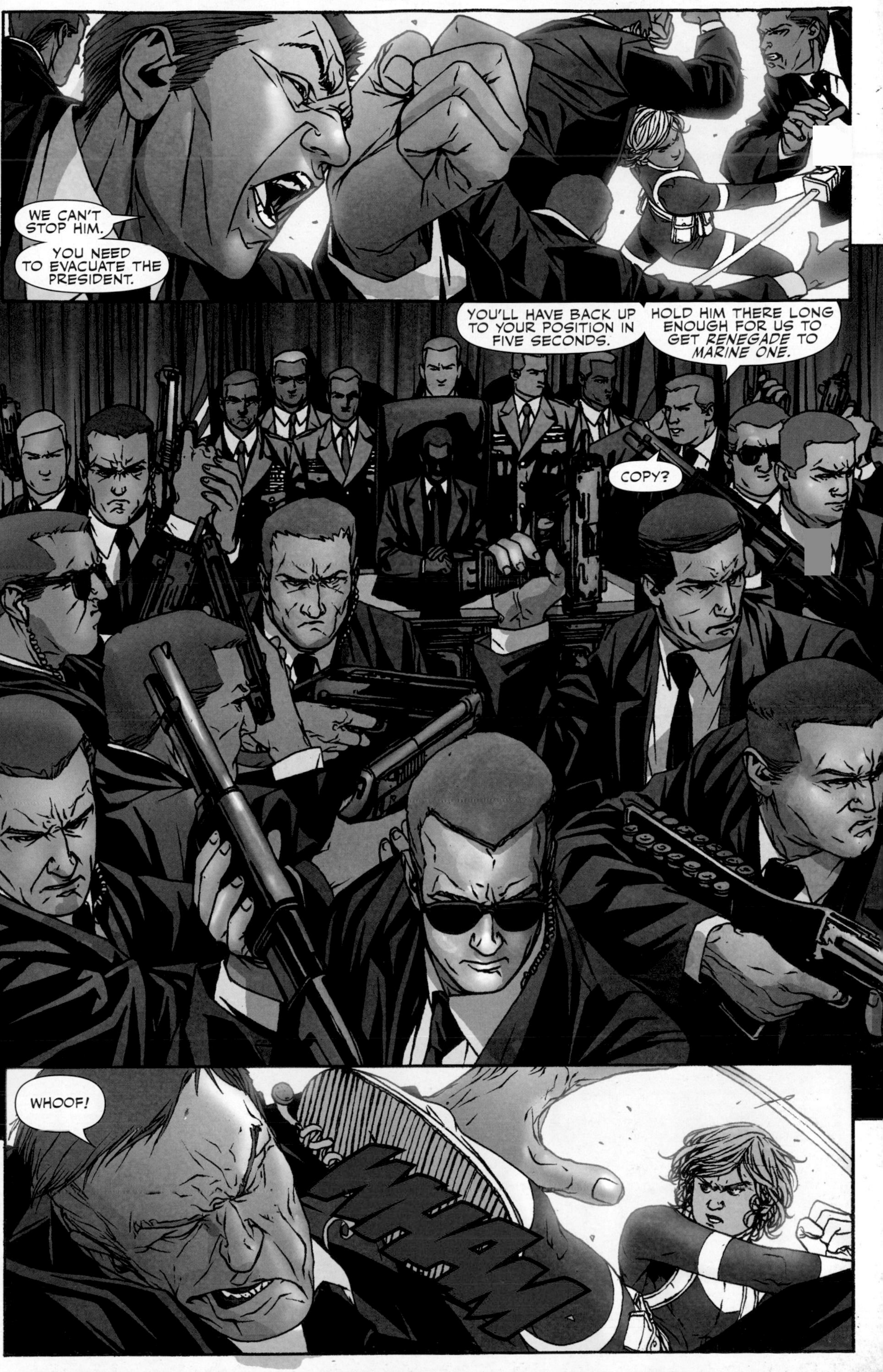
WE CAN'T STOP HIM.
YOU NEED TO EVACUATE THE PRESIDENT.
YOU'LL HAVE BACK UP TO YOUR POSITION IN FIVE SECONDS.
HOLD HIM THERE LONG ENOUGH FOR US TO GET *RENEGADE* TO *MARINE ONE.*
COPY?
WHOOF!
WHAM

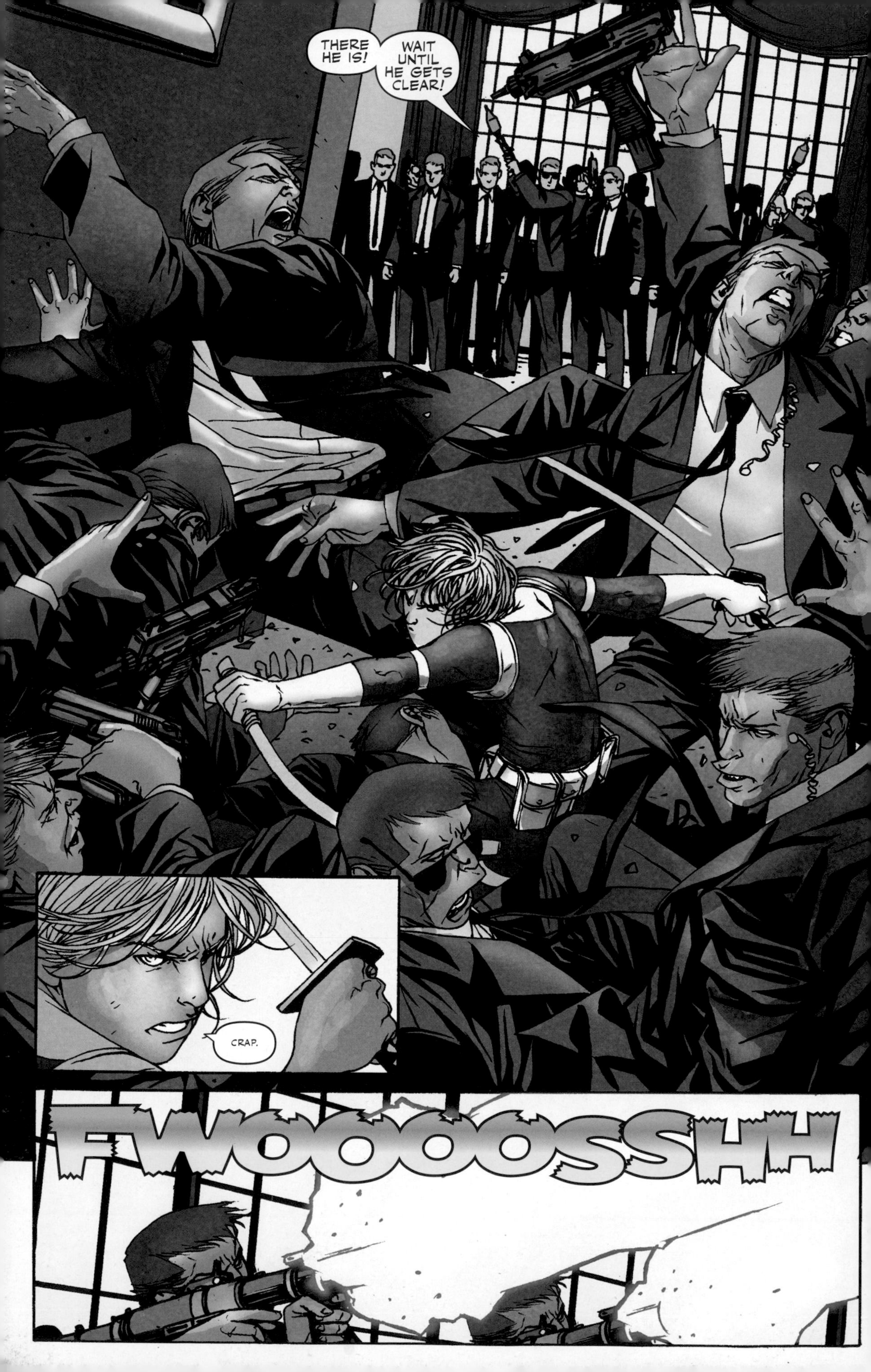
THERE HE IS!
WAIT UNTIL HE GETS CLEAR!
CRAP.
FWOOOOOSSHH

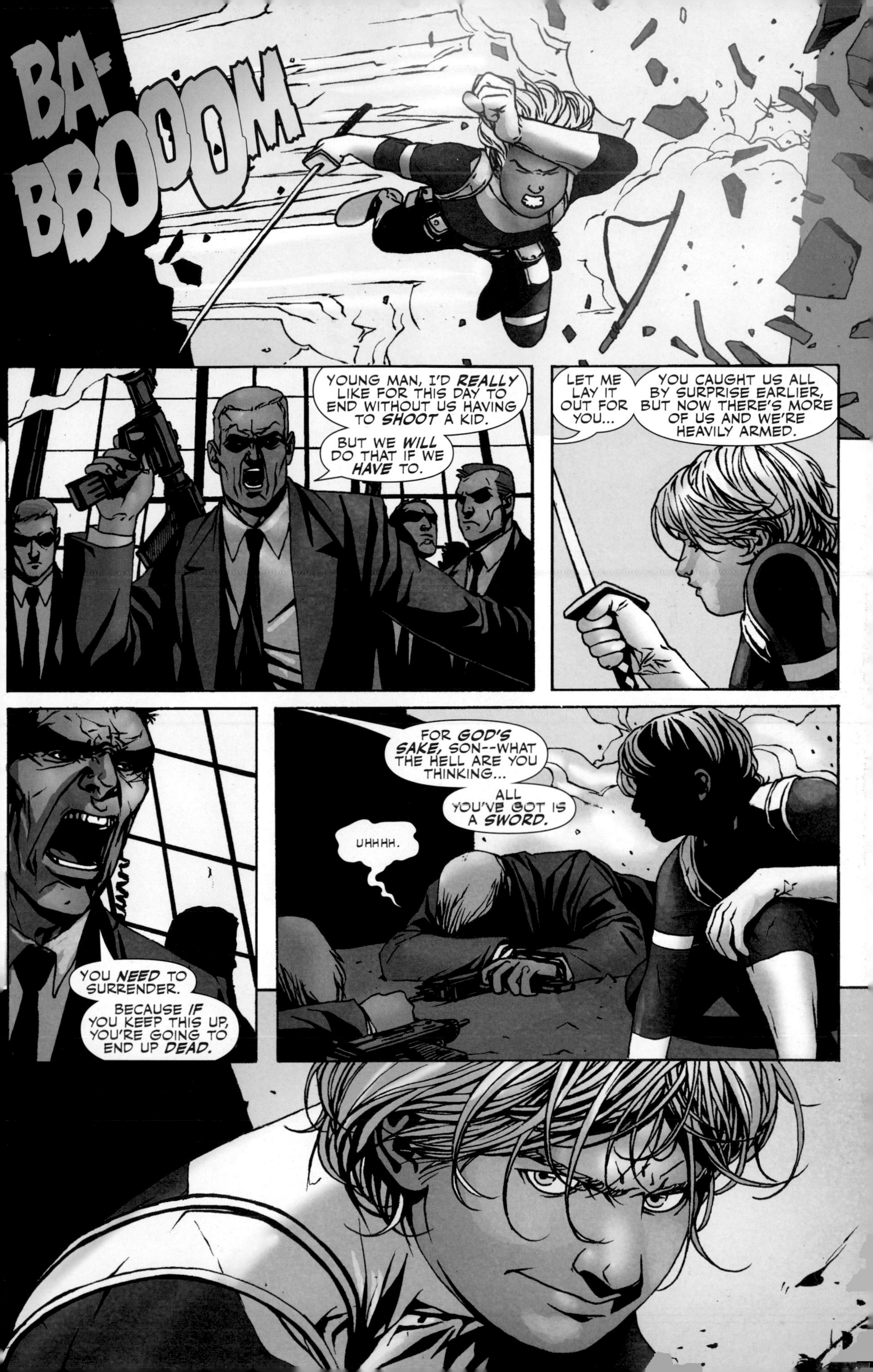
BA-BBOOOM
YOUNG MAN, I'D REALLY LIKE FOR THIS DAY TO END WITHOUT US HAVING TO SHOOT A KID.
BUT WE WILL DO THAT IF WE HAVE TO.
LET ME LAY IT OUT FOR YOU...
YOU CAUGHT US ALL BY SURPRISE EARLIER, BUT NOW THERE'S MORE OF US AND WE'RE HEAVILY ARMED.
YOU NEED TO SURRENDER.
BECAUSE IF YOU KEEP THIS UP, YOU'RE GOING TO END UP DEAD.
FOR GOD'S SAKE, SON--WHAT THE HELL ARE YOU THINKING...
ALL YOU'VE GOT IS A SWORD.
UHHHH.

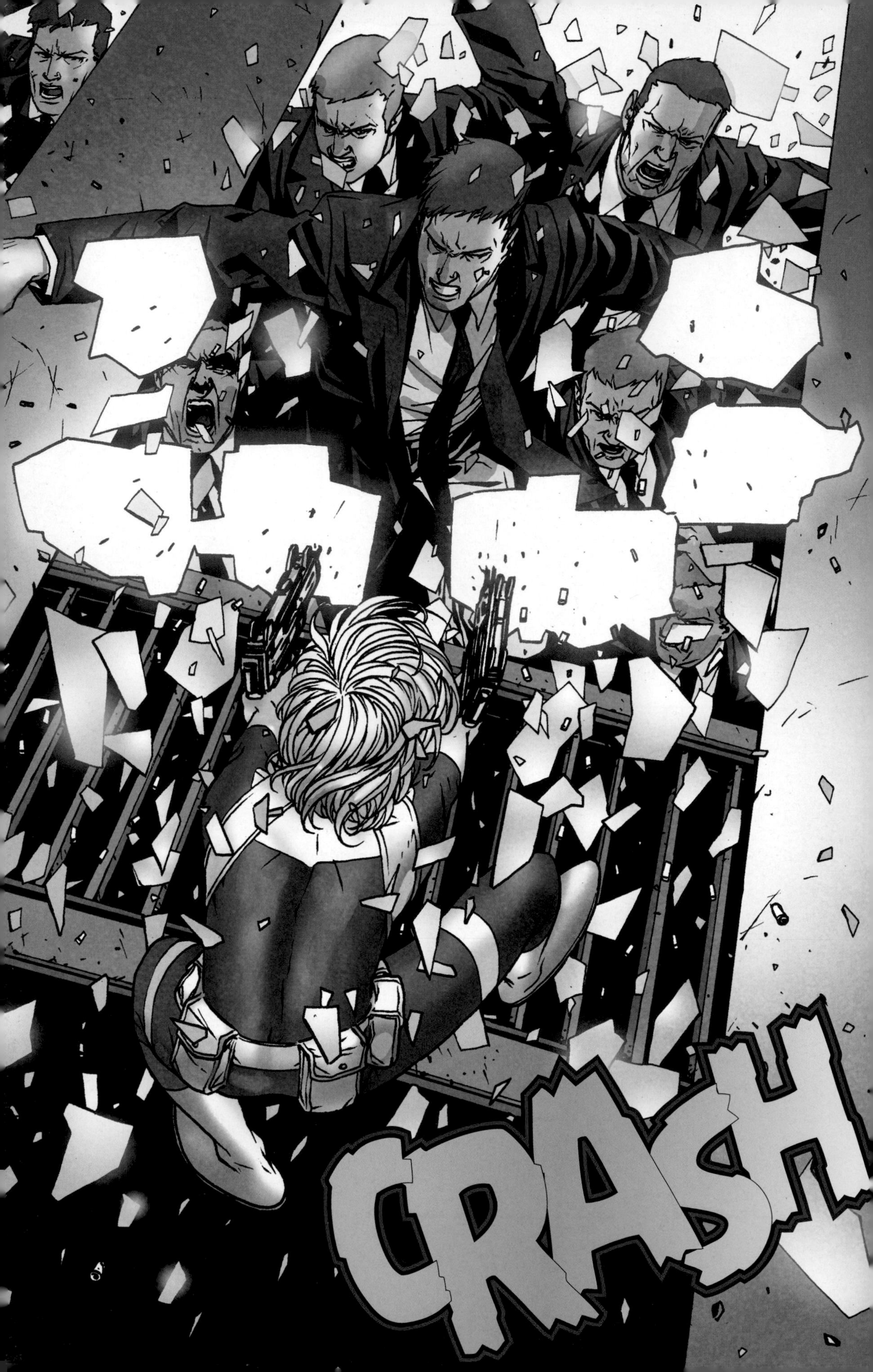
CRASH

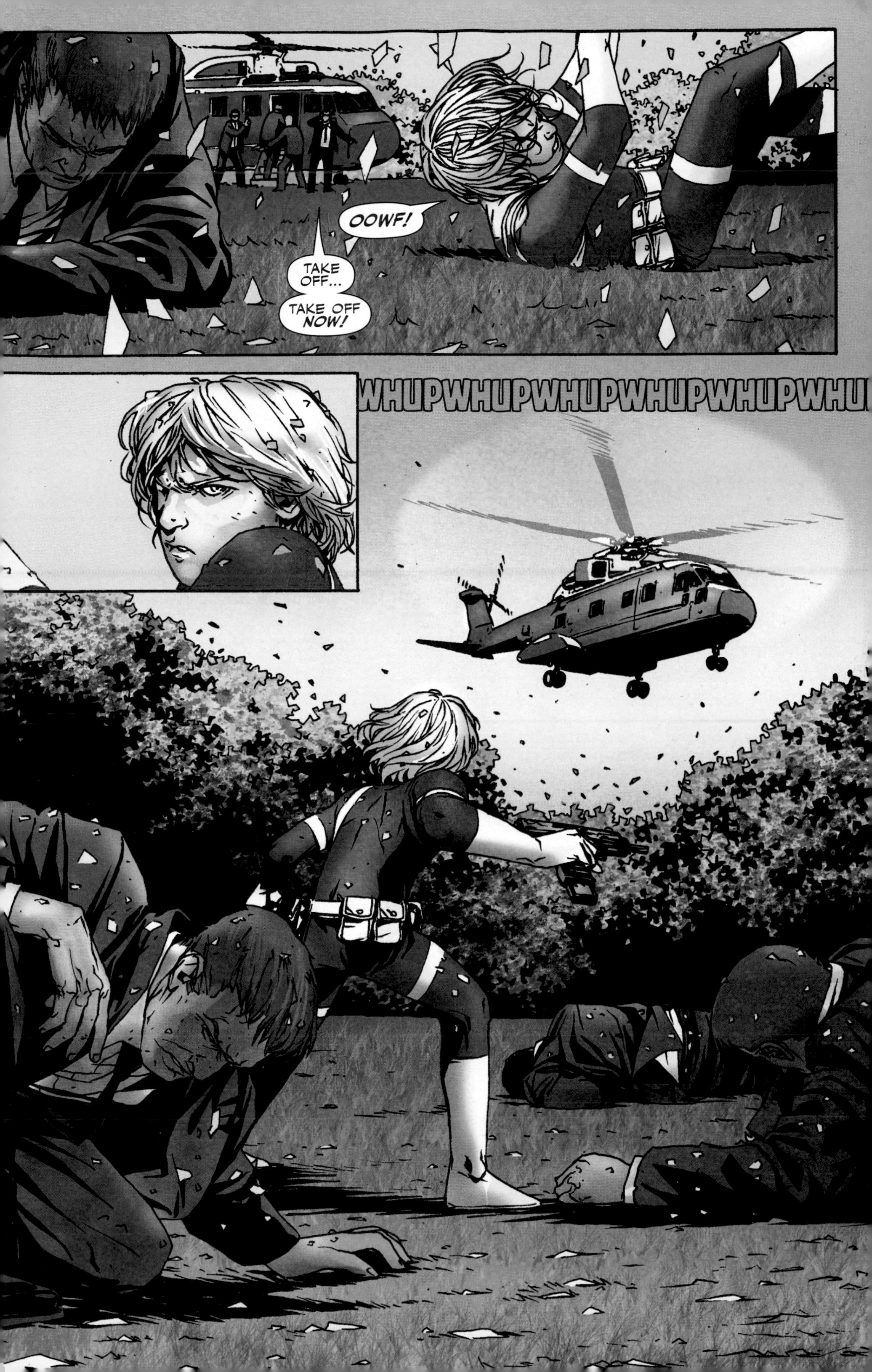
OOWF!
TAKE OFF...
TAKE OFF NOW!
WHUPWHUPWHUPWHUPWHUPWHU

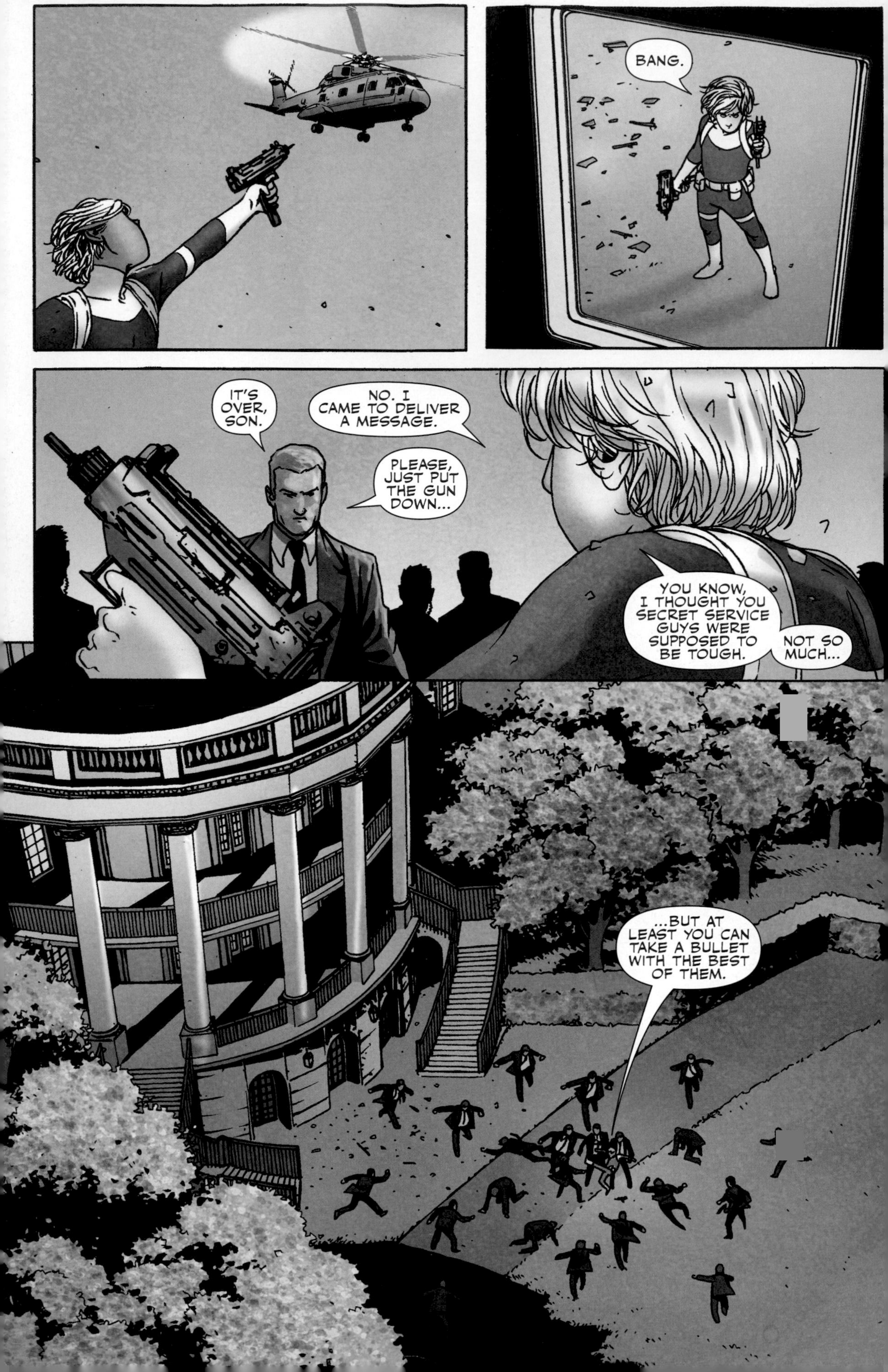
BANG.
IT'S OVER, SON.
NO. I CAME TO DELIVER A MESSAGE.
PLEASE, JUST PUT THE GUN DOWN...
YOU KNOW, I THOUGHT YOU SECRET SERVICE GUYS WERE SUPPOSED TO BE TOUGH.
NOT SO MUCH...
...BUT AT LEAST YOU CAN TAKE A BULLET WITH THE BEST OF THEM.

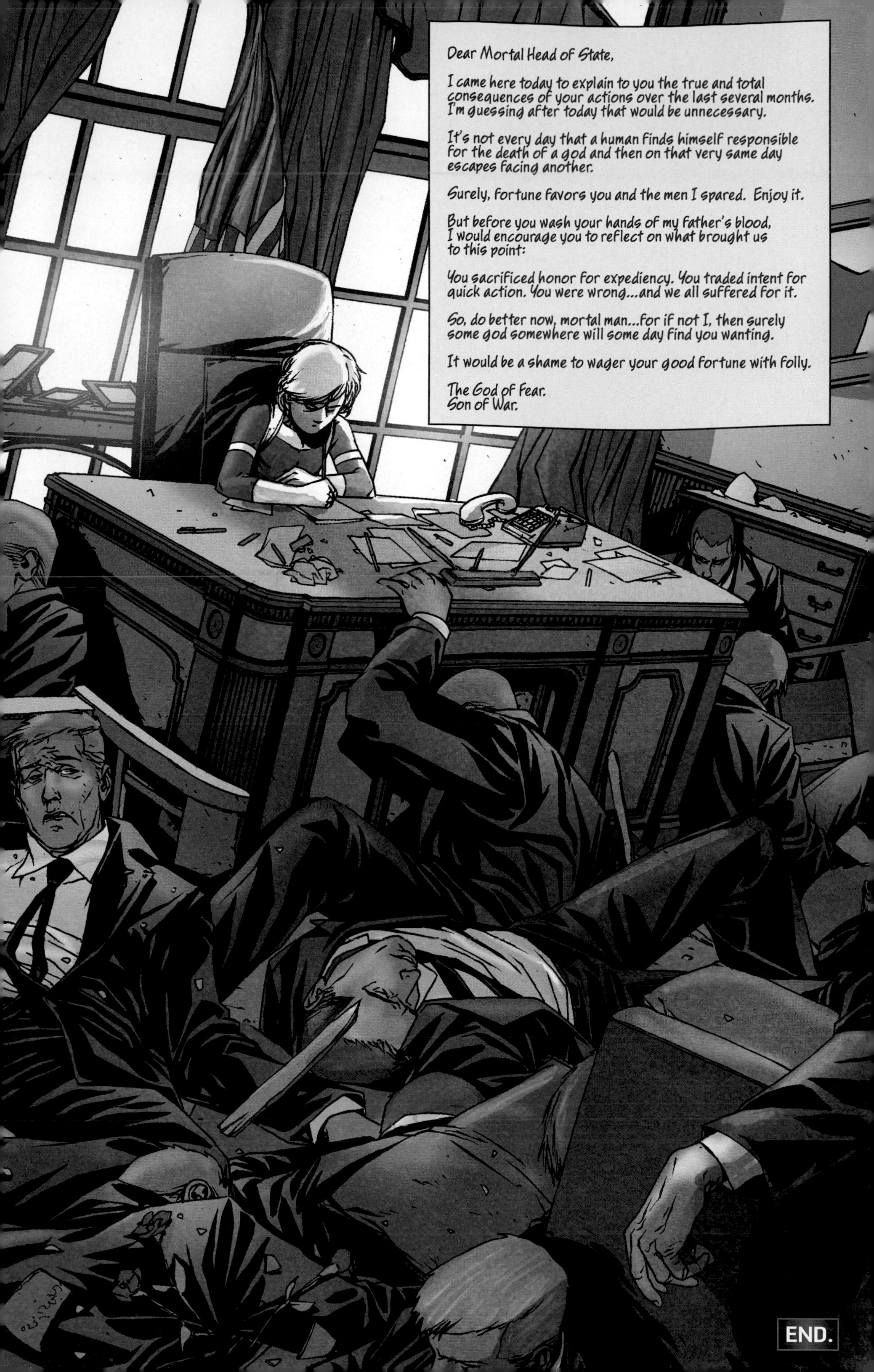
Dear Mortal Head of State,
I came here today to explain to you the true and total consequences of your actions over the last several months. I'm guessing after today that would be unnecessary.
It's not every day that a human finds himself responsible for the death of a god and then on that very same day escapes facing another.
Surely, fortune favors you and the men I spared. Enjoy it.
But before you wash your hands of my father's blood, I would encourage you to reflect on what brought us to this point:
You sacrificed honor for expediency. You traded intent for quick action. You were wrong...and we all suffered for it.
So, do better now, mortal man...for if not I, then surely some god somewhere will some day find you wanting.
It would be a shame to wager your good fortune with folly.
The God of Fear.
Son of War.
END.

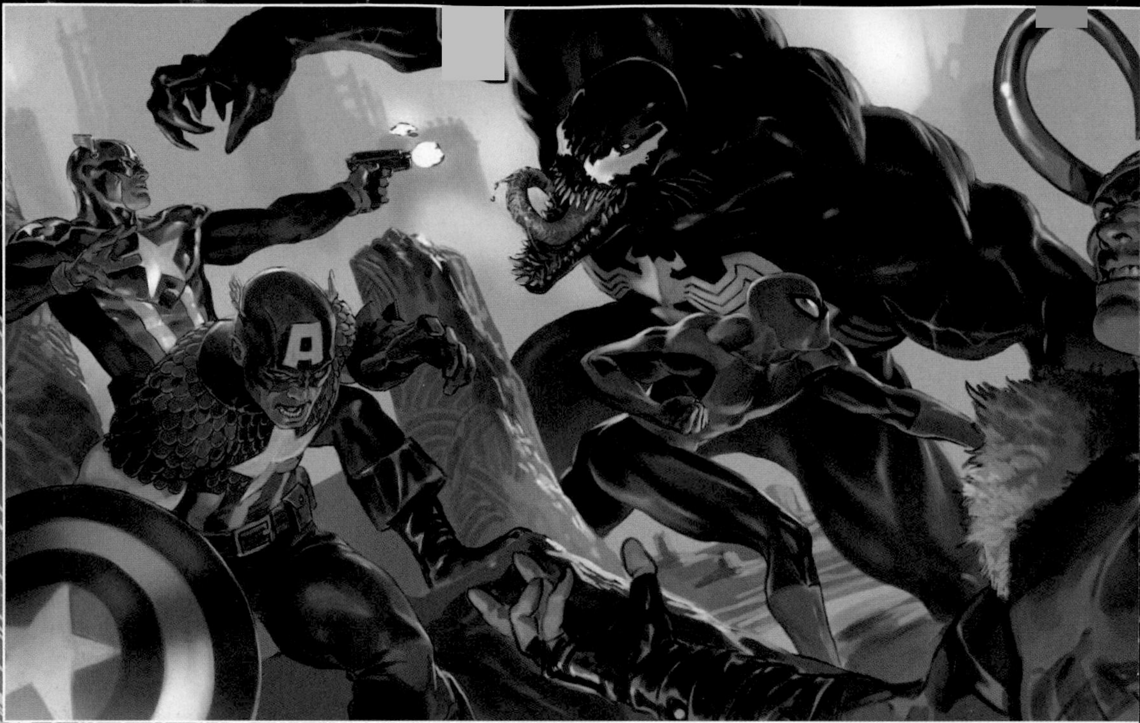

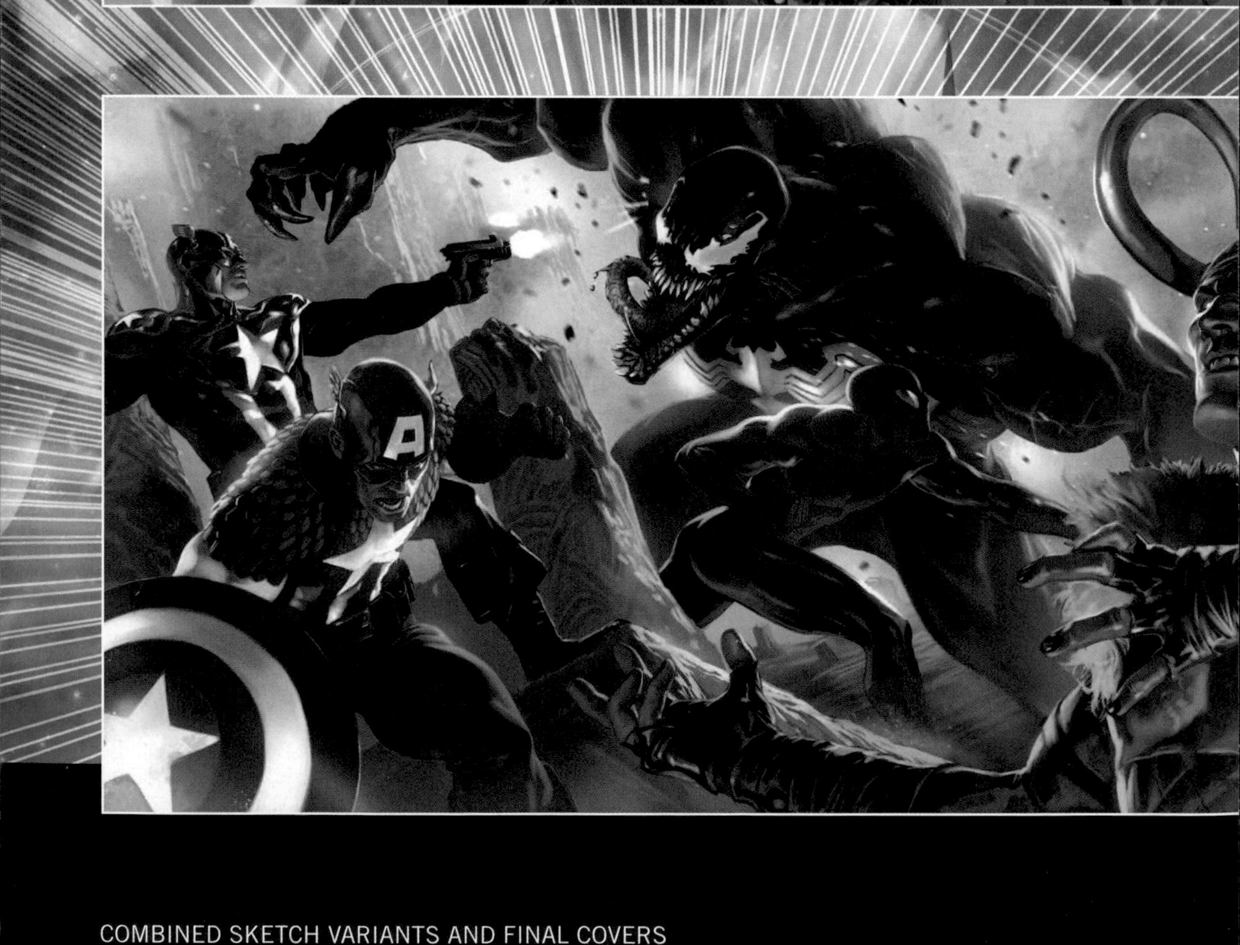

COMBINED SKETCH VARIANTS AND FINAL COVERS

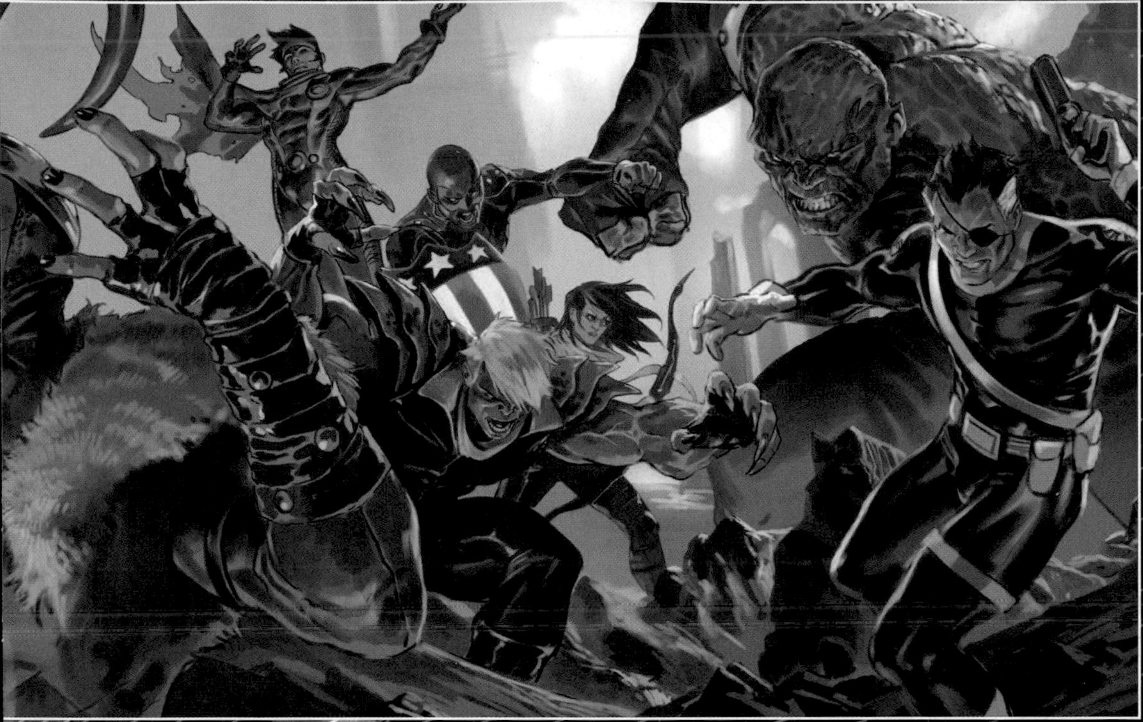

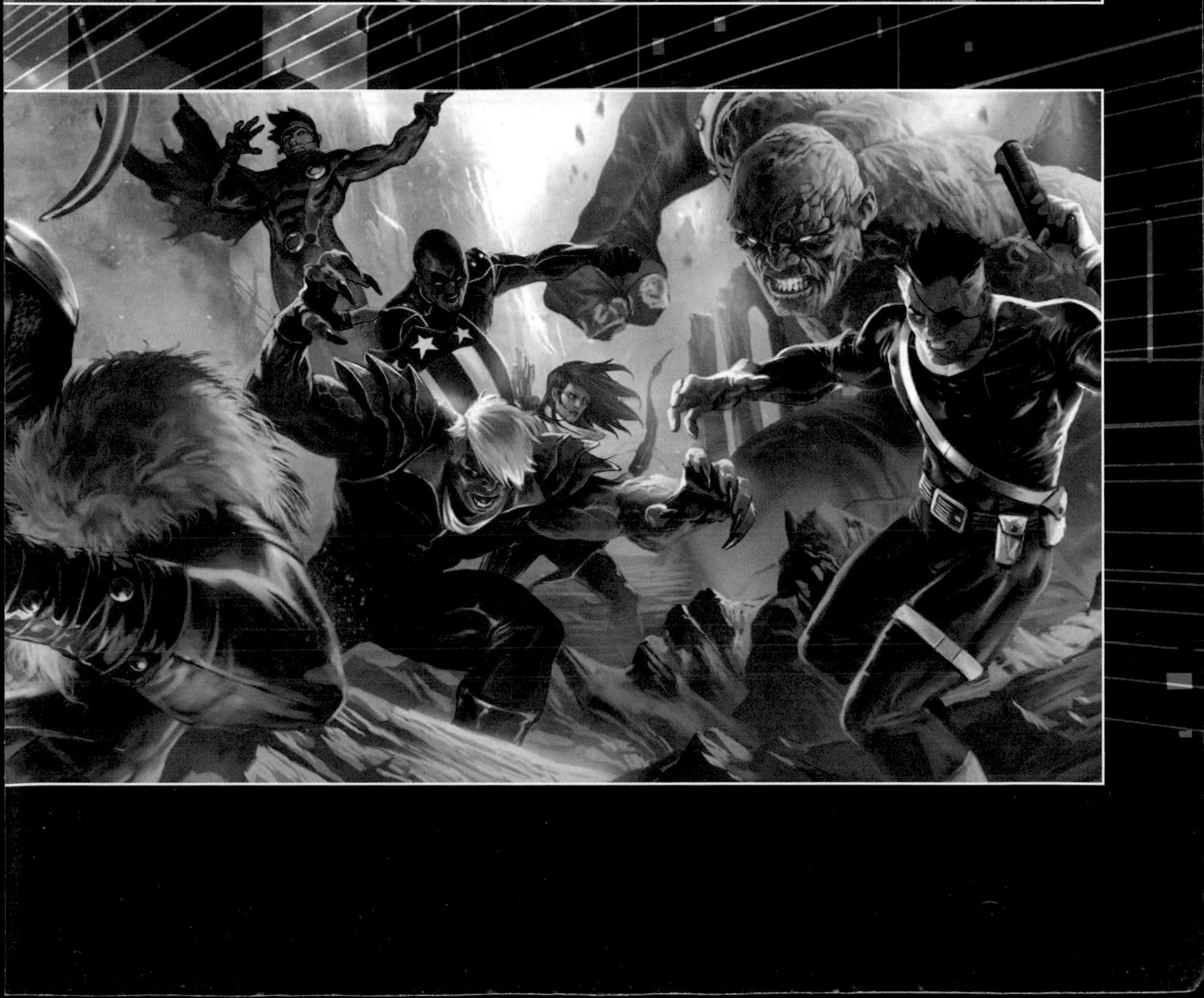

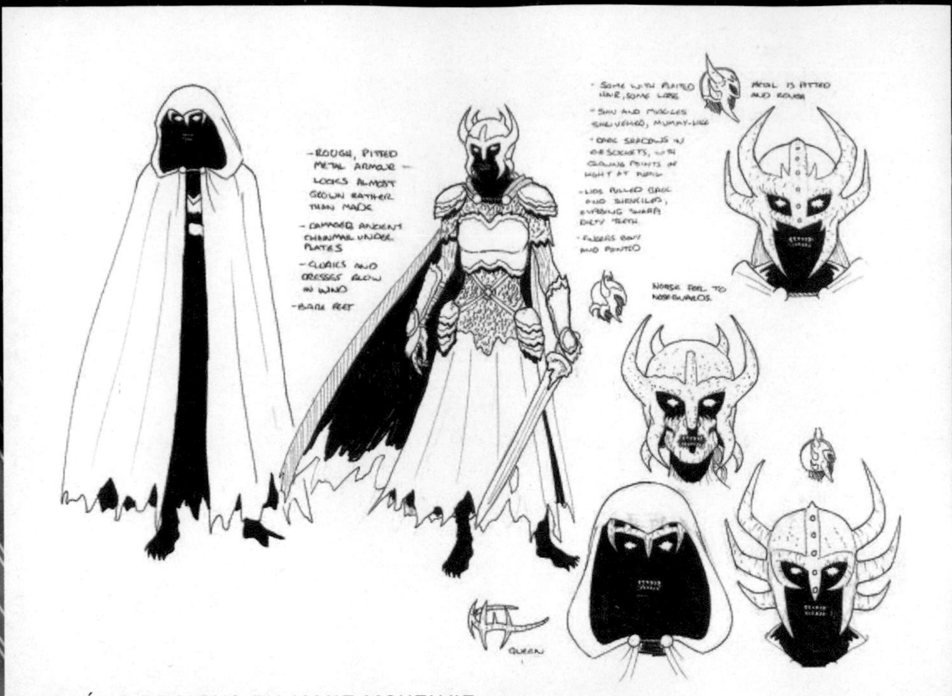

-ROUGH, PITTED METAL ARMOUR -
LOOKS ALMOST GROWN RATHER THAN MADE
- DAMAGED ANCIENT CHAINMAIL UNDER PLATES
- CLOAKS AND DRESSES BLOW IN WIND
- BARE FEET
METAL IS PITTED AND ROUGH
- FINGERS BONY AND POINTED
NORSE FEEL TO NOSEGUARDS.

THE DÍSIR DESIGNS BY JAMIE MCKELVIE

SIEGE: YOUNG AVENGERS, PAGES 13-22 PENCILS BY MAHMUD A. ASRAR

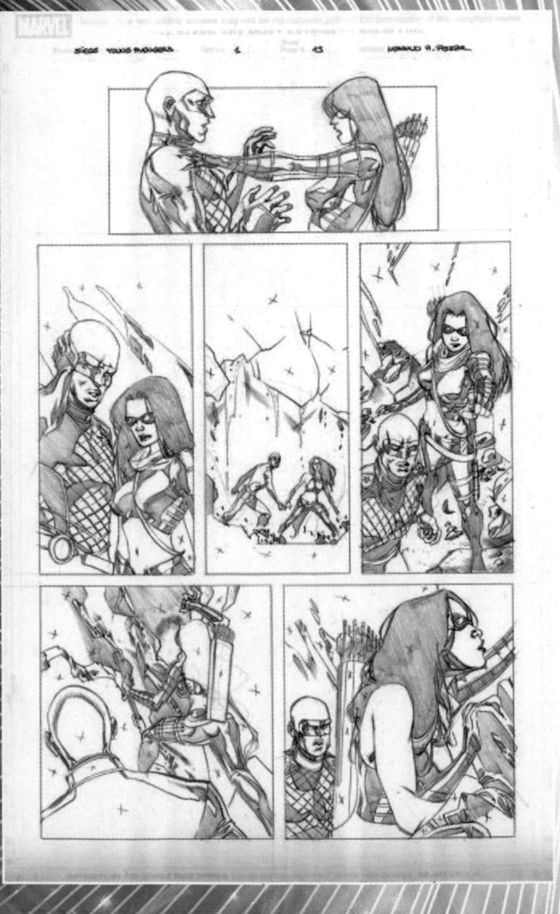

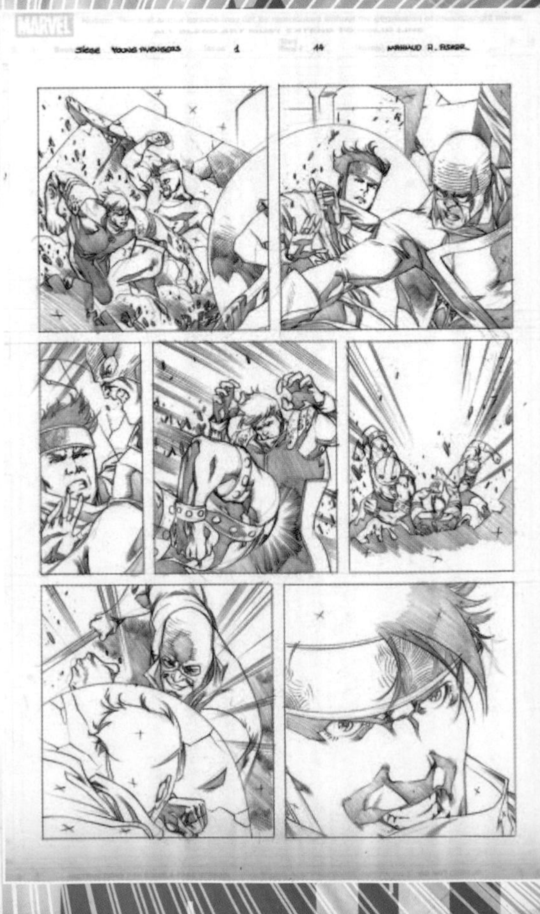

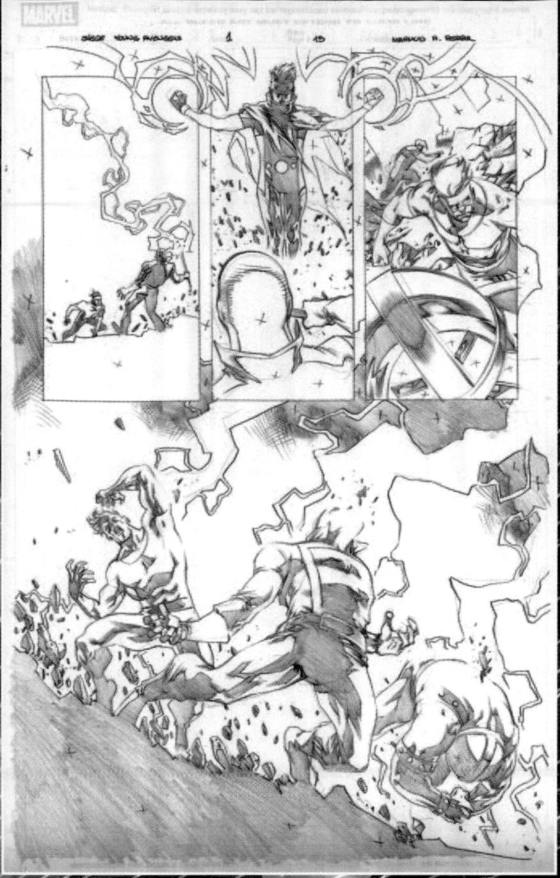

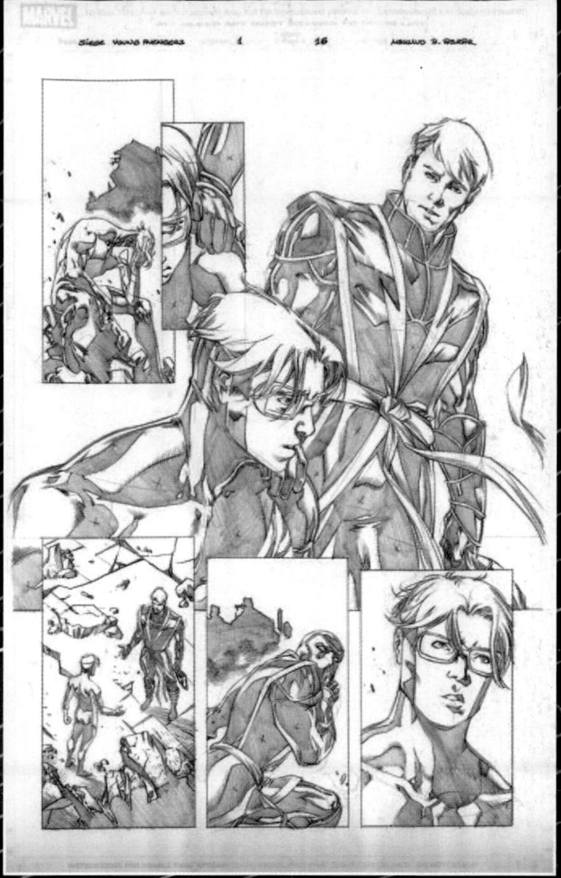

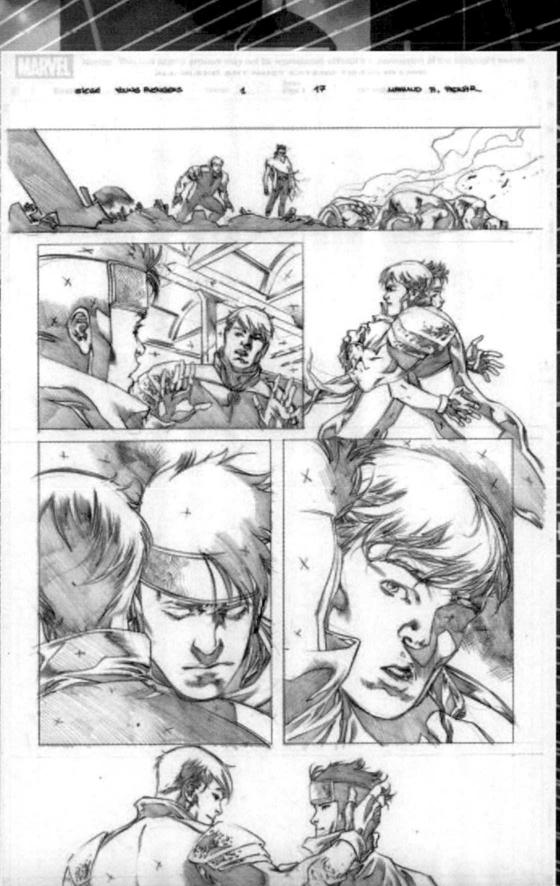

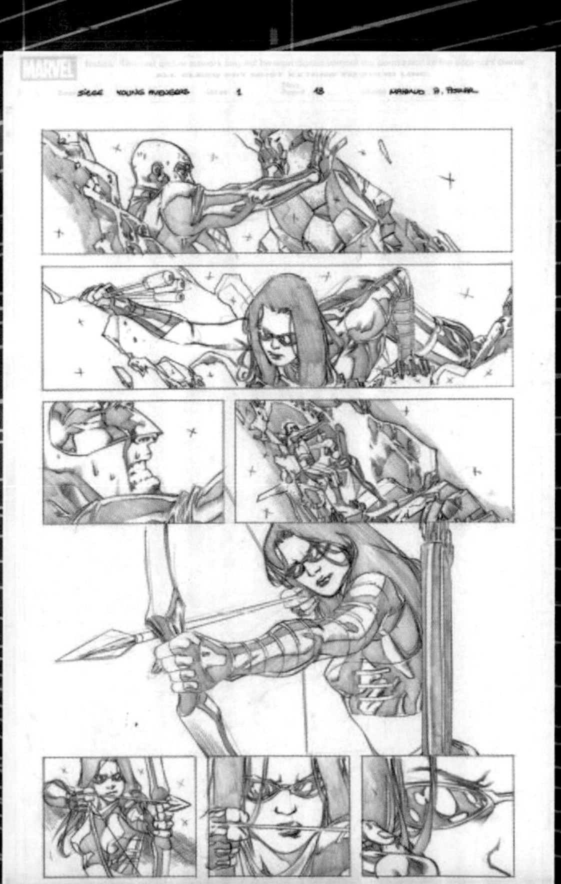

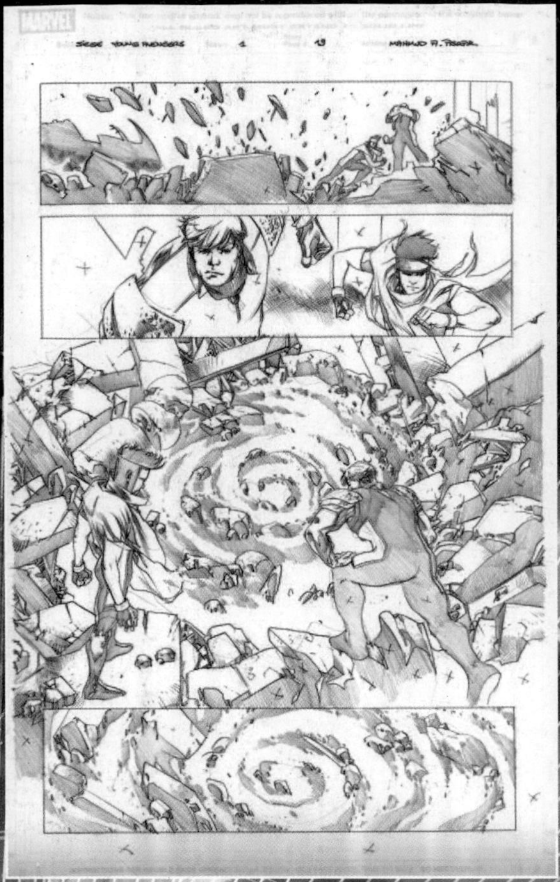

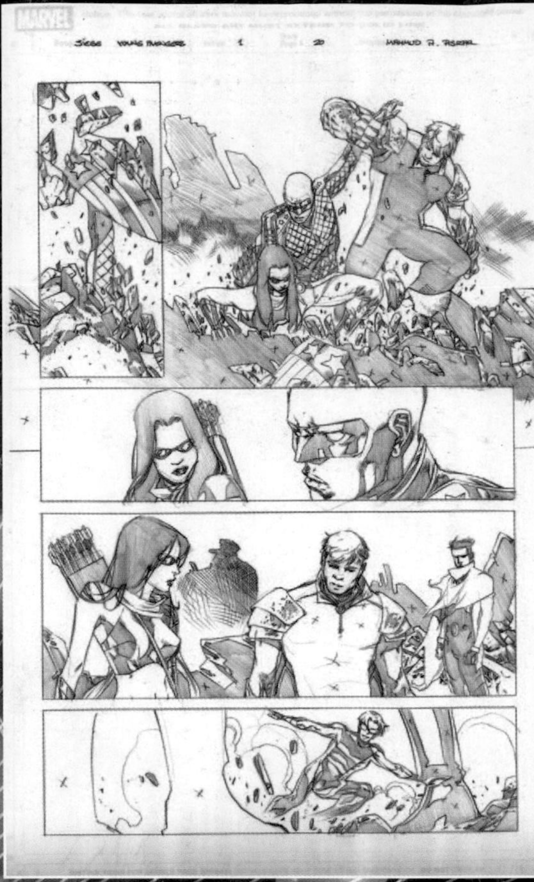

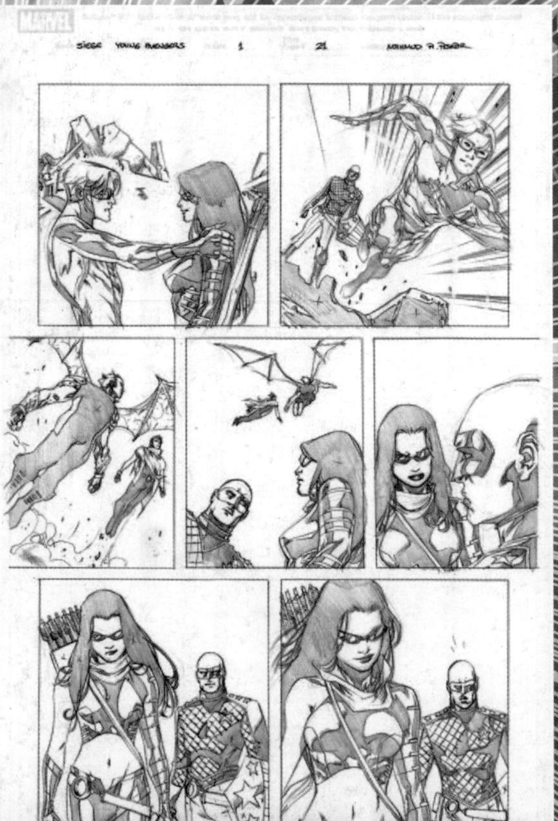

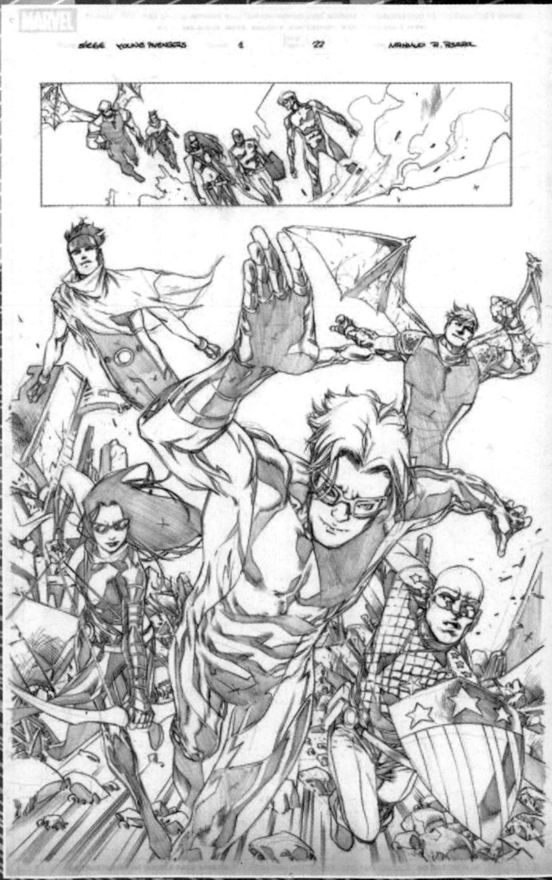

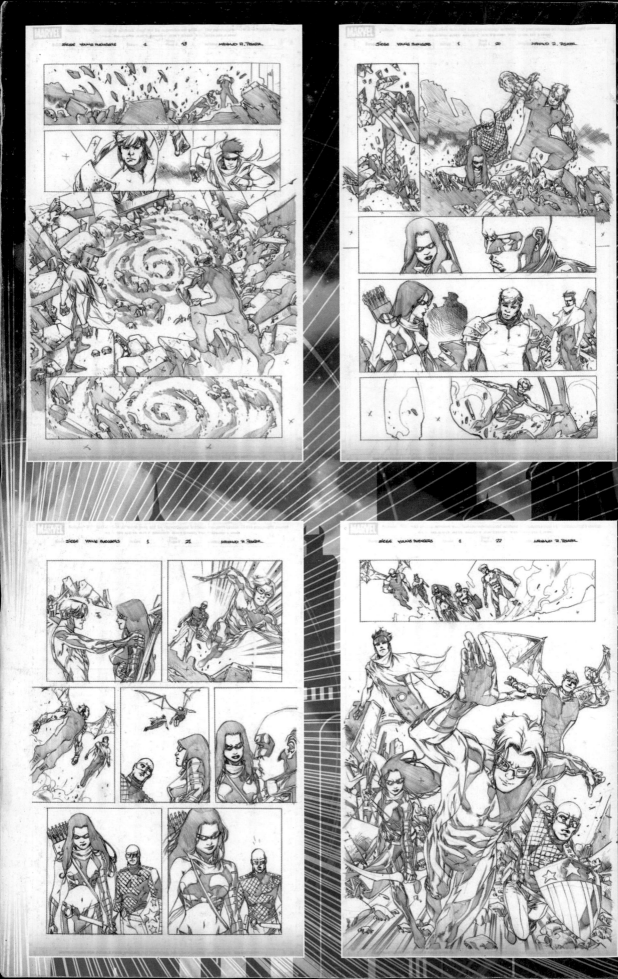